James Scully's poetry has appeared in *Poetry, The New Yorker, The Nation,* and in MODERN POETS, an anthology edited by John Malcolm Brinnin and Bill Read, McGraw-Hill. Mr. Scully is at work on a first book of poems. He has taught at Rutgers and now teaches at the University of Connecticut.

Modern Poetics

James Scully, editor

McGraw-Hill Book Company
New York   Toronto   San Francisco

Library of Congress Catalog Card Number: 65-20415
McGraw-Hill Paperbacks

8910112 MUMU 9876
ISBN 07-055872-8

ACKNOWLEDGMENTS

W. B. Yeats: "A General Introduction for My Work"

Reprinted with permission of The Macmillan Company from ESSAYS AND INTRODUCTIONS by W. B. Yeats. © Mrs. W. B. Yeats 1961. Reprinted by permission of Mrs. W. B. Yeats and Messrs. Macmillan & Co. Ltd.

Ezra Pound: "A Retrospect"

From THE LITERARY ESSAYS OF EZRA POUND. All rights reserved. Reprinted by permission of New Directions, Publishers.

Reprinted by permission of Mr. A. V. Moore, literary agent for Ezra Pound.

Ezra Pound: "The Chinese Ideogram"

From ABC OF READING by Ezra Pound. All rights reserved. Reprinted by permission of the publishers, New Directions.

Reprinted by permission of Mr. A. V. Moore, literary agent for Ezra Pound.

Robert Frost: "Sentence Sounds"

Portion of a letter from Robert Frost to John T. Bartlett reprinted from THE SELECTED LETTERS OF ROBERT FROST edited by Lawrance Thompson. Copyright © 1964 by Lawrance Thompson and Holt, Rinehart and Winston, Inc. Reprinted by permission of Holt, Rinehart and Winston, Inc.

Robert Frost: "The Figure a Poem Makes"

From COMPLETE POEMS OF ROBERT FROST. Copyright 1949 by Holt, Rinehart and Winston, Inc. Reprinted by permission of Holt, Rinehart and Winston, Inc.

Reprinted by permission of Laurence Pollinger Limited, agent for Jonathan Cape Limited, the publisher.

T. S. Eliot: "Tradition and the Individual Talent"

From SELECTED ESSAYS: New Edition by T. S. Eliot, copyright, 1932, 1936, 1950, by Harcourt, Brace & World, Inc.; © 1960, 1964, by T. S. Eliot. Reprinted by permission of the publishers.

Reprinted by permission of Methuen & Co. Ltd., the publishers.

William Carlos Williams: "A New Measure"

From THE SELECTED LETTERS OF WILLIAM CARLOS WILLIAMS, edited by John C. Thirlwall. Copyright © 1957 by William Carlos Williams. Reprinted by permission of Ivan Obolensky, Inc., New York, publishers.

Gerard Manley Hopkins: "Author's Preface"

Reprinted with permission of the Oxford University Press from POEMS OF GERARD MANLEY HOPKINS. Copyright 1948 by Oxford University Press, Inc.

John Crowe Ransom: "Poetry: A Note in Ontology"

Reprinted with permission of Charles Scribner's Sons from THE

Contents

A PREFATORY NOTE

It should be remarked, first, that the following selections obviously do not constitute a poetics; this would be true even if the length and range of the anthology were extended. All selections, however, have been drawn from the prose writings of poets, not from those of theoreticians; the majority are concerned with poetry as a present and future activity, as a "making" or strategy. The anthology might be considered a response to questions posed by Ezra Pound in his *ABC of Reading:*

> If you wanted to know something about an automobile, would you go to a man who had made one and driven it, or to a man who had merely heard about it?
> And of the two men who had made automobiles, would you go to one who had made a good one, or one who had made a botch?

Each essay (letter, journal entry, interview) should open an avenue into the poetic theory implicit in the writer's own poetry. Essays ordinarily form a more neutral medium than do poems. With however little success, one is free to concentrate on the statement of ideas without having to evoke, on the spot, psychological realities—the very realities which in concert with things and ideas may become poetry; although a few of the essays actually do approach the condition of poems. No one is represented as a critic, except casually; each poet addresses himself to his own poetry or his own conception of it. Finally, the essays will prove of value insofar as they orient the reader with respect to that poetry. When Pound went on to ask if his reader would "look at the actual car or only at the specifications," the required answer was evident.

To attempt even a listing of the theoretical prepossessions of the modern poets would be presumptuous, but a few words about depersonalization and the emulation of the scientist, or of some ill-defined image of the scientist, might be relevant and acceptable.

When the great French poet Paul Valéry observed that "it is the very one who wants to write down his dream who is obliged to be extremely wide awake," he was replying, in effect if not in intention, to those who preferred science above poetry. Nevertheless he too presupposed the superiority of science, not because he considered it a more comprehensive repository of knowledge or truth, but because it maintained the most efficient procedure and precise instruments for arriving at a formulation. It was not the body of science that so beguiled him, but the scientific approach. As late as 1939, in a lecture delivered at Oxford he could say: "With every question, before making any deep examination of the content, I take a look at the language; I generally proceed like a surgeon who sterilizes his hands and prepares the area to be operated on. This is what I call *cleaning up the verbal situation*. You must excuse this expression," he momentarily concluded, "equating the words and forms of speech with the hands and instruments of a surgeon." The procedure of a surgeon who sterilizes himself, his instruments, and even his patient, and who generally reduces a situation to its simplest form in order that he may operate more effectively, attested to a scientific attitude. Here, writ large, was the attitude which had insinuated itself into much modern poetry, granting power, imposing limitations, and ultimately declaring itself through the various theories of depersonalization.

10

When Ezra Pound wrote that "his true Penelope was Flaubert," he proposed to embrace the demonic author of a book which purposed "no lyricism, no comments, the author's personality absent," the same author who declared that "the time for Beauty is over. Mankind may return to it, but it has no use for it at present. The more Art develops, the more scientific it will be, just as science will become artistic." Pound praised Ernest Fenollosa's essay on the Chinese written character, also, by calling it "the first definite assertion of the applicability of scientific method to literary criticism." And Marianne Moore went so far as to contend that the poet's work and the scientist's are analogous, for both are willing to waste effort, "each is attentive to clues, each must narrow the choice, must strive for precision"; like poetry, "science is the process of discovering." Biology courses in particular had affected her poetry, for "economy of statement, logic employed to ends that are disinterested, drawing and identifying, liberate—at least have some bearing on—the imagination."

The most famous espousal of depersonalization is T. S. Eliot's. "The progress of an artist is a continual self-sacrifice, a continued extinction of personality," he claims; "it is in this depersonalization that art may be said to approach the condition of science." For an analogy to the creative process he appeals to the laboratory: the poet's mind is like a shred of platinum when the latter is introduced into a chamber containing oxygen and sulphur dioxide; with absolute impunity, it acts as a catalyst. But Eliot's later disclaimer, that "only those who have personality and emotions know what it means to want to escape from those things," implies a curiously "unscientific" involvement. One hears of the traditional costumes and manners of Japanese women, and of the exposed nape of the neck, which is at least as incendiary as the exposure afforded by a bikini on the French Riviera. If some things are truly relative, the reader may sense raw meat in Eliot's essay, "Tradition and the Individual Talent." But whether depersonalization may ever be transcendent, or is fated to remain a mask held against one's pained obsession with personality, may well be an unanswerable question.

Depersonalization has proved less magnetic to those less susceptible to the lure of science. W. B. Yeats complained of "the scientific movement" because it "brought with it a literature which was always tending to lose itself in externalities of all kinds, in opinion, in declamation, in picturesque writing, in word-painting, or in . . . an attempt 'to build in brick and mortar inside the covers of a book.' " The immediate end of all depersonalization theories, however they are modified, is to claim for works of art an objective validity commensurate with scientific formulas, and, on another level, such theories obliquely suggest that a poem is a physical fact in the way that a piece of sculpture or a painting is.

But Yeats did not, for that reason, believe a poet could be justified by the expression of himself—no more than David Jones, who says in his "Preface" that "the workman must be dead to himself while engaged upon the work, otherwise we have that sort of 'self-expression' which is as undesirable in the painter or writer as in the carpenter, the cantor, the half-back, or the cook." Yeats would have the poet put in a formulated, if not necessarily formal, appearance, just as the poem should collect itself under a facing of traditional rhythms, for all art is "a monotony in external things for the sake of an interior variety, a sacrifice of gross effects to subtle effects, an asceticism of the imagination." He would not eradicate personality, which is the source of theme and energy; rather, he would find for it a more-than-casual significance. In Eliot's theory, the poet remains unaffected throughout the changes he effects or substances he instigates, as it were, into existence; for Yeats, the poet's personality is itself a substance, a physical and spiritual complexity which attains, in and through his work, a conclusiveness.

The more openly personal poets, such as e e cummings, are the most hostile to science—to the scientific attitude, that is. Thus Wallace Stevens epitomized the "anti-master-man," who bears a resemblance to Stevens's Freud, as a "floribund ascetic"—the "floribund" casting its novel insight back onto the unstated "moribund," thereby suggesting sterility hemmed in by fecundity, a living death laid out in the midst of flowery profusion. As Stevens envisions it, there could be "no poetry without the personality of the poet, and that, quite simply, is why the definition of poetry has not been found and why, in short, there is none."

Although it necessitates a shift in terminology and perspective (from a consideration of the poet in the poem to a like consideration of the biology in the processes of thought), the issues of depersonalization and the challenge ostensibly posed by science are nicely articulated in Elizabeth Sewall's distinction between "an exclusive mythology which chooses to overlook the body's participation" in thought—which would abstract the perceiver from his perception—and "an inclusive mythology which is prepared in varying degrees to admit the body, the notion of the organism as a whole, as a partner in that . . . operation known as thought."

Exclusive mythology may be illustrated by reference to the ideals of French Symbolism, whereby a poem approximates a mathematical equation or a formula in that a measure of its validity is its inner consistency. Susanne Langer describes mathematical constructions as being "only symbols; they have meanings in terms of relationships, not of substance; something in reality answers to them, but they are not supposed to be items in that reality." A symbolist poem aspires to the condition of a perpetual motion machine, as someone once remarked, vibrating ceaselessly yet doing no work. It denotes nothing. Its validity inheres in an impregnable, formal integrity.

But in an inclusive mythology, according to Miss Sewall, "the inclusion of the participating self (poet or reader, it is all one) is open, deliberate, an active ingredient in what goes on. Poetry is the most inclusive form of thought we have yet devised, a conscious call upon those resources of myth which underlie all language and all thinking. If the self is involved in any working system of thought, whether it is recognized or not, poetry, with its recognition of the self's co-operation, is in fact nearest to reality. Exclusive mythology, in its preoccupation with abstract form, embarks on a wholesale game of make-believe by the exclusion of the self." To this one might only wish to add that make-believe also has its use.

There are no conclusions, certainly; and it is possible to take pleasure in the attitude of Randolph Bourne, who, being most fearful of "premature crystallization," considered it his task "to divide, confuse, disturb, keep the intellectual waters constantly in motion to prevent any . . . ice from ever forming."

Again, to break off on a rhapsodic note, there is D. H. Lawrence's stunning paean to the immediate present, when "there is no perfection, no consummation, nothing finished. The strands are all flying, quivering, intermingling into the web, the waters are shak-

13

A PREFATORY NOTE

ing the moon. There is no round, consummate moon on the face of running water, nor on the face of the unfinished tide. There are no gems in the living plasm." Or, if there are, they flash out only at special moments when "the whole tide of all life and all time suddenly heaves, and appears before us as an apparition, a revelation. We look at the very white quick of nascent creation. A water-lily heaves herself from the flood, looks around, gleams, and is gone."

In the introductory sketches all quotations, unless attributed otherwise, are from writings of the poets themselves. The sole exception is "they are what/they're talking about," which is from John Malcolm Brinnin's poem entitled "Marianne Moore's." Only the footnotes in brackets are the editor's. The contributors appear in chronological order according to the publication dates of their first books of poems.

I wish to thank David McKain for his numerous suggestions, all of them stimulating in one way or another; Rex Warner for enlightening me on a small point bearing on a major cultural ignorance; and my wife, Arlene, for being considerably more than an overseer.

J. S.

Modern Poetics

W. B. Yeats

W. B. Yeats was born in Sandymount, Dublin, on June 13, 1865; he died January 28, 1939, on the French Riviera. During his long productive life he appeared in a number of related guises: as a young Anglo-Irish poet, a founder of the Rhymers' Club, whose verse was notable for its Pre-Raphaelite afterglow; a student of Rosicrucianism and other esoterica, and elaborator of the symbolic system presented in A Vision; a symbolist whose poètry, riding on a "passionate syntax," is substantiated by a colloquial vocabulary; an explorer of Irish mythology; and a founder of the Irish National Theatre, as well as a prime mover in the attempt to revive Ireland's culture and civilization. In each of these roles a truth inheres, although none alone does justice to his complex integrity.

Yeats; believing that no poet is justified by the expression of himself, praised Synge because he "sought for the race, not through the eyes or in the history, or even in the future, but . . . in the depths of the mind, and in all art like his, although it does not command—indeed because it does not—may lie the roots of far-branching events. Only that which does not teach, which does not cry out, which does not persuade, which does not condescend, which does not explain, is irresistible." The poet stands as a species of oracle, a premier of abiding mysteries. His mind is essentially communal; its symbols are drawn from the "Great Memory" where the human realities have accumulated. Whatever his utterance it should transcend mere emotion, which is temporal and personal, so as to assume the weight and validity of passion.

It follows that poetry is an autonomous activity in which argument, theory, erudition, and observation "are merely what Blake called 'little devils who fight for themselves,' illusions of our visible passing life, who must be made to serve the moods, or we have no part in eternity." Even patriotism is more than impure motive in an artist, and "an absorption in fragmentary sensuous beauty or detachable ideas" deprives one of the power "to mould vast material into a single image." According to Yeats, in his ancient Church "there is an altar and no pulpit."

Tradition, then, extends no lesson; rather, it constitutes a kind of ripeness. "When we delight in a spring day there mixes, perhaps, with our personal emotion an emotion Chaucer found in Guillaume de Lorris, who had it from the poetry of Provence; we celebrate our draughty May with an enthusiasm made ripe by more meridian suns; and all our art has its image in the Mass that would lack authority were it not descended from savage ceremonies taught amid what perils and by what spirits to naked savages. The old images, the old emotions, awakened again to overwhelming life, like the gods Heine tells of, by the belief and passion of some new soul, are the only masterpieces." From such grounds, Yeats's own great poetry arises.

A General Introduction for My Work*

I. THE FIRST PRINCIPLE

A poet writes always of his personal life, in his finest work out of its tragedy, whatever it be, remorse, lost love, or mere loneliness; he never speaks directly as to someone at the breakfast table, there is always a phantasmagoria. Dante and Milton had mythologies, Shakespeare the characters of English history or of traditional romance; even when the poet seems most himself, when he is Raleigh and gives potentates the lie, or Shelley 'a nerve o'er which do creep the else unfelt oppressions of this earth,' or Byron when 'the soul wears out the breast' as 'the sword outwears its sheath,' he is never the bundle of accident and incoherence that sits down to breakfast; he has been reborn as an idea, something intended, complete. A novelist might describe his accidence, his incoherence, he must

---

* From *Essays and Introductions* by **W. B. Yeats.**

17

not; he is more type than man, more passion than type. He is Lear, Romeo, Oedipus, Tiresias; he has stepped out of a play, and even the woman he loves is Rosalind, Cleopatra, never The Dark Lady. He is part of his own phantasmagoria and we adore him because nature has grown intelligible, and by so doing a part of our creative power. 'When mind is lost in the light of the Self,' says the Prashna Upanishad, 'it dreams no more; still in the body it is lost in happiness.' 'A wise man seeks in Self,' says the Chandogya Upanishad, 'those that are alive and those that are dead and gets what the world cannot give.' The world knows nothing because it has made nothing, we know everything because we have made everything.

II. SUBJECT-MATTER

It was through the old Fenian leader John O'Leary I found my theme. His long imprisonment, his longer banishment, his magnificent head, his scholarship, his pride, his integrity, all that aristocratic dream nourished amid little shops and little farms, had drawn around him a group of young men; I was but eighteen or nineteen and had already, under the influence of *The Faerie Queene* and *The Sad Shepherd,* written a pastoral play, and under that of Shelley's *Prometheus Unbound* two plays, one staged somewhere in the Caucasus, the other in a crater of the moon; and I knew myself to be vague and incoherent. He gave me the poems of Thomas Davis, said they were not good poetry but had changed his life when a young man, spoke of other poets associated with Davis and *The Nation* newspaper, probably lent me their books. I saw even more clearly than O'Leary that they were not good poetry. I read nothing but romantic literature; hated that dry eighteenth-century rhetoric; but they had one quality I admired and admire: they were not separated individual men; they spoke or tried to speak out of a people to a people; behind them stretched the generations. I knew, though but now and then as young men know things, that I must turn from that modern literature Jonathan Swift compared to the web a spider draws out of its bowels; I hated and still hate with an ever growing hatred the literature of the point of view. I wanted, if my ignorance permitted, to get back to Homer, to those that fed at his table. I wanted to cry as all men cried, to laugh as all men laughed, and the Young Ireland poets when not writing mere politics had the same want, but they did not know that the common and its befitting language is the research of a lifetime and when found may lack popular recognition. Then somebody, not O'Leary, told me of Standish O'Grady and his interpretation of Irish legends. O'Leary had sent me to O'Curry, but his unarranged and uninterpreted history defeated my boyish indolence.

A generation before *The Nation* newspaper was founded the Royal Irish Academy had begun the study of ancient Irish literature. That study was as much a gift from the Protestant aristocracy which had created the Parliament as *The Nation* and its school, though Davis and Mitchel were Protestants; was a gift from the Catholic middle classes who were to create the Irish Free State. The Academy persuaded the English Government to finance an ordnance survey on a large scale; scholars, including that great scholar O'Donovan, were sent from village to village recording names and their legends. Perhaps it was the last moment when such work could be well done, the memory of the people was still intact, the collectors themselves had perhaps heard or seen the banshee; the Royal Irish Academy and its public with equal enthusiasm welcomed Pagan and Christian; thought the Round Towers a commemoration of Persian fire-worship. There was little orthodoxy to take alarm; the Catholics were crushed and cowed; an honoured great-uncle of mine—his portrait by some forgotten master hangs upon my bedroom wall—a Church of Ireland rector, would upon occasion boast that you could not ask a question he could not answer with a perfectly appropriate blasphemy or indecency. When several counties had been surveyed but nothing published, the Government, afraid of rousing dangerous patriotic emotion, withdrew support; large manuscript volumes remain containing much picturesque correspondence between scholars.

When modern Irish literature began, O'Grady's influence predominated. He could delight us with an extravagance we were too critical to share; a day will come, he said, when Slieve-na-mon will be more famous than Olympus, yet he was no Nationalist as we understood the word, but in rebellion, as he was fond of explaining, against the House of Commons, not against the King. His cousin, that great scholar Hayes O'Grady, would not join our non-political Irish Literary Society because he considered it a Fenian body, but boasted that although he had lived in England for forty years he had never made an English friend. He worked at the British Museum compiling their Gaelic catalogue and translating our heroic tales in an eighteenth-century frenzy; his heroine 'fractured her heart,' his hero 'ascended to the apex of the eminence' and there 'vibrated his javelin,' and afterwards took ship upon 'colossal ocean's superficies.' Both O'Gradys considered themselves as representing the old Irish land-owning aristocracy; both probably, Standish O'Grady certainly, thought that England, because decadent and democratic, had betrayed their order. It was another member of that order, Lady Gregory, who was to do for the heroic legends in *Gods and Fighting Men* and in *Cuchulain of Muirthemne* what Lady Charlotte Guest's *Mabinogion* had done with less beauty and style for those of Wales. Standish O'Grady had much modern sentiment, his style, like that of John Mitchel forty years before, shaped by Carlyle; she formed her style upon the Anglo-Irish dialect of her neighbourhood, an old vivid speech with a partly Tudor vocabulary, a syntax partly moulded by men who still thought in Gaelic.

I had heard in Sligo cottages or from pilots at Rosses Point endless stories of apparitions, whether of the recent dead or of the people of history and legend, of that Queen Maeve whose reputed cairn stands on the mountain over the bay. Then at the British Museum I read stories Irish writers of the 'forties and 'fifties had written of such apparitions, but they enraged me more than pleased because they turned the country visions into a joke. But when I went from cottage to cottage with Lady Gregory and watched her hand recording that great collection she has called *Visions and Beliefs* I escaped disfiguring humour.

Behind all Irish history hangs a great tapestry, even Christianity had to accept it and be itself pictured there. Nobody looking at its dim folds can say where Christianity begins and Druidism ends; 'There is one perfect among the birds, one perfect among the fish, and one among men that is perfect.' I can only explain by that suggestion of recent scholars—Professor Burkitt of Cambridge commended it to my attention—that St. Patrick came to Ireland not in the fifth century but towards the end of the second. The great controversies had not begun; Easter was still the first full moon after the Equinox. Upon that day the world had been created, the Ark rested upon Ararat, Moses led the Israelites out of Egypt; the umbilical cord which united Christianity to the ancient world had not yet been cut, Christ was still the half-brother of Dionysus. A man just tonsured by the Druids could learn from the nearest Christian neighbour to sign himself with the Cross without sense of incongruity, nor would his children acquire that sense. The organised clans weakened Church organisation, they could accept the monk but not the bishop.

A modern man, *The Golden Bough* and *Human Personality* in his head, finds much that is congenial in St. Patrick's Creed as recorded in his Confessions, and nothing to reject except the word 'soon' in the statement that Christ will soon judge the quick and the dead. He can repeat it, believe it even, without a thought of the historic Christ, or ancient Judea, or of anything subject to historical conjecture and shifting evidence; I repeat it and think of 'the Self' in the Upanishads. Into this tradition, oral and written, went in later years fragments of Neo-Platonism, cabbalistic words—I have heard the words 'tetragrammaton agla' in Doneraile—the floating debris of mediaeval thought, but nothing that did not please the solitary mind. Even the religious equivalent for Baroque and Rococo could not come to us as thought, perhaps because Gaelic is incapable of abstraction. It came as cruelty. That tapestry filled the scene at the birth of modern Irish literature, it is there in the Synge of *The Well of the Saints,* in James Stephens, and in Lady Gregory throughout, in all of George Russell that did not come from the Upanishads, and in all but my later poetry.

Sometimes I am told in commendation, if the newspaper is Irish, in condemnation if English, that my movement perished under the firing squads of 1916; sometimes that those firing squads made our realistic movement possible. If that statement is true, and it is only so in part, for romance was everywhere receding, it is because in the imagination of Pearse and his fellow soldiers the Sacrifice of the Mass had found the Red Branch in the tapestry; they went out to die calling upon Cuchulain:—

Fall, Hercules, from Heaven in tempests hurled
To cleanse the beastly stable of this world.

In one sense the poets of 1916 were not of what the newspapers call my school. The Gaelic League, made timid by a modern popularisation of Catholicism sprung from the aspidistra and not from the root of Jesse, dreaded intellectual daring and stuck to dictionary and grammar. Pearse and MacDonagh and others among the executed men would have done, or attempted, in Gaelic what we did or attempted in English.

Our mythology, our legends, differ from those of other European countries because down to the end of the seventeenth century they had the attention, perhaps the unquestioned belief, of peasant and noble alike; Homer belongs to sedentary men, even to-day our ancient queens, our mediaeval soldiers and lovers, can make a pedlar shudder. I can put my own thought, despair perhaps from the study of present circumstance in the light of ancient philosophy, into the mouth of rambling poets of the seventeenth century, or even of some imagined ballad singer of to-day, and the deeper my thought the more credible, the more peasant-like, are ballad singer and rambling poet. Some modern poets contend that jazz and music-hall songs are the folk art of our time, that we should mould our art upon them; we Irish poets, modern men also, reject every folk art that does not go back to Olympus. Give me time and a little youth and I will prove that even 'Johnny, I hardly knew ye' goes back.

Mr. Arnold Toynbee in an annex to the second volume of *The Study of History* describes the birth and decay of what he calls the Far Western Christian culture; it lost at the Synod of Whitby its chance of mastering Europe, suffered final ecclesiastical defeat in the twelfth century with 'the thoroughgoing incorporation of the Irish Christendom into the Roman Church. In the political and literary spheres' it lasted unbroken till the seventeenth century. He then insists that if 'Jewish Zionism and Irish Nationalism succeed in achieving their aims, then Jewry and Irishry will each fit into its own tiny niche . . . among sixty or seventy national communities', find life somewhat easier, but cease to be 'the relic of an independent society . . . the romance of Ancient Ireland has at last come to an end . . . Modern Ireland has made up her mind, in our generation, to find her level as a willing inmate in our workaday Western world.'

If Irish literature goes on as my generation planned it, it may do something to keep the 'Irishry' living, nor will the work of the realists hinder, nor the figures they imagine, nor those described in memoirs of the revolution. These last especially, like certain great political predecessors, Parnell, Swift, Lord Edward, have stepped back into the tapestry. It may be indeed that certain characteristics of the 'Irishry' must grow in importance. When Lady Gregory asked me to annotate her *Visions and Beliefs* I began, that I might understand what she had taken down in Galway, an investigation of contemporary spiritualism. For several years I frequented those mediums who in various poor parts of London instruct artisans or their wives for a few pence upon their relations to their dead, to their employers, and to their children; then I compared what she had heard in Galway, or I in London, with the visions of Swedenborg, and, after my inadequate notes had been published, with Indian belief. If Lady Gregory had not said when we passed an old man in the woods, 'That man may know the secret of the

ages,' I might never have talked with Shri Purohit Swámi nor made
him translate his Master's travels in Tibet, nor helped him translate
the Upanishads. I think I now know why the gamekeeper at Coole
heard the footsteps of a deer on the edge of the lake where no deer
had passed for a hundred years, and why a certain cracked old
priest said that nobody had been to hell or heaven in his time, mean-
ing thereby that the Rath had got them all; that the dead stayed
where they had lived, or near it, sought no abstract region of blessing
or punishment but retreated, as it were, into the hidden character
of their neighbourhood. I am convinced that in two or three genera-
tions it will become generally known that the mechanical theory
has no reality, that the natural and supernatural are knit together,
that to escape a dangerous fanaticism we must study a new science;
at that moment Europeans may find something attractive in a
Christ posed against a background not of Judaism but of Druidism,
not shut off in dead history, but flowing, concrete, phenomenal.

I was born into this faith, have lived in it, and shall die in it;
my Christ, a legitimate deduction from the Creed of St. Patrick as
I think, is that Unity of Being Dante compared to a perfectly pro-
portioned human body, Blake's 'Imagination,' what the Upanishads
have named 'Self': nor is this unity distant and therefore intellec-
tually understandable, but imminent, differing from man to man
and age to age, taking upon itself pain and ugliness, 'eye of newt,
and toe of frog.'

Subconscious preoccupation with this theme brought me *A
Vision,* its harsh geometry an incomplete interpretation. The
'Irishry' have preserved their ancient 'deposit' through wars which,
during the sixteenth and seventeenth centuries, became wars of
extermination; no people, Lecky said at the opening of his *Ireland
in the Eighteenth Century,* have undergone greater persecution, nor
did that persecution altogether cease up to our own day. No people
hate as we do in whom that past is always alive, there are moments
when hatred poisons my life and I accuse myself of effeminacy be-
cause I have not given it adequate expression. It is not enough to
have put it into the mouth of a rambling peasant poet. Then I re-
mind myself that though mine is the first English marriage I know
of in the direct line, all my family names are English, and that I
owe my soul to Shakespeare, to Spenser and to Blake, perhaps to
William Morris, and to the English language in which I think, speak,
and write, that everything I love has come to me through English;
my hatred tortures me with love, my love with hate. I am like the

Tibetan monk who dreams at his initiation that he is eaten by a wild beast and learns on waking that he himself is eater and eaten. This is Irish hatred and solitude, the hatred of human life that made Swift write *Gulliver* and the epitaph upon his tomb, that can still make us wag between extremes and doubt our sanity.

Again and again I am asked why I do not write in Gaelic. Some four or five years ago I was invited to dinner by a London society and found myself among London journalists, Indian students, and foreign political refugees. An Indian paper says it was a dinner in my honour; I hope not; I have forgotten, though I have a clear memory of my own angry mind. I should have spoken as men are expected to speak at public dinners; I should have paid and been paid conventional compliments; then they would speak of the refugees; from that on all would be lively and topical, foreign tyranny would be arraigned, England seem even to those confused Indians the protector of liberty; I grew angrier and angrier; Wordsworth, that typical Englishman, had published his famous sonnet to François Dominique Toussaint, a Santo Domingo Negro:—

There's not a breathing of the common wind
That will forget thee

in the year when Emmet conspired and died, and he remembered that rebellion as little as the half hanging and the pitch cap that preceded it by half a dozen years. That there might be no topical speeches I denounced the oppression of the people of India; being a man of letters, not a politician, I told how they had been forced to learn everything, even their own Sanskrit, through the vehicle of English till the first discoverer of wisdom had become bywords for vague abstract facility. I begged the Indian writers present to remember that no man can think or write with music and vigour except in his mother tongue. I turned a friendly audience hostile, yet when I think of that scene I am unrepentant and angry.

I could no more have written Gaelic than can those Indians write in English; Gaelic is my national language, but it is not my mother tongue.

III. STYLE AND ATTITUDE

Style is almost unconscious. I know what I have tried to do, little what I have done. Contemporary lyric poems, even those that moved me—*The Stream's Secret, Dolores*—seemed too long, but an Irish preference for a swift current might be mere indolence, yet Burns may have felt the same when he read Thomson and Cowper. The English mind is meditative, rich, deliberate; it may remember the Thames valley. I planned to write short lyrics or poetic drama where every speech would be short and concentrated, knit by dramatic tension, and I did so with more confidence because young English poets were at that time writing out of emotion at the moment of crisis, though their old slow-moving meditation returned almost at once. Then, and in this English poetry has followed my lead, I tried to make the language of poetry coincide with that of passionate, normal speech. I wanted to write in whatever language comes most naturally when we soliloquise, as I do all day long, upon the events of our own lives or of any life where we can see ourselves for the moment. I sometimes compare myself with the mad old slum women I hear denouncing and remembering; 'How dare you,' I heard one say of some imaginary suitor, 'and you without health or a home!' If I spoke my thoughts aloud they might be as angry and as wild. It was a long time before I had made a language to my liking; I began to make it when I discovered some twenty years ago that I must seek, not as Wordsworth thought, words in common use, but a powerful and passionate syntax, and a complete coincidence between period and stanza. Because I need a passionate syntax for passionate subject-matter I compel myself to accept those traditional metres that have developed with the language. Ezra Pound, Turner, Lawrence wrote admirable free verse, I could not. I would lose myself, become joyless like those mad old women. The translators of the Bible, Sir Thomas Browne, certain translators from the Greek when translators still bothered about rhythm, created a form midway between prose and verse that seems natural to impersonal meditation; but all that is personal soon rots; it must be packed in ice or salt. Once when I was in delirium from pneumonia I dictated a letter to George Moore telling him to eat salt because it was a symbol of eternity; the delirium passed, I had no memory of that letter, but I must have meant what I now mean. If I wrote of personal love or sorrow in free verse, or in any rhythm that left it unchanged, amid all its accidence, I would be full of self-contempt because of my egotism and indiscretion, and foresee the boredom of my reader. I must choose a traditional stanza, even what I alter must seem traditional. I commit my emotion to shepherds, herdsmen, camel-drivers, learned men, Milton's

or Shelley's Platonist, that tower Palmer drew. Talk to me of origi-
nality and I will turn on you with rage. I am a crowd, I am a lonely
man, I am nothing. Ancient salt is best packing. The heroes of
Shakespeare convey to us through their looks, or through the
metaphorical patterns of their speech, the sudden enlargement of
their vision, their ecstasy at the approach of death: 'She should
have died hereafter,' 'Of many thousand kisses, the poor last,' 'Ab-
sent thee from felicity awhile.' They have become God or Mother
Goddess, the pelican, 'My baby at my breast,' but all must be cold;
no actress has ever sobbed when she played Cleopatra, even the
shallow brain of a producer has never thought of such a thing.
The supernatural is present, cold winds blow across our hands, upon
our faces, the thermometer falls, and because of that cold we are
hated by journalists and groundlings. There may be in this or that
detail painful tragedy, but in the whole work none. I have heard
Lady Gregory say, rejecting some play in the modern manner sent
to the Abbey Theatre, 'Tragedy must be a joy to the man who dies.'
Nor is it any different with lyrics, songs, narrative poems; neither
scholars nor the populace have sung or read anything generation
after generation because of its pain. The maid of honour whose
tragedy they sing must be lifted out of history with timeless pattern,
she is one of the four Maries, the rhythm is old and familiar, imagi-
nation must dance, must be carried beyond feeling into the ab-
original ice. Is ice the correct word? I once boasted, copying the
phrase from a letter of my father's, that I would write a poem 'cold
and passionate as the dawn.'

When I wrote in blank verse I was dissatisfied; my vaguely
mediaeval *Countess Cathleen* fitted the measure, but our Heroic
Age went better, or so I fancied, in the ballad metre of *The Green
Helmet*. There was something in what I felt about Deirdre, about
Cuchulain, that rejected the Renaissance and its characteristic
metres, and this was a principal reason why I created in dance
plays the form that varies blank verse with lyric metres. When I
speak blank verse and analyse my feelings, I stand at a moment of
history when instinct, its traditional songs and dances, its general
agreement, is of the past. I have been cast up out of the whale's
belly though I still remember the sound and sway that came from
beyond its ribs, and, like the Queen in Paul Fort's ballad, I smell
of the fish of the sea. The contrapuntal structure of the verse, to
employ a term adopted by Robert Bridges, combines the past and
present. If I repeat the first line of *Paradise Lost* so as to emphasise

its five feet I am among the folk singers—'Of mán's first dísobédience ánd the frúit,' but speak it as I should I cross it with another emphasis, that of passionate prose—'Of mán's fírst disobédience and the frúit,' or 'Of mán's fírst dísobedience and the frúit'; the folk song is still there, but a ghostly voice, an unvariable possibility, an unconscious norm. What moves me and my hearer is a vivid speech that has no laws except that it must not exorcise the ghostly voice. I am awake and asleep, at my moment of revelation, self-possessed in self-surrender; there is no rhyme, no echo of the beaten drum, the dancing foot, that would overset my balance. When I was a boy I wrote a poem upon dancing that had one good line: 'They snatch with their hands at the sleep of the skies.' If I sat down and thought for a year I would discover that but for certain syllabic limitations, a rejection or acceptance of certain elisions, I must wake or sleep.

The Countess Cathleen could speak a blank verse which I had loosened, almost put out of joint, for her need, because I thought of her as mediaeval and thereby connected her with the general European movement. For Deirdre and Cuchulain and all the other figures of Irish legend are still in the whale's belly.

IV.   WHITHER?

The young English poets reject dream and personal emotion; they have thought out opinions that join them to this or that political party; they employ an intricate psychology, action in character, not as in the ballads character in action, and all consider that they have a right to the same close attention that men pay to the mathematician and the metaphysician. One of the more distinguished has just explained that man has hitherto slept but must now awake. They are determined to express the factory, the metropolis, that they may be modern. Young men teaching school in some picturesque cathedral town, or settled for life in Capri or in Sicily, defend their type of metaphor by saying that it comes naturally to a man who travels to his work by Tube. I am indebted to a man of this school who went through my work at my request, crossing out all conventional metaphors, but they seem to me to have rejected also those dream associations which were the whole art of Mallarmé. He had topped a previous wave. As they express not what the Upanishads call "that ancient Self" but individual intellect, they have the right to choose the man in the Tube because of his objective importance. They attempt to kill the whale, push the Renaissance higher yet, out-think Leonardo; their verse kills the folk ghost and yet would remain verse. I am joined to the 'Irishry' and I expect a counter-Renaissance. No doubt it is part of the game to push that Renaissance; I make no complaint; I am accustomed to the geometrical arrangement of history in *A Vision,* but I go deeper than 'custom' for my convictions. When I stand upon O'Connell Bridge in the half-light and notice that discordant architecture, all those electric signs, where modern heterogeneity has taken physical form, a vague hatred comes up out of my own dark and I am certain that wherever in Europe there are minds strong enough to lead others the same vague hatred rises; in four or five or in less generations this hatred will have issued in violence and imposed some kind of rule of kindred. I cannot know the nature of that rule, for its opposite fills the light; all I can do to bring it nearer is to intensify my hatred. I am no Nationalist, except in Ireland for passing reasons; State and Nation are the work of intellect, and when you consider what comes before and after them they are, as Victor Hugo said of something or other, not worth the blade of grass God gives for the nest of the linnet.

1937

Ezra Pound

"To break the pentameter, that was the first heave"—but only one of the many destructions that permitted Ezra Pound to reform the features of modern poetry. And his speech, archaic or immediately colloquial, shoulders its way through the fixations of traditional English metrics. The syntax is natural, if discontinuous, but the logical progression of his thought is often riddled with ellipses, a fact prompting him to be obliquely repetitive; as in the "Jamesian parenthesis: you realize that the person you are talking to hasn't got the different steps, and you go back over them." In contemporary life, the absence of a common cultural ground occasions "the struggle that one has, when one meets another man who has had a lot of experience, to find the point where the two experiences touch, so that he really knows what you are talking about."

Pound's notions of language have been oriented, or at least corroborated, by the Chinese ideogram, which is in effect "a vivid shorthand picture of the operations of nature." As an early sponsor of Imagism, a seminal movement in modern poetry, he had presented natural symbols, or words corresponding to things, without embroidering them with commentary and regardless of whether those "things" were moving or static, objective or subjective. By extension, such theories and practices passed into the ideogrammatic method of the Cantos, *a work of epic proportions, where "the juxtaposition of scenes, images, episodes . . . sparks off an abstract idea." An objective reality has a complex or complicated significance; and a single historical personage may represent, as G. S. Fraser expresses it, "a whole cluster of attitudes."*

Born "in a half savage country, out of date"—Hailey, Idaho, on October 30, 1885—Pound, despite his languages, remains the classicist who casts about "for the least possible variant that would turn the most worn-out and commonest phrases of journalism into something distinguished." That is, he pares the fuzz off our daily idiom. His search for an efficient, accurate language, for an expression proportionate to its meaning, is intended to reflect the larger quest for civilization, for permanence, for a social order beyond the pale of egoism.

A Retrospect*

There has been so much scribbling about a new fashion in poetry, that I may perhaps be pardoned this brief recapitulation and retrospect.

In the spring or early summer of 1912, 'H. D.', Richard Aldington and myself decided that we were agreed upon the three principles following:

1. Direct treatment of the 'thing' whether subjective or objective.

2. To use absolutely no word that does not contribute to the presentation.

3. As regarding rhythm: to compose in the sequence of the musical phrase, not in sequence of a metronome.

Upon many points of taste and of predilection we differed, but

---

* **A group of early essays and notes which appeared under this title in** *Pavannes and Divisions* **(1918). 'A Few Don'ts' was first printed in** *Poetry,* **I: 6 (March, 1913). From** *The Literary Essays of Ezra Pound.*

agreeing upon these three positions we thought we had as much right to a group name, at least as much right, as a number of French 'schools' proclaimed by Mr. Flint in the August number of Harold Monro's magazine for 1911.

This school has since been 'joined' or 'followed' by numerous people who, whatever their merits, do not show any signs of agreeing with the second specification. Indeed *vers libre* has become as prolix and as verbose as any of the flaccid varieties that preceded it. It has brought faults of its own. The actual language and phrasing is often as bad as that of our elders without even the excuse that the words are shovelled in to fill a metric pattern or to complete the noise of a rhyme-sound. Whether or no the phrases followed by the followers are musical must be left to the reader's decision. At times I can find a marked metre in 'vers libres', as stale and hackneyed as any pseudo-Swinburnian, at times the writers seem to follow no musical structure whatever. But it is, on the whole, good that the field should be ploughed. Perhaps a few good poems have come from the new method, and if so it is justified.

Criticism is not a circumscription or a set of prohibitions. It provides fixed points of departure. It may startle a dull reader into alertness. That little of it which is good is mostly in stray phrases; or if it be an older artist helping a younger it is in great measure but rules of thumb, cautions gained by experience.

I set together a few phrases on practical working about the time the first remarks on imagisme were published. The first use of the word 'Imagiste' was in my note to T. E. Hulme's five poems, printed at the end of my 'Ripostes' in the autumn of 1912. I reprint my cautions from *Poetry* for March, 1913.

A FEW DON'TS

An 'Image' is that which presents an intellectual and emotional complex in an instant of time. I use the term 'complex' rather in the technical sense employed by the newer psychologists, such as Hart, though we might not agree absolutely in our application.

It is the presentation of such a 'complex' instantaneously which gives that sense of sudden liberation; that sense of freedom from time limits and space limits; that sense of sudden growth, which we experience in the presence of the greatest works of art.

It is better to present one Image in a lifetime than to produce voluminous works.

All this, however, some may consider open to debate. The

immediate necessity is to tabulate A LIST OF DON'TS for those beginning to write verses. I can not put all of them into Mosaic negative.

To begin with, consider the three propositions (demanding direct treatment, economy of words, and the sequence of the musical phrase), not as dogma—never consider anything as dogma—but as the result of long contemplation, which, even if it is some one else's contemplation, may be worth consideration.

Pay no attention to the criticism of men who have never themselves written a notable work. Consider the discrepancies between the actual writing of the Greek poets and dramatists, and the theories of the Graeco-Roman grammarians, concocted to explain their metres.

LANGUAGE

Use no superfluous word, no adjective which does not reveal something.

Don't use such an expression as 'dim lands *of peace*'. It dulls the image. It mixes an abstraction with the concrete. It comes from the writer's not realizing that the natural object is always the *adequate* symbol.

Go in fear of abstractions. Do not retell in mediocre verse what has already been done in good prose. Don't think any intelligent person is going to be deceived when you try to shirk all the difficulties of the unspeakably difficult art of good prose by chopping your composition into line lengths.

What the expert is tired of today the public will be tired of tomorrow.

Don't imagine that the art of poetry is any simpler than the art of music, or that you can please the expert before you have spent at least as much effort on the art of verse as the average piano teacher spends on the art of music.

Be influenced by as many great artists as you can, but have the decency either to acknowledge the debt outright, or to try to conceal it.

Don't allow "influence' to mean merely that you mop up the particular decorative vocabulary of some one or two poets whom you happen to admire. A Turkish war correspondent was recently caught red-handed babbling in his despatches of 'dove-grey' hills, or else it was 'pearl-pale', I can not remember.

Use either no ornament or good ornament.

RHYTHM AND RHYME

Let the candidate fill his mind with the finest cadences he can discover, preferably in a foreign language,[1] so that the meaning of the words may be less likely to divert his attention from the movement; e.g. Saxon charms, Hebridean Folk Songs, the verse of Dante, and the lyrics of Shakespeare—if he can dissociate the vocabulary from the cadence. Let him dissect the lyrics of Goethe coldly into their component sound values, syllables long and short, stressed and unstressed, into vowels and consonants.

It is not necessary that a poem should rely on its music, but if it does rely on its music that music must be such as will delight the expert.

Let the neophyte know assonance and alliteration, rhyme immediate and delayed, simple and polyphonic, as a musician would expect to know harmony and counterpoint and all the minutiae of his craft. No time is too great to give to these matters or to any one of them, even if the artist seldom have need of them.

Don't imagine that a thing will 'go' in verse just because it's too dull to go in prose.

Don't be 'viewy'—leave that to the writers of pretty little philosophic essays. Don't be descriptive; remember that the painter can describe a landscape much better than you can, and that he has to know a deal more about it.

When Shakespeare talks of the 'Dawn in russet mantle clad' he presents something which the painter does not present. There is in this line of his nothing that one can call description; he presents.

Consider the way of the scientists rather than the way of an advertising agent for a new soap.

The scientist does not expect to be acclaimed as a great scientist until he has *discovered* something. He begins by learning what has been discovered already. He goes from that point onward. He does not bank on being a charming fellow personally. He does not expect his friends to applaud the results of his freshman class work. Freshmen in poetry are unfortunately not confined to a definite and recognizable class room. They are 'all over the shop'. Is it any wonder 'the public is indifferent to poetry?'

Don't chop your stuff into separate *iambs*. Don't make each line stop dead at the end, and then begin every next line with a

---

[1] This is for rhythm, his vocabulary must of course be found in his native tongue.

heave. Let the beginning of the next line catch the rise of the rhythm wave, unless you want a definite longish pause.

In short, behave as a musician, a good musician, when dealing with that phase of your art which has exact parallels in music. The same laws govern, and you are bound by no others.

Naturally, your rhythmic structure should not destroy the shape of your words, or their natural sound, or their meaning. It is improbable that, at the start, you will be able to get a rhythm-structure strong enough to affect them very much, though you may fall a victim to all sorts of false stopping due to line ends and cæsurae.

The Musician can rely on pitch and the volume of the orchestra. You can not. The term harmony is misapplied in poetry; it refers to simultaneous sounds of different pitch. There is, however, in the best verse a sort of residue of sound which remains in the ear of the hearer and acts more or less as an organ-base.

A rhyme must have in it some slight element of surprise if it is to give pleasure; it need not be bizarre or curious, but it must be well used if used at all.

Vide further Vildrac and Duhamel's notes on rhyme in *'Technique Poétique'*.

That part of your poetry which strikes upon the imaginative *eye* of the reader will lose nothing by translation into a foreign tongue; that which appeals to the ear can reach only those who take it in the original.

Consider the definiteness of Dante's presentation, as compared with Milton's rhetoric. Read as much of Wordsworth as does not seem too unutterably dull.[2]

If you want the gist of the matter go to Sappho, Catullus, Villon, Heine when he is in the vein, Gautier when he is not too frigid; or, if you have not the tongues, seek out the leisurely Chaucer. Good prose will do you no harm, and there is good discipline to be had by trying to write it.

Translation is likewise good training, if you find that your original matter 'wobbles' when you try to rewrite it. The meaning of the poem to be translated can not 'wobble.'

If you are using a symmetrical form, don't put in what you want to say and then fill up the remaining vacuums with slush.

Don't mess up the perception of one sense by trying to define

---

[2] Vide infra.

it in terms of another. This is usually only the result of being too lazy to find the exact word. To this clause there are possibly exceptions.

The first three simple prescriptions will throw out nine-tenths of all the bad poetry now accepted as standard and classic; and will prevent you from many a crime of production.

'. . . *Mais d'abord il faut être un poète*', as MM. Duhamel and Vildrac have said at the end of their little book, *'Notes sur la Technique Poétique.'*

Since March 1913, Ford Madox Hueffer has pointed out that Wordsworth was so intent on the ordinary or plain word that he never thought of hunting for *le mot juste*.

John Butler Yeats has handled or man-handled Wordsworth and the Victorians, and his criticism, contained in letters to his son, is now printed and available.

I do not like writing *about* art, my first, at least I think it was my first essay on the subject, was a protest against it.

PROLEGOMENA[3]

Time was when the poet lay in a green field with his head against a tree and played his diversion on a ha'penny whistle, and Caesar's predecessors conquered the earth, and the predecessors of golden Crassus embezzled, and fashions had their say, and let him alone. And presumably he was fairly content in this circumstance, for I have small doubt that the occasional passerby, being attracted by curiosity to know why any one should lie under a tree and blow diversion on a ha'penny whistle, came and conversed with him, and that among these passers-by there was on occasion a person of charm or a young lady who had not read *Man and Superman;* and looking back upon this naïve state of affairs we call it the age of gold.

Metastasio, and he should know if any one, assures us that this age endures—even though the modern poet is expected to holloa his verses down a speaking tube to the editors of cheap magazines—S. S. McClure, or some one of that sort—even though hordes of authors meet in dreariness and drink healths to the 'Copyright Bill'; even though these things be, the age of gold pertains.

---

[3] *Poetry and Drama* (then the *Poetry Review,* edited by Harold Monro), Feb. 1912.

Imperceivably, if you like, but pertains. You meet unkempt Amyclas in a Soho restaurant and chant together of dead and forgotten things—it is a manner of speech among poets to chant of dead, half-forgotten things, there seems no special harm in it; it has always been done—and it's rather better to be a clerk in the Post Office than to look after a lot of stinking, verminous sheep—and at another hour of the day one substitutes the drawing-room for the restaurant and tea is probably more palatable than mead and mare's milk, and little cakes than honey. And in this fashion one survives the resignation of Mr Balfour, and the iniquities of the American customs-house, *e quel bufera infernal,* the periodical press. And then in the middle of it, there being apparently no other person at once capable and available one is stopped and asked to explain oneself.

I begin on the chord thus querulous, for I would much rather lie on what is left of Catullus' parlour floor and speculate the azure beneath it and the hills off to Salo and Riva with their forgotten gods moving unhindered amongst them, than discuss any processes and theories of art whatsover. I would rather play tennis. I shall not argue.

CREDO

Rhythm.—I believe in an 'absolute rhythm', a rhythm, that is, in poetry which corresponds exactly to the emotion or shade of emotion to be expressed. A man's rhythm must be interpretative, it will be, therefore, in the end, his own, uncounterfeiting, uncounterfeitable.

Symbols.—I believe that the proper and perfect symbol is the natural object, that if a man use 'symbols' he must so use them that their symbolic function does not obtrude; so that *a* sense, and the poetic quality of the passage, is not lost to those who do not understand the symbol as such, to whom, for instance, a hawk is a hawk.

Technique.—I believe in technique as the test of a man's sincerity; in law when it is ascertainable; in the trampling down of every convention that impedes or obscures the determination of the law, or the precise rendering of the impulse.

Form.—I think there is a 'fluid' as well as a 'solid' content, that some poems may have form as a tree has form, some as water poured into a vase. That most symmetrical forms have certain uses.

That a vast number of subjects cannot be precisely, and therefore not properly rendered in symmetrical forms.

'Thinking that alone worthy wherein the whole art is employed'.[4] I think the artist should master all known forms and systems of metric, and I have with some persistence set about doing this, searching particularly into those periods wherein the systems came to birth or attained their maturity. It has been complained, with some justice, that I dump my note-books on the public. I think that only after a long struggle will poetry attain such a degree of development, or, if you will, modernity, that it will vitally concern people who are accustomed, in prose, to Henry James and Anatole France, in music to Debussy. I am constantly contending that it took two centuries of Provence and one of Tuscany to develop the media of Dante's masterwork, that it took the latinists of the Renaissance, and the Pleiade, and his own age of painted speech to prepare Shakespeare his tools. It is tremendously important that great poetry be written, it makes no jot of difference who writes it. The experimental demonstrations of one man may save the time of many—hence my furore over Arnaut Daniel—if a man's experiments try out one new rime, or dispense conclusively with one iota of currently accepted nonsense, he is merely playing fair with his colleagues when he chalks up his result.

No man ever writes very much poetry that 'matters.' In bulk, that is, no one produces much that is final, and when a man is not doing this highest thing, this saying the thing once for all and perfectly; when he is not matching Ποικιλόθρον', ἀθάνατ' 'Αφρόδιτα,[5] or 'Hist—said Kate the Queen', he had much better be making the sorts of experiment which may be of use to him in his later work, or to his successors.

'The lyf so short, the craft so long to lerne.' It is a foolish thing for a man to begin his work on a too narrow foundation, it is a disgraceful thing for a man's work not to show steady growth and increasing fineness from first to last.

As for 'adaptations'; one finds that all the old masters of painting recommend to their pupils that they begin by copying masterwork, and proceed to their own composition.

As for 'Every man his own poet', the more every man knows about poetry the better. I believe in every one writing poetry

---

4 Dante, *De Volgari Eloquio*.

5 ["Splendid-throned, deathless Aphrodite": the opening line of Sappho's famous invocation.]

who wants to; most do. I believe in every man knowing enough of music to play 'God bless our home' on the harmonium, but I do not believe in every man giving concerts and printing his sin. The mastery of any art is the work of a lifetime. I should not discriminate between the 'amateur' and the 'professional'. Or rather I should discriminate quite often in favour of the amateur, but I should discriminate between the amateur and the expert. It is certain that the present chaos will endure until the Art of poetry has been preached down the amateur gullet, until there is such a general understanding of the fact that poetry is an art and not a pastime; such a knowledge of technique; of technique of surface and technique of content, that the amateurs will cease to try to drown out the masters.

If a certain thing was said once for all in Atlantis or Arcadia, in 450 Before Christ or in 1290 after, it is not for us moderns to go saying it over, or to go obscuring the memory of the dead by saying the same thing with less skill and less conviction.

My pawing over the ancients and semi-ancients has been one struggle to find out what has been done, once for all, better than it can ever be done again, and to find out what remains for us to do, and plenty does remain, for if we still feel the same emotions as those which launched the thousand ships, it is quite certain that we come on these feelings differently, through different nuances, by different intellectual gradations. Each age has its own abounding gifts yet only some ages transmute them into matter of duration. No good poetry is ever written in a manner twenty years old, for to write in such a manner shows conclusively that the writer thinks from books, convention and *cliché,* and not from life, yet a man feeling the divorce of life and his art may naturally try to resurrect a forgotten mode if he finds in that mode some leaven, or if he think he sees in it some element lacking in contemporary art which might unite that art again to its sustenance, life.

In the art of Daniel and Cavalcanti, I have seen that precision which I miss in the Victorians, that explicit rendering, be it of external nature, or of emotion. Their testimony is of the eyewitness, their symptoms are first hand.

As for the nineteenth century, with all respect to its achievements, I think we shall look back upon it as a rather blurry, messy sort of a period, a rather sentimentalistic, mannerish sort of a period. I say this without any self-righteousness, with no self-satisfaction.

As for there being a 'movement' or my being of it, the conception of poetry as a 'pure art' in the sense in which I use the term, revived with Swinburne. From the puritanical revolt to Swinburne, poetry had been merely the vehicle—yes, definitely, Arthur Symon's scruples and feelings about the word not withholding—the ox-cart and post-chaise for transmitting thoughts poetic or otherwise. And perhaps the 'great Victorians', though it is doubtful, and assuredly the 'nineties' continued the development of the art, confining their improvements, however, chiefly to sound and to refinements of manner.

Mr Yeats has once and for all stripped English poetry of its perdamnable rhetoric. He has boiled away all that is not poetic—and a good deal that is. He has become a classic in his own lifetime and *nel mezzo del cammin*. He has made our poetic idiom a thing pliable, a speech without inversions.

Robert Bridges, Maurice Hewlett and Frederic Manning are[6] in their different ways seriously concerned with overhauling the metric, in testing the language and its adaptability to certain modes. Ford Hueffer is making some sort of experiments in modernity. The Provost of Oriel continues his translation of the *Divina Commedia*.

As to Twentieth century poetry, and the poetry which I expect to see written during the next decade or so, it will, I think, move against poppy-cock, it will be harder and saner, it will be what Mr Hewlett calls 'nearer the bone'. It will be as much like granite as it can be, its force will lie in its truth, its interpretative power (of course, poetic force does always rest there); I mean it will not try to seem forcible by rhetorical din, and luxurious riot. We will have fewer painted adjectives impeding the shock and stroke of it. At least for myself, I want it so, austere, direct, free from emotional slither.

What is there now, in 1917, to be added?

RE VERS LIBRE

I think the desire for vers libre is due to the sense of quantity reasserting itself after years of starvation. But I doubt if we can take over, for English, the rules of quantity laid down for Greek and Latin, mostly by Latin grammarians.

---

[6] (Dec. 1911).

I think one should write vers libre only when one 'must', that is to say, only when the 'thing' builds up a rhythm more beautiful than that of set metres, or more real, more a part of the emotion of the 'thing', more germane, intimate, interpretative than the measure of regular accentual verse; a rhythm which discontents one with set iambic or set anapæstic.

Eliot has said the thing very well when he said, 'No *vers* is *libre* for the man who wants to do a good job.'

As a matter of detail, there is vers libre with accent heavily marked as a drum-beat (as par example my 'Dance Figure'), and on the other hand I think I have gone as far as can profitably be gone in the other direction (and perhaps too far). I mean I do not think one can use to any advantage rhythms much more tenuous and imperceptible than some I have used. I think progress lies rather in an attempt to approximate classical quantitative metres (NOT to copy them) than in a carelessness regarding such things.[7]

I agree with John Yeats on the relation of beauty to certitude. I prefer satire, which is due to emotion, to any sham of emotion.

I have had to write, or at least I have written a good deal about art, sculpture, painting and poetry. I have seen what seemed to me the best of contemporary work reviled and obstructed. Can any one write prose of permanent or durable interest when he is merely saying for one year what nearly every one will say at the end of three or four years? I have been battistrada for a sculptor, a painter, a novelist, several poets. I wrote also of certain French writers in *The New Age* in nineteen twelve or eleven.

I would much rather that people would look at Brzeska's sculpture and Lewis's drawings, and that they would read Joyce, Jules Romains, Eliot, than that they should read what I have said of these men, or that I should be asked to republish argumentative essays and reviews.

All that the critic can do for the reader or audience or spectator is to focus his gaze or audition. Rightly or wrongly I think my blasts and essays have done their work, and that more people are now likely to go to the sources than are likely to read this book.

Jammes's 'Existences' in *'La Triomphe de la Vie'* is available. So are his early poems. I think we need a convenient anthology rather than descriptive criticism. Carl Sandburg wrote me from Chicago, 'It's hell when poets can't afford to buy each other's

---

[7] Let me date this statement 20 Aug. 1917.

books.' Half the people who care, only borrow. In America so few people know each other that the difficulty lies more than half in distribution. Perhaps one should make an anthology: Romains's 'Un Etre en Marche' and 'Prières', Vildrac's 'Visite'. Retrospectively the fine wrought work of Laforgue, the flashes of Rimbaud, the hard-bit lines of Tristan Corbière, Tailhade's sketches in 'Poèmes Aristophanesques', the 'Litanies' of De Gourmont.

It is difficult at all times to write of the fine arts, it is almost impossible unless one can accompany one's prose with many reproductions. Still I would seize this chance or any chance to reaffirm my belief in Wyndham Lewis's genius, both in his drawings and his writings. And I would name an out of the way prose book, the *'Scenes and Portraits'* of Frederic Manning, as well as James Joyce's short stories and novel, 'Dubliners' and the now well known 'Portrait of the Artist' as well as Lewis' 'Tarr', if, that is, I may treat my strange reader as if he were a new friend come into the room, intent on ransacking my bookshelf.

ONLY EMOTION ENDURES

'Only emotion endures.' Surely it is better for me to name over the few beautiful poems that still ring in my head than for me to search my flat for back numbers of periodicals and rearrange all that I have said about friendly and hostile writers.

The first twelve lines of Padraic Colum's 'Drover'; his 'O Woman shapely as a swan, on your account I shall not die'; Joyce's 'I hear an army'; the lines of Yeats that ring in my head and in the heads of all young men of my time who care for poetry: Braseal and the Fisherman, 'The fire that stirs about her when she stirs'; the later lines of 'The Scholars', the faces of the Magi; William Carlos Williams's 'Postlude', Aldington's version of 'Atthis', and 'H. D.'s' waves like pine tops, and her verse in 'Des Imagistes' the first anthology; Hueffer's 'How red your lips are' in his translation from Von der Vogelweide, his 'Three Ten', the general effect of his 'On Heaven'; his sense of the prose values or prose qualities in poetry; his ability to write poems that half-chant and are spoiled by a musician's additions; beyond these a poem by Alice Corbin, 'One City Only', and another ending 'But sliding water over a stone'. These things have worn smooth in my head and I am not through with them, nor with Aldington's 'In Via Sestina' nor his other poems in

'Des Imagistes', though people have told me their flaws. It may be that their content is too much embedded in me for me to look back at the words.

I am almost a different person when I come to take up the argument for Eliot's poems.

The Chinese Ideogram*

Fenollosa's essay was perhaps too far ahead of his time to be easily comprehended. He did not proclaim his method as a method. He was trying to explain the Chinese ideograph as a means of transmission and registration of thought. He got to the root of the matter, to the root of the difference between what is valid in Chinese thinking and invalid or misleading in a great deal of European thinking and language.

The simplest statement I can make of his meaning is as follows:

In Europe, if you ask a man to define anything, his definition always moves away from the simple things that he knows perfectly well, it recedes into an unknown region, that is a region of remoter and progressively remoter abstraction.

* From *ABC of Reading* by Ezra Pound. This is a summary statement of Professor Ernest Fenollosa's "The Chinese Written Character as a Medium for Poetry," an invaluable essay which was adopted and published, posthumously, by Pound.

Thus if you ask him what red is, he says it is a 'colour'.

If you ask him what a colour is, he tells you it is a vibration or a refraction of light, or a division of the spectrum.

And if you ask him what vibration is, he tells you it is a mode of energy, or something of that sort, until you arrive at a modality of being, or non-being, or at any rate you get in beyond your depth, and beyond his depth.

In the middle ages when there wasn't any material science, as we now understand it, when human knowledge could not make automobiles run, or electricity carry language through the air, etc., etc., in short, when learning consisted in little more than splitting up of terminology, there was a good deal of care for terminology, and the general exactitude in the use of abstract terms may have been (probably was) higher.

I mean a mediaeval theologian took care not to define a dog in terms that would have applied just as well to a dog's tooth or its hide, or the noise it makes when lapping water; but all your teachers will tell you that science developed more rapidly after Bacon had suggested the direct examination of phenomena, and after Galileo and others had stopped discussing things so much, and had begun really to look at them, and to invent means (like the telescope) of seeing them better.

The most useful living member of the Huxley family has emphasized the fact that the telescope wasn't merely an idea, but that it was very definitely a technical achievement.

By contrast to the method of abstraction, or of defining things in more and still more general terms, Fenollosa emphasizes the method of science, 'which is the method of poetry', as distinct from that of 'philosophic discussion', and is the way the Chinese go about it in their ideograph or abbreviated picture writing.

To go back to the beginning of history, you probably know that there is spoken language and written language, and that there are two kinds of written language, one based on sound and the other on sight.

You speak to an animal with a few simple noises and gestures. Levy-Bruhl's account of primitive languages in Africa records languages that are still bound up with mimicry and gesture.

The Egyptians finally used abbreviated pictures to represent sounds, but the Chinese still use abbreviated pictures AS pictures, that is to say, Chinese ideogram does not try to be the picture of a sound, or to be a written sign recalling a sound, but it is still the picture of a thing; of a thing in a given position or relation, or of a combination of things. It *means* the thing or the action or situation, or quality germane to the several things that it pictures.

Gaudier Brzeska, who was accustomed to looking at the real shape of things, could read a certain amount of Chinese writing without ANY STUDY. He said, 'Of course, you can *see* it's a horse' (or a wing or whatever).

In tables showing primitive Chinese characters in one column and the present 'conventionalized' signs in another, anyone can see how the ideogram for man or tree or sunrise developed, or 'was simplified from', or was reduced to the essentials of the first picture of man, tree or sunrise.

Thus

人   man

木   tree

日   sun

東   sun tangled in the tree's branches, as at sunrise, meaning
       now the East.

But when the Chinaman wanted to make a picture of something more complicated, or of a general idea, how did he go about it?

He is to define red. How can he do it in a picture that isn't painted in red paint?

He puts (or his ancestor put) together the abbreviated pictures of

    ROSE   CHERRY

  IRON RUST   FLAMINGO

That, you see, is very much the kind of thing a biologist does (in a very much more complicated way) when he gets together a few hundred or thousand slides, and picks out what is necessary for his general statement. Something that fits the case, that applies in all of the cases.

The Chinese 'word' or ideogram for red is based on something everyone KNOWS.

(If ideogram had developed in England, the writers would possibly have substituted the front side of a robin, or something less exotic than a flamingo.)

Fenollosa was telling how and why a language written in this way simply HAD TO STAY POETIC; simply couldn't help being and staying poetic in a way that a column of English type might very well not stay poetic.

He died before getting round to publishing and proclaiming a 'method'.

This is nevertheless the RIGHT WAY to study poetry, or literature, or painting. It is in fact the way the more intelligent members of the general public DO study painting. If you want to find out something about painting you go to the National Gallery, or the Salon Carré, or the Brera, or the Prado, and LOOK at the pictures.

For every reader of books on art, 1,000 people go to LOOK at the paintings. Thank heaven!

Robert Frost

*In calling Robert Frost "the quirky medium of so many truths,"
John Berryman commemorated the man's incorrigible caginess, as
well as the poet's findings. Basic and elusive, Frost claimed that he
wrote to keep "the over curious" out of the secret places of his
mind. This might be impertinent, though interesting, had he not
virtually apotheosized such diffidence into an aesthetic criterion.
Poetry becomes profound, by sleight of mind and tongue, as it
provides "the one permissible way of saying one thing and meaning
another."*

*Frost once described his poems as the unforced expression of
a life he was forced to live. The cruder the raw material, and the
more idiomatic the voice that talks it into shape, the better. As for
"poetical" tones: "You can get enough of those sentence tones
that suggest grandeur and sweetness everywhere in poetry. What
bothers people in my blank verse is that I have tried to see what
I could do with boasting tones and quizzical tones and shrugging
tones (for there are such) and forty eleven other tones. All I care
a cent for is to catch sentence tones that haven't been brought to*

book. I don't say to make them, mind you, but to catch them. No one makes them or adds to them. They are always there—living in the cave of the mouth. They are real cave things: they were before words were. And they are as definitely things as any image of sight." So phanopoeia, or image making, recedes before some age-old nuance that quickens the living voice. But before it may be metamorphosed into poetry, that voice must be counterpointed against a traditional metre, a sustaining ground rhythm: "there are the very regular preestablished accent and measure of blank verse, and there are the very irregular accent and measure of speaking intonation," the poet's pleasure being to "drag and break the intonation across the meter as waves first comb and then break stumbling on the shingle."

Determined never to take any "character's" side in anything he wrote, Frost thought that we would be judged, finally, "by the delicacy of our feeling of where to stop short." As would be true for any respecter of persons or epistemology, discretion is all. Even the beauty of metaphor is that it "breaks down somewhere;" poetry, indeed knowledge, keeps pace with one's ability to sense— and come to a tentative conclusion before—the point where disintegration actually occurs. Each poem is a daily walk with a cliff's-edge prospect toward the ending. "My poems," he wrote to an acquaintance, "are all set to trip the reader head foremost into the boundless. Ever since infancy I have had the habit of leaving my blocks carts chairs and such like ordinaries where people would be pretty sure to fall forward over them in the dark. Forward, you understand, and in the dark. I may leave my toys in the wrong place and so in vain. It is my intention we are speaking of—my innate mischievousness."

Robert Frost was born March 26, 1875, in San Francisco, California. He died in Boston, in the winter of 1963.

Sentence Sounds*

I want to write down here two or three cardinal principles that I wish you would think over and turn over now and again till we *can* protract talk.

I give you a new definition of a sentence:

A sentence is a sound in itself on which other sounds called words may be strung.

You may string words together without a sentence-sound to string them on just as you may tie clothes together by the sleeves and stretch them without a clothes line between two trees, but—it is bad for the clothes.

The number of words you may string on one sentence-sound is not fixed but there is always danger of over loading.

The sentence-sounds are very definite entities. (This is no

* **Portion of a letter from Robert Frost to John T. Bartlett reprinted from** *The Selected Letters of Robert Frost* **edited by Lawrance Thompson.**

literary mysticism I am preaching.) They are as definite as words. It is not impossible that they could be collected in a book though I don't at present see on what system they would be catalogued.

They are apprehended by the ear. They are gathered by the ear from the vernacular and brought into books. Many of them are already familiar to us in books. I think no writer invents them. The most original writer only catches them fresh from talk, where they grow spontaneously.

A man is all a writer if *all* his words are strung on definite recognizable sentence sounds. The voice of the imagination, the speaking voice must know certainly how to behave how to posture in every sentence he offers.

A man is a marked writer if his words are largely strung on the more striking sentence sounds.

A word about recognition: In literature it is our business to give people the thing that will make them say, "Oh yes I know what you mean." It is never to tell them something they dont know, but something they know and hadnt thought of saying. It must be something they recognize.

A PATCH OF OLD SNOW

In the corner of the wall where the bushes haven't been trimmed, there is a patch of old snow like a blow-away newspaper that has come to rest there. And it is dirty as with the print and news of a day I have forgotten, if I ever read it.

Now that is no good except for what I may call certain points of recognition in it: patch of old snow in a corner of the wall,— you know what that is. You know what a blow-away newspaper is. You know the curious dirt on old snow and last of all you know how easily you forget what you read in papers.

Now for the sentence sounds. We will look for the marked ones because they are easiest to discuss. The first sentence sound will do but it is merely ordinary and bookish: it is entirely subordinate in interest to the meaning of the words strung on it. But half the effectiveness of the second sentence is in the very special tone with which you must say—news of a day I have forgotten— if I ever read it. You must be able to say Oh yes one knows how that goes. (There is some adjective to describe the intonation or cadence, but I won't hunt for it.)

One of the least successful of the poems in my book is almost saved by a final striking sentence-sound (Asking for Roses.)

Not caring so very much *what* she supposes.
Take My November Guest. Did you know at once how we say such sentences as these when we talk?
She thinks I have no eye for these.

———

Not yesterday I learned etc.

———

But it were vain to tell her so

———

Get away from the sing-song. You must hear and recognize in the last line the sentence sound that supports, No use in telling him so.

Let's have some examples pell-mell in prose and verse because I don't want you to think I am setting up as an authority on verse alone.
My father used to say—
You're a liar!
If a hen and a half lay an egg and a half etc.
A long long time ago—
Put it there, old man! (Offering your hand)
I aint a going [to] hurt you, so you needn't be scared.
Suppose Henry Horne says something offensive to a young lady named Rita when her brother Charles is by to protect her. Can you hear the two different tones in which she says their respective names. "Henry Horne! Charles!" I can hear it better than I can say it. And by oral practice I get further and further away from it.
Never you say a thing like that to a man!
And such they are and such they will be found.
Well I swan!
Unless I'm greatly mistaken——
Hence with denial vain and coy excuse
A soldier and afraid (afeared)
Come, child, come home.
The thing for me to do is to get right out of here while I am able.
No fool like an old fool.
It is so and not otherwise that we get the variety that makes it fun to write and read. *The ear does it.* The ear is the only true writer and the only true reader. I have known people who could read without hearing the sentence sounds and they were the fastest readers. Eye readers we call them. They can get the meaning by

glances. But they are bad readers because they miss the best part of what a good writer puts into his work.

Remember that the sentence sound often says more than the words. It may even as in irony convey a meaning opposite to the words.

I wouldn't be writing all this if I didn't think it the most important thing I know. I write it partly for my own benefit, to clarify my ideas for an essay or two I am going to write some fine day (not far distant.)

To judge a poem or piece of prose you go the same way to work—apply the one test—greatest test. You listen for the sentence sounds. If you find some of those not bookish, caught fresh from the mouths of people, some of them striking, all of them definite and recognizable, so recognizable that with a little trouble you can place them and even name them, you know you have found a writer.

The Figure a Poem Makes*

Abstraction is an old story with the philosophers, but it has been like a new toy in the hands of the artists of our day. Why can't we have any one quality of poetry we choose by itself? We can have in thought. Then it will go hard if we can't in practice. Our lives for it.

Granted no one but a humanist much cares how sound a poem is if it is only *a* sound. The sound is the gold in the ore. Then we will have the sound out alone and dispense with the inessential. We do till we make the discovery that the object in writing poetry is to make all poems sound as different as possible from each other, and the resources for that of vowels, consonants, punctuation, syntax, words, sentences, meter are not enough. We need the help of context—meaning—subject matter. That is the greatest help towards variety. All that can be done with words is soon told. So also with meters—particularly in our language where there are

* **From** *Complete Poems of Robert Frost.*

virtually but two, strict iambic and loose iambic. The ancients with many were still poor if they depended on meters for all tune. It is painful to watch our sprung-rhythmists straining at the point of omitting one short from a foot for relief from monotony. The possibilities for tune from the dramatic tones of meaning struck across the rigidity of a limited meter are endless. And we are back in poetry as merely one more art of having something to say, sound or unsound. Probably better if sound, because deeper and from wider experience.

Then there is this wildness whereof it is spoken. Granted again that it has an equal claim with sound to being a poem's better half. If it is a wild tune, it is a poem. Our problem then is, as modern abstractionists, to have the wildness pure; to be wild with nothing to be wild about. We bring up as aberrationists, giving way to undirected associations and kicking ourselves from one chance suggestion to another in all directions as of a hot afternoon in the life of a grasshopper. Theme alone can steady us down. Just as the first mystery was how a poem could have a tune in such a straightness as meter, so the second mystery is how a poem can have wildness and at the same time a subject that shall be fulfilled.

It should be of the pleasure of a poem itself to tell how it can. The figure a poem makes. It begins in delight and ends in wisdom. The figure is the same as for love. No one can really hold that the ecstasy should be static and stand still in one place. It begins in delight, it inclines to the impulse, it assumes direction with the first line laid down, it runs a course of lucky events, and ends in a clarification of life—not necessarily a great clarification, such as sects and cults are founded on, but in a momentary stay against confusion. It has denouement. It has an outcome that though unforeseen was predestined from the first image of the original mood—and indeed from the very mood. It is but a trick poem and no poem at all if the best of it was thought of first and saved for the last. It finds its own name as it goes and discovers the best waiting for it in some final phrase at once wise and sad—the happy-sad blend of the drinking song.

No tears in the writer, no tears in the reader. No surprise for the writer, no surprise for the reader. For me the initial delight is in the surprise of remembering something I didn't know I knew. I am in a place, in a situation, as if I had materialized from cloud or risen out of the ground. There is a glad recognition of the long lost and the rest follows. Step by step the wonder of unexpected supply keeps growing. The impressions most useful to my purpose seem always those I was unaware of and so made no note of at the time when taken, and the conclusion is come to that like giants we are always hurling experience ahead of us to pave the future with against the day when we may want to strike a line of purpose across it for somewhere. The line will have the more charm for not being mechanically straight. We enjoy the straight crookedness of a good walking stick. Modern instruments of precision are being used to make things crooked as if by eye and hand in the old days.

I tell how there may be a better wildness of logic than of inconsequence. But the logic is backward, in retrospect, after the act. It must be more felt than seen ahead like prophecy. It must be a revelation, or a series of revelations, as much for the poet as for the reader. For it to be that there must have been the greatest freedom of the material to move about in it and to establish relations in it regardless of time and space, previous relation, and everything but affinity. We prate of freedom. We call our schools free because we are not free to stay away from them till we are sixteen years of age. I have given up my democratic prejudices and now willingly set the lower classes free to be completely taken care of by the upper classes. Political freedom is nothing to me. I bestow it right and left. All I would keep for myself is the freedom of my material—the condition of body and mind now and then to summons aptly from the vast chaos of all I have lived through.

Scholars and artists thrown together are often annoyed at the puzzle of where they differ. Both work from knowledge; but I suspect they differ most importantly in the way their knowledge is come by. Scholars get theirs with conscientious thoroughness along projected lines of logic; poets theirs cavalierly and as it happens in and out of books. They stick to nothing deliberately, but let what will stick to them like burrs where they walk in the fields. No acquirement is on assignment, or even self-assignment. Knowledge of the second kind is much more available in the wild free ways of wit and art. A schoolboy may be defined as one who can tell you what he knows in the order in which he learned it. The artist must value himself as he snatches a thing from some previous order in time and space into a new order with not so much as a ligature clinging to it of the old place where it was organic.

More than once I should have lost my soul to radicalism if it had been the originality it was mistaken for by its young converts. Originality and initiative are what I ask for my country. For myself the originality need be no more than the freshness of a poem run in the way I have described: from delight to wisdom. The figure is the same as for love. Like a piece of ice on a hot stove the poem must ride on its own melting. A poem may be worked over once it is in being, but may not be worried into being. Its most previous quality will remain its having run itself and carried away the poet with it. Read it a hundred times: it will forever keep its freshness as a metal keeps its fragrance. It can never lose its sense of a meaning that once unfolded by surprise as it went.

T. S. Eliot

T. S. Eliot was born September 26, 1888, in St. Louis, Missouri. After studying at Harvard and the Sorbonne, he emigrated to England in 1914 and in 1927 became a British subject. Long before his death on January 4, 1965, he had become the most celebrated and influential man of letters in the English-speaking world.

With his contemporaries, Eliot matured during "a period of search for a proper modern colloquial idiom." Poetry, he held, must not stray too far from ordinary everyday language; most poetic revolutions, such as those materialized in Dryden or Wordsworth, signal a return to common speech. Yet the poet's mind must be uncommon in its capacity for "amalgamating disparate experience." The ordinary man "falls in love, or reads Spinoza, and these two experiences have nothing to do with each other, or with the noise of the typewriter or the smell of cooking; in the mind of the poet these experiences are always forming new wholes." Further, each amalgam of experiences is a new emotion which the poet must "realize" for an audience, or a succession of audiences, no two of which will be entirely alike. He accomplishes his purpose by finding or creating a stable, intrinsically efficacious "objective correlative": that is, "a set of objects, a situation, a chain of events which shall be the formula of that particular *emotion; such that when the external facts, which must terminate in sensory experience, are given, the emotion is immediately evoked."*

Poetry is a constant reminder of all the things that can only be said in one language and are untranslatable. Even within a language only a part of the meaning can be conveyed by paraphrase, itself a kind of translation, because "the poet is occupied with frontiers of consciousness beyond which words fail, though meanings still exist." Those meanings are inextricable from what Eliot calls the "music" of poetry, the vibration arising partly from each word's accumulated associations, and partly from the immediate context that qualifies it. Or, to consider this from a more intimate perspective, poetry is revealed in and through the "auditory imagination," which is the "feeling for syllable and rhythm, penetrating far below the conscious levels of thought and feeling, invigorating every word; sinking to the most primitive and forgotten, returning to the origin and bringing something back, seeking the beginning and the end. It works through meanings, certainly, or not without meanings in the ordinary sense, and fuses the old and obliterated and trite, the current and the new and surprising, the most ancient and the most civilized mentality." Here, too, one may sense how readily, in Eliot's mind, words press toward a resolution in the Word.

Tradition and the Individual Talent*

I

In English writing we seldom speak of tradition, though we occasionally apply its name in deploring its absence. We cannot refer to "the tradition" or to "a tradition"; at most, we employ the adjective in saying that the poetry of So-and-so is "traditional" or even "too traditional." Seldom, perhaps, does the word appear except in a phrase of censure. If otherwise, it is vaguely approbative, with the implication, as to the work approved, of some pleasing archæological reconstruction. You can hardly make the word agreeable to English ears without this comfortable reference to the reassuring science of archæology.

Certainly the word is not likely to appear in our appreciations of living or dead writers. Every nation, every race, has not only its own creative, but its own critical turn of mind; and is even more

* From *Selected Essays*: **New Edition by T. S. Eliot.**

oblivious of the shortcomings and limitations of its critical habits than of those of its creative genius. We know, or think we know, from the enormous mass of critical writing that has appeared in the French language the critical method or habit of the French; we only conclude (we are such unconscious people) that the French are "more critical" than we, and sometimes even plume ourselves a little with the fact, as if the French were the less spontaneous. Perhaps they are; but we might remind ourselves that criticism is as inevitable as breathing, and that we should be none the worse for articulating what passes in our minds when we read a book and feel an emotion about it, for criticizing our own minds in their work of criticism. One of the facts that might come to light in this process is our tendency to insist, when we praise a poet, upon those aspects of his work in which he least resembles anyone else. In these aspects or parts of his work we pretend to find what is individual, what is the peculiar essence of the man. We dwell with satisfaction upon the poet's difference from his predecessors, especially his immediate predecessors; we endeavour to find something that can be isolated in order to be enjoyed. Whereas if we approach a poet without his prejudice we shall often find that not only the best, but the most individual parts of his work may be those in which the dead poets, his ancestors, assert their immortality most vigorously. And I do not mean the impressionable period of adolescence, but the period of full maturity.

Yet if the only form of tradition, of handing down, consisted in following the ways of the immediate generation before us in a blind or timid adherence to its successes, "tradition" should positively be discouraged. We have seen many such simple currents soon lost in the sand; and novelty is better than repetition. Tradition is a matter of much wider significance. It cannot be inherited, and if you want it you must obtain it by great labour. It involves, in the first place, the historical sense, which we may call nearly indispensable to anyone who would continue to be a poet beyond his twenty-fifth year; and the historical sense involves a perception, not only of the pastness of the past, but of its presence; the historical sense compels a man to write not merely with his own generation in his bones, but with a feeling that the whole of the literature of Europe from Homer and within it the whole of the literature of his own country has a simultaneous existence and composes a simultaneous order. This historical sense, which is a sense of the timeless as well as of the temporal and of the timeless and of the temporal together, is what makes a writer traditional.

And it is at the same time what makes a writer most acutely conscious of his place in time, of his contemporaneity.

No poet, no artist of any art, has his complete meaning alone. His significance, his appreciation is the appreciation of his relation to the dead poets and artists. You cannot value him alone; you must set him, for contrast and comparison, among the dead. I mean this as a principle of æsthetic, not merely historical, criticism. The necessity that he shall conform, that he shall cohere, is not one-sided; what happens when a new work of art is created is something that happens simultaneously to all the works of art which preceded it. The existing monuments form an ideal order among themselves, which is modified by the introduction of the new (the really new) work of art among them. The existing order is complete before the new work arrives; for order to persist after the supervention of novelty, the *whole* existing order must be, if ever so slightly, altered; and so the relations, proportions, values of each work of art toward the whole are readjusted; and this is conformity between the old and the new. Whoever has approved this idea of order, of the form of European, of English literature, will not find it preposterous that the past should be altered by the present as much as the present is directed by the past. And the poet who is aware of this will be aware of great difficulties and responsibilities.

In a peculiar sense he will be aware also that he must inevitably be judged by the standards of the past. I say judged, not amputated, by them; not judged to be as good as, or worse or better than, the dead; and certainly not judged by the canons of dead critics. It is a judgment, a comparison, in which two things are measured by each other. To conform merely would be for the new work not really to conform at all; it would not be new, and would therefore not be a work of art. And we do not quite say that the new is more valuable because it fits in; but its fitting in is a test of its value—a test, it is true, which can only be slowly and cautiously applied, for we are none of us infallible judges of conformity. We say: it appears to conform, and is perhaps individual, or it appears individual, and may conform; but we are hardly likely to find that it is one and not the other.

To proceed to a more intelligible exposition of the relation of the poet to the past: he can neither take the past as a lump, an indiscriminate bolus, nor can he form himself wholly on one or two private admirations, nor can he form himself wholly upon one preferred period. The first course is inadmissible, the second is an important experience of youth, and the third is a pleasant and highly desirable supplement. The poet must be very conscious of the main current, which does not at all flow invariably through the most distinguished reputations. He must be quite aware of the obvious fact that art never improves, but that the material of art is never quite the same. He must be aware that the mind of Europe—the mind of his own country—a mind which he learns in time to be much more important than his own private mind—is a mind which changes, and that this change is a development which abandons nothing *en route,* which does not superannuate either Shakespeare, or Homer, or the rock drawing of the Magdalenian draughtsmen. That this development, refinement perhaps, complication certainly, is not, from the point of view of the artist, any improvement. Perhaps not even an improvement from the point of view of the psychologist or not to the extent which we imagine; perhaps only in the end based upon a complication in economics and machinery. But the difference between the present and the past is that the conscious present is an awareness of the past in a way and to an extent which the past's awareness of itself cannot show.

Some one said: "The dead writers are remote from us because we *know* so much more than they did." Precisely, and they are that which we know.

I am alive to a usual objection to what is clearly part of my programme for the *métier* of poetry. The objection is that the doctrine requires a ridiculous amount of erudition (pedantry), a claim which can be rejected by appeal to the lives of poets in any pantheon. It will even be affirmed that much learning deadens or perverts poetic sensibility. While, however, we persist in believing that a poet ought to know as much as will not encroach upon his necessary receptivity and necessary laziness, it is not desirable to confine knowledge to whatever can be put into a useful shape for examinations, drawing-rooms, or the still more pretentious modes of publicity. Some can absorb knowledge, the more tardy must sweat for it. Shakespeare acquired more essential history from Plutarch than most men could from the whole British Museum. What is to be insisted upon is that the poet must develop or procure the consciousness of the past and that he should continue to develop this consciousness throughout his career.

What happens is a continual surrender of himself as he is at the moment to something which is more valuable. The progress of an artist is a continual self-sacrifice, a continual extinction of personality.

There remains to define this process of depersonalization and its relation to the sense of tradition. It is in this depersonalization that art may be said to approach the condition of science. I shall, therefore, invite you to consider, as a suggestive analogy, the action which takes place when a bit of finely filiated platinum is introduced into a chamber containing oxygen and sulphur dioxide.

II

Honest criticism and sensitive appreciation is directed not upon the poet but upon the poetry. If we attend to the confused cries of the newspaper critics and the susurrus of popular repetition that follows, we shall hear the names of poets in great numbers; if we seek not Blue-book knowledge but the enjoyment of poetry, and ask for a poem, we shall seldom find it. In the last article I tried to point out the importance of the relation of the poem to other poems by other authors, and suggested the conception of poetry as a living whole of all the poetry that has ever been written. The other aspect of this Impersonal theory of poetry is the relation of the poem to its author. And I hinted, by an analogy, that the mind of the mature poet differs from that of the immature one not precisely in any valuation of "personality," not being necessarily more interesting, or having "more to say," but rather by being a more finely perfected medium in which special, or very varied, feelings are at liberty to enter into new combinations.

The analogy was that of the catalyst. When the two gases previously mentioned are mixed in the presence of a filament of platinum, they form sulphurous acid. This combination takes place only if the platinum is present; nevertheless the newly formed acid contains no trace of platinum, and the platinum itself is apparently unaffected; has remained inert, neutral, and unchanged. The mind of the poet is the shred of platinum. It may partly or exclusively operate upon the experience of the man himself; but, the more perfect the artist, the more completely separate in him will be the man who suffers and the mind which creates; the more perfectly will the mind digest and transmute the passions which are its material.

The experience, you will notice, the elements which enter the presence of the transforming catalyst, are of two kinds: emotions and feelings. The effect of a work of art upon the person who enjoys it is an experience different in kind from any experience not of art. It may be formed out of one emotion, or may be a combination of several; and various feelings, inhering for the writer in particular words or phrases or images, may be added to compose the final result. Or great poetry may be made without the direct use of any emotion whatever: composed out of feelings solely. Canto XV of the *Inferno* (Brunetto Latini) is a working up of the emotion evident in the situation; but the effect, though single as that of any work of art, is obtained by considerable complexity of detail. The last quatrain gives an image, a feeling attaching to an image, which "came," which did not develop simply out of what precedes, but which was probably in suspension in the poet's mind until the proper combination arrived for it to add itself to. The poet's mind is in fact a receptacle for seizing and storing up numberless feelings, phrases, images, which remain there until the particles which can unite to form a new compound are present together.

If you compare several representative passages of the greatest poetry you see how great is the variety of types of combination, and also how completely any semi-ethical criterion of "sublimity" misses the mark. For it is not the "greatness," the intensity, of the emotions, the components, but the intensity of the artistic process, the pressure, so to speak, under which the fusion takes place, that counts. The episode of Paolo and Francesca employs a definite emotion, but the intensity of the poetry is something quite different from whatever intensity in the supposed experience it may give the impression of. It is no more intense, furthermore, than Canto XXVI, the voyage of Ulysses, which has not the direct dependence upon an emotion. Great variety is possible in the process of transmutation of emotion: the murder of Agamemnon, or the agony of Othello, gives an artistic effect apparently closer to a possible original than the scenes from Dante. In the *Agamemnon,* the artistic emotion approximates to the emotion of an actual spectator; in *Othello* to the emotion of the protagonist himself. But the difference between art and the event is always absolute; the combination which is the murder of Agamemnon is probably as complex as that which is the voyage of Ulysses. In either case there has been a fusion of elements. The ode of Keats contains a number of feelings which have nothing particular to do with the nightingale, but which the nightingale, partly, perhaps, because of its attractive name, and partly because of its reputation, served to bring together.

The point of view which I am struggling to attack is perhaps related to the metaphysical theory of the substantial unity of the soul: for my meaning is, that the poet has, not a "personality" to express, but a particular medium, which is only a medium and not a personality, in which impressions and experiences combine in peculiar and unexpected ways. Impressions and experiences which are important for the man may take no place in the poetry, and those which become important in the poetry may play quite a negligible part in the man, the personality.

I will quote a passage which is unfamiliar enough to be regarded with fresh attention in the light—or darkness—of these observations:

> And now methinks I could e'en chide myself
> For doating on her beauty, though her death
> Shall be revenged after no common action.
> Does the silkworm expend her yellow labours
> For thee? For thee does she undo herself?
> Are lordships sold to maintain ladyships
> For the poor benefit of a bewildering minute?
> Why does yon fellow falsify highways,
> And put his life between the judge's lips,
> To refine such a thing—keeps horse and men
> To beat their valours for her? . . .

In this passage (as is evident if it is taken in its context) there is a combination of positive and negative emotions: an intensely strong attraction toward beauty and an equally intense fascination by the ugliness which is contrasted with it and which destroys it. This balance of contrasted emotion is in the dramatic situation to which the speech is pertinent, but that situation alone is inadequate to it. This is, so to speak, the structural emotion, provided by the drama. But the whole effect, the dominant tone, is due to the fact that a number of floating feelings, having an affinity to this emotion by no means superficially evident, have combined with it to give us a new art emotion.

It is not in his personal emotions, the emotions provoked by particular events in his life, that the poet is in any way remarkable or interesting. His particular emotions may be simple, or crude, or flat. The emotion in his poetry will be a very complex thing, but not with the complexity of the emotions of people who have very complex or unusual emotions in life. One error, in fact, of eccentricity in poetry is to seek for new human emotions to express; and in this search for novelty in the wrong place it discovers the perverse. The business of the poet is not to find new emotions, but to use the ordinary ones and, in working them up into poetry, to express feelings which are not in actual emotions at all. And emotions which he has never experienced will serve his turn as well as those familiar to him. Consequently, we must believe that "emotion recollected in tranquillity" is an inexact formula. For it is neither emotion, nor recollection, nor, without distortion of meaning, tranquillity. It is a concentration, and a new thing resulting from the concentration, of a very great number of experiences which to the practical and active person would not seem to be experiences at all; it is a concentration which does not happen consciously or of deliberation. These experiences are not "recollected," and they finally unite in an atmosphere which is "tranquil" only in that it is a passive attending upon the event. Of course this is not quite the whole story. There is a great deal, in the writing of poetry, which must be conscious and deliberate. In fact, the bad poet is usually unconscious where he ought to be conscious, and conscious where he ought to be unconscious. Both errors tend to make him "personal." Poetry is not a turning loose of emotion, but an escape from emotion; it is not the expression of personality, but an escape from personality. But, of course, only those who have personality and emotions know what it means to want to escape from these things.

III

ὁ δὲ νοῦς ἴσως θειότερόν τι καὶ ἀπαθές ἐστιν [1]

This essay proposes to halt at the frontier of metaphysics or mysticism, and confine itself to such practical conclusions as can be applied by the responsible person interested in poetry. To divert interest from the poet to the poetry is a laudable aim: for it would conduce to a juster estimation of actual poetry, good and bad. There are many people who appreciate the expression of sincere emotion in verse, and there is a smaller number of people who can appreciate technical excellence. But very few know when there is expression of *significant* emotion, emotion which has its life in the poem and not in the history of the poet. The emotion of art is impersonal. And the poet cannot reach this impersonality without surrendering himself wholly to the work to be done. And he is not likely to know what is to be done unless he lives in what is not merely the present, but the present moment of the past, unless he is conscious, not of what is dead, but of what is already living.

[1] ["The mind is undoubtedly something more divine and unimpressionable." From Aristotle's *De Anima*, I, 4.]

William Carlos Williams

The son of an Englishman and a Puerto Rican of French and Basque ancestry, William Carlos Williams was born September 17, 1883, in Rutherford, New Jersey. Having studied medicine at the University of Pennsylvania, where he met Ezra Pound and H. D., Williams travelled to Leipzig for postgraduate work in pediatrics, which he then practiced in the Rutherford area until a few years before his death in 1963.

Williams is an American writer insofar as America has claimed a tradition of revolution, because he believes that the truth, or what passes for truth, must be periodically redressed, reexamined, and reaffirmed in a new mode. Ready-made forms are sinister cookie cutters impressed on the daily flux; or, as he says, "I was early in life sick to my very pit with order that cuts off the crab's feelers to make it fit into the box." Before creation may evolve, there must be a destruction of the box—the rhyme scheme mesmerized by the pendulum's swing, perhaps, or the "fascistic" sonnet form. The type of the modern artist is Whitman, who "broke through the deadness of copied forms which keep shouting above

69

everything that wants to get said today, drowning out one man with the accumulated weight of a thousand voices in the past. . . ."

In his recognition that "the secret of much that we might tell" lingers in "the monotony of our intonation," there is little chauvinism and less resignation. Williams simply wishes to find his own language, "for everything we know and do is tied up with words, with the phrases words make, with the grammar which stultifies, the prose or poetical rhythms which bind us to our pet indolences and medievalisms. To Americans especially, those who no longer speak English, this is especially important. We need too often a burst of air in at the window of our prose. It is absolutely indispensable that we get this before we can even begin to think straight again. It's the words, the words we need to get back to, words washed clean. . . . This is a moral question at base, surely, but a technical one also and first."

The materia poetica *is (in a remarkable phrase) anything "seen, smelt, touched, apprehended and understood to be what it is —the flesh of a constantly repeated permanence." In poetry the objective is not to teach or communicate, but to reveal. "To be an artist, as to be a good artisan," Williams wrote, "a man must know his materials. But in addition he must possess that really glandular perception of their uniqueness which realizes in them an end in itself, each piece irreplaceable by a substitute, not to be broken down to other meaning. Not to pull out, transubstantiate, boil, unglue, hammer, melt, digest and psychoanalyze, not even to distill but to see and keep what the understanding touches intact—as grapes are round and come in bunches."*

A New Measure*

I have never been one to write by rule, even by my own rules. Let's begin with the rule of counted syllables, in which all poems have been written hitherto. That has become tiresome to my ear.

Finally, the stated syllables, as in the best of present-day free verse, have become entirely divorced from the beat, that is the measure. The musical pace proceeds without them.

Therefore the measure, that is to say, the count, having got rid of the words, which held it down, is returned to the *music*.

The words, having been freed, have been allowed to run all over the map, "free," as we have mistakenly thought. This has amounted to no more (in Whitman and others) than no discipline at all.

But if we keep in mind the *tune* which the lines (not necessarily the words) make in our ears, we are ready to proceed.

---

* From a letter written to Richard Eberhart, May 23, 1954.

By measure I mean musical pace. Now, with music in our ears the words need only be taught to keep as distinguished an order, as chosen a character, as regular, according to the music, as in the best of prose.

By its *music* shall the best of modern verse be known and the *resources* of the music. The refinement of the poem, its subtlety, is not to be known by the elevation of the words but—the words don't so much matter—by the resources of the *music*.

To give you an example from my own work—not that I know anything about what I have myself written:

(count):—not that I ever count when writing but, at best, the lines must be capable of being counted, that is to say, *measured*—(believe it or not).—At that I may, half consciously, even count the measure under my breath as I write.—

(approximate example)

    (1)　The smell of the heat is boxwood
        (2)　when rousing us
            (3)　a movement of the air
    (4)　stirs our thoughts
        (5)　that had no life in them
            (6)　to a life, a life in which

(or)

    (1)　Mother of God! Our Lady!
        (2)　the heart
            (3)　is an unruly master:
    (4)　Forgive us our sins
        (5)　as we
            (6)　forgive
    (7)　those who have sinned against

Count a single beat to each numeral. You may not agree with my ear, but that is the way I count the line. Over the whole poem it gives a pattern to the meter that can be felt as a new measure. It gives resources to the ear which result in a language which we hear spoken about us every day.

Gerard Manley Hopkins

Gerard Manley Hopkins was born June 11, 1844, in Stratford, Essex. While at Oxford he became a convert to Roman Catholicism, subsequently entering the priesthood as a Jesuit; but although he was one of the great technical and perceptual innovators, or renovators, of poetry in modern times, Hopkins had little opportunity to exert influence until the posthumous publication of his poems in 1918, almost thirty years after his death on June 8, 1889.

As a viable technique is the handiwork of vision, so Hopkins's manipulation of prosody, idiom, and aural coincidence is an attempt to re-create the dynamic essence of the world along with his perception of it. Every natural object has a unique, intrinsic form, an "inscape," which is maintained by "instress," a kind of artful, gravitational force centered within. (Occasionally "instress" may refer to the sensation of "inscape," as though the latter were a flashbulb filament and the former its beam-print striding onto the mind.) From a religious perspective this theory was confirmed by Duns Scotus, the medieval theologian who emphasized the individuality or "Thisness," the distinctive presence, both of men and natural objects, so that Hopkins named him not a traveller but an "unraveller" who had pursued a way into the hearts of things.

Hopkins's inward fusion of thought and feeling has its counterpart in the constellations of sound and meaning which he "explodes" like fireworks displays. Curiously, his configurations of language anticipate Ezra Pound's definition of the "Image" as "that which presents an intellectual and emotional complex in an instant of time." At any given moment, human reality harbors more crystallizations and confusions than are admitted by the processes of reason. Even unresolved dialectical tension, because it requires that its constituents be identified, is inadequate to that reality; thus, F. R. Leavis has called attention to a manuscript alteration where Hopkins's original "black, white; wrong, right" had been changed by him to read "black, white; right, wrong." Surely, the waters of life have seldom emerged in a muddier condition.

As outlined in the "Author's Preface," Hopkins's strong-stress prosody frees the speaking voice, detaching it from the more rigid metrics that ordinarily would serve as its foil; the fact borders on poignancy when one considers that the only formal discipline Hopkins may not have broached, although he felt severely tried by it, was that imposed by his chosen mode of life as a member of the Society of Jesus.

Author's Preface*

The poems in this book[1] are written some in Running Rhythm, the common rhythm in English use, some in Sprung Rhythm, and some in a mixture of the two. And those in the common rhythm are some counterpointed, some not.

Common English rhythm, called Running Rhythm above, is measured by feet of either two or three syllables (putting aside the imperfect feet at the beginning and end of lines and also some unusual measures, in which feet seem to be paired together and double or composite feet to arise) never more or less.

Every foot has one principal stress or accent, and this or the syllable it falls on may be called the Stress of the foot and the other part, the one or two unaccented syllables, the Slack. Feet (and the rhythms made out of them) in which the stress comes first are called Falling Feet and Falling Rhythms, feet and rhythm in which

---

* **From _Poems of Gerard Manley Hopkins_.**

[1] [A manuscript collection in the possession of Robert Bridges.]

the slack comes first are called Rising Feet and Rhythms, and if the stress is between two slacks there will be Rocking Feet and Rhythms. These distinctions are real and true to nature; but for purposes of scanning it is a great convenience to follow the example of music and take the stress always first, as the accent or the chief accent always comes first in a musical bar. If this is done there will be in common English verse only two possible feet—the so-called accentual Trochee and Dactyl, and correspondingly only two possible uniform rhythms, the so-called Trochaic and Dactylic. But they may be mixed and then what the Greeks called a Logaoedic Rhythm arises.[2] These are the facts and according to these the scanning of ordinary regularly-written English verse is very simple indeed and to bring in other principles is here unnecessary.

But because verse written strictly in these feet and by these principles will become same and tame the poets have brought in licences and departures from rule to give variety, and especially when the natural rhythm is rising, as in the common ten-syllable or five-foot verse, rhymed or blank. These irregularities are chiefly Reversed Feet and Reversed or Counterpoint Rhythm, which two things are two steps or degrees of licence in the same kind. By a reversed foot I mean the putting the stress where, to judge by the rest of the measure, the slack should be and the slack where the stress, and this is done freely at the beginning of a line and, in the course of a line, after a pause; only scarcely ever in the second foot or place and never in the last, unless when the poet designs some extraordinary effect; for these places are characteristic and sensitive and cannot well be touched. But the reversal of the first foot and of some middle foot after a strong pause is a thing so natural that our poets have generally done it, from Chaucer down, without remark and it commonly passes unnoticed and cannot be said to amount to a formal change of rhythm, but rather is that irregularity which all natural growth and motion shews. If however the reversal is repeated in two feet running, especially so as to include the sensitive second foot, it must be due either to great want of ear or else is a calculated effect, the superinducing or *mounting* of a new rhythm upon the old; and since the new or mounted rhythm is actually heard and at the same time the mind naturally supplies the natural or standard foregoing rhythm, for we do not forget what the

---

2 [It may also arise when anapests are combined with iambs. More importantly, the Greeks considered Logaoedic Rhythm as hovering between speech and song.]

rhythm is that by rights we should be hearing, two rhythms are in some manner running at once and we have something answerable to counterpoint in music, which is two or more strains of tune going on together, and this is Counterpoint Rhythm.[3] Of this kind of verse Milton is the great master and the choruses of *Samson Agonistes* are written throughout in it—but with the disadvantage that he does not let the reader clearly know what the ground-rhythm is meant to be and so they have struck most readers as merely irregular. And in fact if you counterpoint throughout, since one only of the counter rhythms is actually heard, the other is really destroyed or cannot come to exist, and what is written is one rhythm only and probably Sprung Rhythm, of which I now speak.

Sprung Rhythm, as used in this book, is measured by feet of from one to four syllables, regularly, and for particular effects any number of weak or slack syllables may be used. It has one stress, which falls on the only syllable, if there is only one, or, if there are more, then scanning as above, on the first, and so gives rise to four sorts of feet, a monosyllable and the so-called accentual Trochee, Dactyl, and the First Paeon.[4] And there will be four corresponding natural rhythms; but nominally the feet are mixed and any one may follow any other. And hence Sprung Rhythm differs from Running Rhythm in having or being only one nominal rhythm, a mixed or 'logaoedic' one, instead of three, but on the other hand in having twice the flexibility of foot, so that any two stresses may follow one another running or be divided by one, two, or three slack syllables. But strict Sprung Rhythm cannot be counterpointed. In Sprung Rhythm, as in logaoedic rhythm generally, the feet are assumed to be equally long or strong and their seeming inequality is made up by pause or stressing.

Remark also that it is natural in Sprung Rhythm for the lines to be *rove over*,[5] that is for the scanning of each line immediately to take up that of the one before, so that if the first has one or more syllables at its end the other must have so many the less at its beginning; and in fact the scanning runs on without break from the

---

[3] [When one of its rhythms, presumably the base, is removed or has atrophied, then Counterpoint Rhythm modulates into Sprung Rhythm.]

[4] [The first Paeon is a foot consisting of one stressed syllable followed by three slack ones.]

[5] [Hopkins speaks as though the lines or verses were lengths of rope to be looped over and secured, one to the other, so as to form a continuum within the stanza.]

beginning, say, of a stanza to the end and all the stanza is one long strain, though written in lines asunder.

Two licences are natural to Sprung Rhythm. The one is rests, as in music; but of this an example is scarcely to be found in this book, unless in the *Echos,* second line.[6] The other is *hangers* or *outrides,* that is one, two, or three slack syllables added to a foot and not counting in the nominal scanning. They are so called because they seem to hang below the line or ride forward or backward from it in another dimension than the line itself, according to a principle needless to explain here.[7] These outriding half feet or hangers are marked by a loop underneath them, and plenty of them will be found.

The other marks are easily understood, namely accents, where the reader might be in doubt which syllable should have the stress; slurs, that is loops *over* syllables, to tie them together into the time of one; little loops at the end of a line to shew that the rhyme goes on to the first letter of the next line; what in music are called pauses ⌒, to shew that the syllable should be dwelt on; and twirls ~, to mark reversed or counterpointed rhythm.[8]

Note on the nature and history of Sprung Rhythm—Sprung Rhythm is the most natural of things. For (1) it is the rhythm of common speech and of written prose, when rhythm is perceived in them. (2) It is the rhythm of all but the most monotonously regular music, so that in the words of choruses and refrains and in songs written closely to music it arises. (3) It is found in nursery rhymes, weather saws, and so on; because, however these may have been once made in running rhythm, the terminations having dropped off by the change of language, the stresses come together and so the rhythm is sprung. (4) It arises in common verse when reversed or counterpointed, for the same reason.

But nevertheless in spite of all this and though Greek and Latin lyric verse, which is well known, and the old English verse seen in 'Pierce Ploughman' are in sprung rhythm, it has in fact ceased to be used since the Elizabethan age, Greene being the last writer

---

6 ["The Leaden Echo And The Golden Echo."]

7 [Elsewhere, Hopkins wrote that "an outriding foot is, by a sort of contradiction, a recognized extra-metrical effect; it is and it is not part of the metre; not part of it, not being counted, but part of it by producing a calculated effect which tells in the general success." Also, see W. H. Gardner's *Gerard Manley Hopkins: A Study of Poetic Idiosyncrasy in Relation to Poetic Tradition,* vol. I, pp. 84–90.]

8 [The twirl, misrepresented here, should be ⌒.]

who can be said to have recognized it. For perhaps there was not, down to our days, a single, even short, poem in English in which sprung rhythm is employed—not for single effects or in fixed places —but as the governing principle of the scansion. I say this because the contrary has been asserted: if it is otherwise the poem should be cited.

Some of the sonnets in this book are in five-foot, some in six-foot or Alexandrine lines.

Nos. 13 and 22[9] are Curtal-Sonnets, that is they are constructed in proportions resembling those of the sonnet proper, namely, 6+4 instead of 8+6, with however a halfline tailpiece (so that the equation is rather $1\frac{1}{2} + \frac{1}{2} - 2\frac{1}{2} = 10\frac{1}{2}$).

[9] ["Pied Beauty" and "Peace," respectively.]

John Crowe Ransom

Born April 30, 1888, in Pulaski, Tennessee, John Crowe Ransom was educated at Vanderbilt University and at Oxford, which he attended as a Rhodes scholar. A founder and editor of The Fugitive *(1922–1925), and later founder and editor of* The Kenyon Review, *he became nominating spokesman for the New Criticism. Perhaps more revealing, because less reasoned, is his earlier association with the Fugitives, a group of Southern writers appreciative of T. S. Eliot's poetry and criticism as well as certain French poetry, that of Paul Valéry for example—but who, as poets, favored agrarian or fabulous bodies couched in traditional forms, and who were themselves informed by a well-defined heritage of Southern customs, values, apprehensions, and history. Over some of them, perhaps, the North cast as long a shadow as the Negro. But as indigenes of a defunct romance, an inextricable tapestry of Southern illusion and reality, they evolved their own humane posture, one more durably aristocratic than genteel.*

The spoor of Ransom's poetics might be traced to his ethics, his social values, specifically to decency or decorum, the means by which life aspires to the condition of art. Such decorum does not follow from exclusion, from the drawing down of an eyelid: for it is a horrid as well as a beautiful world, "but without the horror we should never focus the beauty." His prizing of "the artificial" is implicit testimony to the natural man whom art has a canon to restrain, to keep firmly though not despotically in check, in a paradoxical freedom-under-the-law. So Prospero, the former and future duke, with the assistance of Ariel may overrule Caliban, while in Ransom's own poetry a vibrant tension arises from his classical entertainment of unruly subjects. He affects composure by withdrawing into anonymity; or the poem is conceived as a little drama in which the poet, under a cloak of pseudonymity, has cast himself. Metre becomes a kind of artificial language concealing the poet's actual identity, whereas self-protective irony is the inflection which at once withholds and suggests his actual feelings. Finally, dramatic propriety gives form to this activity and makes it an art, just as decorum circumscribes or rounds out human life, momentarily distinguishing it within the great sea of being, of brute appetency.

Poetry: A Note in Ontology*

A poetry may be distinguished from a poetry by virtue of subject-matter, and subject-matter may be differentiated with respect to its ontology, or the reality of its being. An excellent variety of critical doctrine arises recently out of this differentiation, and thus perhaps criticism leans again upon ontological analysis as it was meant to do by Kant. The recent critics remark in effect that some poetry deals with things, while some other poetry deals with ideas. The two poetries will differ from each other as radically as a thing differs from an idea.

The distinction in the hands of critics is a fruitful one. There is apt to go along with it a principle of valuation, which is the consequence of a temperament, and therefore basic. The critic likes things and intends that his poet shall offer them; or likes ideas and intends that he shall offer them; and approves him as he does the one or the other. Criticism cannot well go much deeper than this.

---

* From *The World's Body* by **John Crowe Ransom.**

The critic has carried to the last terms his analysis of the stuff of which poetry is made, and valued it frankly as his temperament or his need requires him to value it.

So philosophical a critic seems to be highly modern. He is; but this critic as a matter of fact is peculiarly on one side of the question. (The implication is unfavorable to the other side of the question.) He is in revolt against the tyranny of ideas, and against the poetry which celebrates ideas, and which may be identified—so far as his usual generalization may be trusted—with the hateful poetry of the Victorians. His bias is in favor of the things. On the other hand the critic who likes Victorian verse, or the poetry of ideas, has probably not thought of anything of so grand a simplicity as electing between the things and the ideas, being apparently not quite capable of the ontological distinction. Therefore he does not know the real or constitutional ground of his liking, and may somewhat ingenuously claim that his predilection is for those poets who give him inspiration, or comfort, or truth, or honest metres, or something else equally "worth while." But Plato, who was not a modern, was just as clear as we are about the basic distinction between the ideas and the things, and yet stands far apart from the aforesaid conscious modern in passionately preferring the ideas over the things. The weight of Plato's testimony would certainly fall on the side of the Victorians, though they may scarcely have thought of calling him as their witness. But this consideration need not conclude the hearing.

1. PHYSICAL POETRY

The poetry which deals with things was much in favor a few years ago with the resolute body of critics. And the critics affected the poets. If necessary, they became the poets, and triumphantly illustrated the new mode. The Imagists were important figures in the history of our poetry, and they were both theorists and creators. It was their intention to present things in their thinginess, or *Dinge* in their *Dinglichkeit;* and to such an extent had the public lost its sense of *Dinglichkeit* that their redirection was wholesome. What the public was inclined to seek in poetry was ideas, whether large ones or small ones, grand ones or pretty ones, certainly ideas to live by and die by, but what the Imagists identified with the stuff of poetry was, simply, things.

Their application of their own principle was sufficiently

heroic, though they scarcely consented to be as extreme in the practice as in the theory. They had artistic talent, every one of the original group, and it was impossible that they should make of poetry so simple an exercise as in doctrine they seemed to think it was. Yet Miss Lowell wrote a poem on "Thompson's Lunch Room, Grand Central Station"; it is admirable if its intention is to show the whole reach of her courage. Its detail goes like this:

Jagged greenwhite bowls of pressed glass
Rearing snow-peaks of chipped sugar
Above the lighthouse-shaped castors
Of gray pepper and gray-white salt.

For most of us as for the public idealist, with his "values," this is inconsequential. Unhappily it seems that the things as things do not necessarily interest us, and that in fact we are not quite constructed with the capacity for a disinterested interest. But it must be noted even here that the things are on their good behavior, looking rather well, and arranged by lines into something approaching a military formation. More technically, there is cross-imagery in the snow-peaks of sugar and in the lighthouse-shaped castors, and cross-imagery involves association, and will presently involve dissociation and thinking. The metre is but a vestige, but even so it means something, for metre is a powerful intellectual determinant marshalling the words and, inevitably, the things. The *Dinglichkeit* of this Imagist specimen, or the realism, was therefore not pure. But it was nearer pure than the world was used to in poetry, and the exhibit was astonishing.

For the purpose of this note I shall give to such poetry, dwelling as exclusively as it dares upon physical things, the name Physical Poetry. It is to stand opposite to that poetry which dwells as firmly as it dares upon ideas.

But perhaps thing *versus* idea does not seem to name an opposition precisely. Then we might phrase it a little differently: image *versus* idea. The idealistic philosophies are not sure that things exist, but they mean the equivalent when they refer to images. (Or they may consent to perceptions; or to impressions, following Hume, and following Croce, who remarks that they are preintellectual and independent of concepts. It is all the same, unless we are extremely technical.) It is sufficient if they concede that image is the raw material of idea. Though it may be an unwieldy and useless affair for the idealist as it stands, much needing to be licked into shape, nevertheless its relation to idea is that of a material cause, and it cannot be dispossessed of its priority. It cannot be dispossessed of a primordial freshness, which idea can never claim. An idea is derivative and tamed. The image is in the natural or wild state, and it has to be discovered there, not put there, obeying its own law and none of ours. We think we can lay hold of image and take it captive, but the docile captive is not the real image but only the idea, which is the image with its character beaten out of it.

But we must be very careful: idealists are nothing if not dialectical. They object that an image in an original state of innocence is a delusion and cannot exist, that no image ever comes to us which does not imply the world of ideas, that there is "no precept without a concept." There is something in it. Every property discovered in the image is a universal property, and nothing discovered in the image is marvelous in kind though it may be pinned down historically or statistically as a single instance. But there is this to be understood too: the image which is not remarkable in any particular property is marvellous in its assemblage of many properties, a manifold of properties, like a mine or a field, something to be explored for the properties; yet science can manage the image, which is infinite in properties, only by equating it to the one property with which the science is concerned; for science at work is always *a science,* and committed to a special interest. It is not by refutation but by abstraction that science destroys the image. It means to get its "value" out of the image, and we may be sure that it has no use for the image in its original state of freedom. People who are engrossed with their pet "values" become habitual killers. Their game is the images, or the things, and they acquire the ability to shoot them as far off as they can be seen, and do. It is thus that we lose the power of imagination, or whatever faculty it is by which we are able to contemplate things as they are in their rich and contingent materiality. But our dreams reproach us, for in dreams they come alive again. Likewise our memory; which makes light of our science by recalling the images in their panoply of circumstance and with their morning freshness upon them.

It is the dream, the recollection, which compels us to poetry, and to deliberate æsthetic experience. It can hardly be argued, I think, that the arts are constituted automatically out of original images, and arise in some early age of innocence. (Though Croce seems to support this view, and to make art a pre-adult stage of experience.) Art is based on second love, not first love. In it we make a return to something which we had wilfully alienated. The child is occupied mostly with things, but it is because he is still unfurnished with systematic ideas, not because he is a ripe citizen by nature and comes along already trailing clouds of glory. Images are clouds of glory for the man who has discovered that ideas are a sort of darkness. Imagism, that is, the recent historical movement, may resemble a naïve poetry of mere things, but we can read the theoretical pronouncements of Imagists, and we can learn that Imagism is motivated by a distaste for the systematic abstractedness of thought. It presupposes acquaintance with science; that famous activity which is "constructive" with respect to the tools of our economic role in this world, and destructive with respect to nature. Imagists wish to escape from science by immersing themselves in images.

Not far off the simplicity of Imagism was, a little later, the subtler simplicity of Mr. George Moore's project shared with several others, in behalf of "pure poetry." In Moore's house on Ebury Street they talked about poetry, with an after-dinner warmth if not an early-morning discretion, and their tastes agreed almost perfectly and reinforced one another. The fruit of these conversations was the volume *Pure Poetry*. It must have been the most exclusive anthology of English poetry that had yet appeared, since its room was closed to all the poems that dallied visibly with ideas, so that many poems that had been coveted by all other anthologists do not appear there. Nevertheless the book is delicious, and something more deserves to be said for it.

First, that "pure poetry" is a kind of Physical Poetry. Its visible content is a thing-content. Technically, I suppose, it is effective in this character if it can exhibit its material in such a way that an image or set of images and not an idea must occupy the foreground of the reader's attention. Thus:

> **Full fathom five thy father lies**
> **Of his bones are coral made.**

Here it is difficult for anybody (except the perfect idealist who is always theoretically possible and who would expect to take a return from anything whatever) to receive any experience except that of a very distinct image, or set of images. It has the configuration of image, which consists in being sharp of edges, and the modality of image, which consists in being given and non-negotiable, and the density, which consists in being full, a plenum of qualities. What is to be done with it? It is pure exhibit; it is to be contemplated; perhaps it is to be enjoyed. The art of poetry depends more frequently on this faculty than on any other in its repertory; the faculty of presenting images so whole and clean that they resist the catalysis of thought.

And something else must be said, going in the opposite direction. "Pure poetry," all the same, is not as pure as it is claimed to be, though on the whole it is Physical Poetry. (All true poetry is a phase of Physical Poetry.) It is not as pure as Imagism is, or at least it is not as pure as Imagism would be if it lived up to its principles; and in fact it is significant that the volume does not contain any Imagist poems, which argues a difference in taste somewhere. Imagism may take trifling things for its material, presumably it will take the first things the poet encounters, since "importance" and "interest" are not primary qualities which a thing possesses but secondary or tertiary ones which the idealist attributes to it by virtue of his own requirements. "Pure poetry" as Moore conceives it, and as the lyrics of Poe and Shakespeare offer it, deals with the more dramatic materials, and here dramatic means human, or at least capable of being referred to the critical set of human interests. Employing this sort of material the poet cannot exactly intend to set the human economists in us actually into motion, but perhaps he does intend to comfort us with the fleeting sense that it is potentially our kind of material.

In the same way "pure poetry" is nicely metred, whereas Imagism was free. Technique is written on it. And by the way the anthology contains no rugged anonymous Scottish ballad either, and probably for a like reason; because it would not be technically finished. Now both Moore and De La Mare are accomplished conservative artists, and what they do or what they approve may be of limited range but it is sure to be technically admirable, and it is certain that they understand what technique in poetry is though they do not define it. Technique takes the thing-content and meters and orders it. Metre is not an original property of things. It is artificial, and conveys the sense of human control, even if it does not wish to impair the thinginess of the things. Metric is a science, and so far as we attend to it we are within the scientific atmosphere. Order is the logical arrangement of things. It involves the dramatic "form" which selects the things, and brings out their appropriate qualities, and carries them through a systematic course of predication until the total impression is a unit of logic and not merely a solid lump of thing-content. The "pure poems" which Moore admires are studied, though it would be fatal if they looked studious. A sustained effort of ideation effected these compositions. It is covered up, and communicates itself only on a subliminal plane of consciousness. But experienced readers are quite aware of it; they know at once what is the matter when they encounter a realism shamelessly passing for poetry, or a well-planned but blundering poetry.

As critics we should have every good will toward Physical Poetry: it is the basic constituent of any poetry. But the product is always something short of a pure or absolute existence, and it cannot quite be said that it consists of nothing but physical objects. The fact is that when we are more than usually satisfied with a Physical Poetry our analysis will probably disclose that it is more than usually impure.

2. PLATONIC POETRY

The poetry of ideas I shall denominate: Platonic Poetry. This also has grades of purity. A discourse which employed only abstract ideas with no images would be a scientific document and not a poem at all, not even a Platonic poem. Platonic Poetry dips heavily into the physical. If Physical Poetry tends to employ some ideation surreptitiously while still looking innocent of idea, Platonic Poetry more than returns the compliment, for it tries as hard as it can to look like Physical Poetry, as if it proposed to conceal its medicine, which is the idea to be propagated, within the sugar candy of objectivity and *Dinglichkeit*. As an instance, it is almost inevitable that I quote a famous Victorian utterance:

> The year's at the spring
> And day's at the morn;
> Morning's at seven;
> The hill-side's dew-pearled;
> The lark's on the wing;
> The snail's on the thorn:
> God's in his heaven—
> All's right with the world!

which is a piece of transparent homiletics; for in it six pretty, co-ordinate images are marched, like six little lambs to the slaughter, to a colon and a powerful text. Now the exhibits of this poetry in the physical kind are always large, and may take more of the attention of the reader than is desired, but they are meant mostly to be illustrative of the ideas. It is on this ground that idealists like Hegel detect something unworthy, like a pedagogical trick, in poetry after all, and consider that the race will abandon it when it has outgrown its childishness and is enlightened.

The ablest arraignment of Platonic Poetry that I have seen, as an exercise which is really science but masquerades as poetry by affecting a concern for physical objects, is that of Mr. Allen Tate in a series of studies recently in *The New Republic*. I will summarize. Platonic Poetry is allegory, a discourse in things, but on the understanding that they are translatable at every point into ideas. (The usual ideas are those which constitute the popular causes, patriotic, religious, moral or social.) Or Platonic Poetry is the elaboration of ideas as such, but in proceeding introduces for ornament some physical properties after the style of Physical Poetry; which is rhetoric. It is positive when the poet believes in the efficacy of the ideas. It is negative when he despairs of their efficacy, because they have conspicuously failed to take care of him, and utters his personal wail:

I fall upon the thorns of life! I bleed!

This is "Romantic Irony," which comes at occasional periods to interrupt the march of scientific optimism. But it still falls under the category of Platonism; it generally proposes some other ideas to take the place of those which are in vogue.

But why Platonism? To define Platonism we must remember that it is not the property of the historical person who reports dialogues about it in an Academy, any more than "pure poetry" is the property of the talkers who describe it from a house on Ebury Street. Platonism, in the sense I mean, is the name of an impulse that is native to us all, frequent, tending to take a too complete possession of our minds. Why should the spirit of mortal be proud? The chief explanation is that modern mortal is probably a Platonist. We are led to believe that nature is rational and that by the force of reasoning we shall possess it. I have read upon high authority: "Two great forces are persistent in Plato: the love of truth and zeal for human improvement." The forces are one force. We love to view the world under universal or scientific ideas to which we give the name truth; and this is because the ideas seem to make not for righteousness but for mastery. The Platonic view of the world is ultimately the predatory, for it reduces to the scientific, which we know. The Platonic Idea becomes the Logos which science worships, which is the Occidental God, whose minions we are, and whose children, claiming a large share in His powers for patrimony.

Now the fine Platonic world of ideas fails to coincide with the original world of perception, which is the world populated by the stubborn and contingent objects, and to which as artists we fly in shame. The sensibility manifested by artists makes fools of scientists, if the latter are inclined to take their special and quite useful form of truth as the whole and comprehensive article. A dandified pagan worldling like Moore can always defeat Platonism; he does it every hour; he can exhibit the savor of his fish and wines, the fragrance of his coffee and cigars, and the solidity of the images in his favorite verse. These are objects which have to be experienced, and cannot be reported, for what is their simple essence that the Platonist can abstract? Moore may sound mystical but he is within the literal truth when he defends "pure poetry" on the ground that the things are constant, and it is the ideas which change—changing according to the latest mode under which the species indulges its grandiose expectation of subjugating nature. The things are constant in the sense that the ideas are never emancipated from the necessity of referring back to them as their original; and the sense that they are not altered nor diminished no matter which ideas may take off from them as a point of departure. The way to obtain the true *Dinglichkeit* of a formal dinner or a landscape or a beloved person is to approach the object as such, and in humility; then it unfolds a nature which we are unprepared for if we have put our trust in the simple idea which attempted to represent it.

The special antipathy of Moore is to the ideas as they put on their moral complexion, the ideas that relate everything to that insignificant centre of action, the human "soul" in its most Platonic and Pharisaic aspect. Nothing can darken perception better than a repetitive moral earnestness, based on the reputed superiority and higher destiny of the human species. If morality is the code by which we expect the race to achieve the more perfect possession of nature, it is an incitement to a more heroic science, but not to

æsthetic experience, nor religious; if it is the code of humility, by
which we intend to know nature as nature is, that is another mat-
ter; but in an age of science morality is inevitably for the general
public the former; and so transcendent a morality as the latter is
now unheard of. And therefore:

> O love, *they* die in yon rich sky,
>   *They* faint on hill or field or river;
> *Our* echoes roll from soul to soul,
>   And grow forever and forever.

The italics are mine. These lines conclude an otherwise innocent
poem, a candidate for the anthology, upon which Moore remarks:
"The Victorian could never reconcile himself to finishing a poem
without speaking about the soul, and the lines are particularly vin-
dictive." Vindictive is just. By what right did the Laureate exult
in the death of the physical echoes and call upon his love to witness
it, but out of the imperiousness of his savage Platonism? Plato him-
self would have admired this ending, and considered that it
redeemed an otherwise vicious poem.

Why do persons who have ideas to promulgate risk the trial
by poetry? If the poets are hired to do it, which is the polite con-
ception of some Hegelians, why do their employers think it worth
the money, which they hold in public trust for the cause? Does a
science have to become a poetry too? A science is the less effective
as a science when it muddies its clear waters with irrelevance, a
sermon becomes less cogent when it begins to quote the poets. The
moralist, the scientist, and the prophet of idealism think evidently
that they must establish their conclusions in poetry, though they
reach these conclusions upon quite other evidence. The poetry is
likely to destroy the conclusions with a sort of death by drowning,
if it is a free poetry.

When that happens the Platonists may be cured of Platonism.
There are probably two cures, of which this is the better. One cure
is by adversity, by the failure of the ideas to work, on account of
treachery or violence, or the contingencies of weather, constitu-
tion, love, and economics; leaving the Platonist defeated and bewil-
dered, possibly humbled, but on the other hand possibly turned
cynical and worthless. Very much preferable is the cure which
comes by education in the fine arts, erasing his Platonism more
gently, leading him to feel that that is not a becoming habit of
mind which dulls the perceptions.

The definition which some writers have given to art is: the reference of the idea to the image. The implication is that the act is not for the purpose of honest comparison so much as for the purpose of proving the idea by the image. But in the event the idea is not disproved so much as it is made to look ineffective and therefore foolish. The ideas will not cover the objects upon which they are imposed, they are too attenuated and threadlike; for ideas have extension and objects have intension, but extension is thin while intension is thick.

There must be a great deal of genuine poetry which started in the poet's mind as a thesis to be developed, but in which the characters and the situations have developed faster than the thesis, and of their own accord. The thesis disappears; or it is recaptured here and there and at the end, and lodged sententiously with the reader, where every successive reading of the poem will dislodge it again. Like this must be some plays, even some play out of Shakespeare, whose thesis would probably be disentangled with difficulty out of the crowded pageant; or some narrative poem with a moral plot but much pure detail; perhaps some "occasional" piece by a Laureate or official person, whose purpose is compromised but whose personal integrity is saved by his wavering between the sentiment which is a public duty and the experience which he has in his own right; even some proclaimed allegory, like Spenser's, unlikely as that may seem, which does not remain transparent and everywhere translatable into idea but makes excursions into the territory of objectivity. These are hybrid performances. They cannot possess beauty of design, though there may be a beauty in detailed passages. But it is common enough, and we should be grateful. The mind is a versatile agent, and unexpectedly stubborn in its determination not really to be hardened in Platonism. Even in an age of science like the nineteenth century the poetic talents are not so loyal to its apostolic zeal as they and it suppose, and do not deserve the unqualified scorn which it is fashionable to offer them, now that the tide has turned, for their performance is qualified.

But this may be not stern enough for concluding a note on Platonic Poetry. I refer again to that whose Platonism is steady and malignant. This poetry is an imitation of Physical Poetry, and not really a poetry. Platonists practise their bogus poetry in order to show that an image will prove an idea, but the literature which succeeds in this delicate mission does not contain real images but illustrations.

3. METAPHYSICAL POETRY

"Most men," Mr. Moore observes, "read and write poetry between fifteen and thirty and afterwards very seldom, for in youth we are attracted by ideas, and modern poetry being concerned almost exclusively with ideas we live on duty, liberty, and fraternity as chameleons are said to live on light and air, till at last we turn from ideas to things, thinking that we have lost our taste for poetry, unless, perchance, we are classical scholars."

Much is conveyed in this characteristic sentence, even in proportion to its length. As for the indicated chronology, the cart is put after the horse, which is its proper sequence. And it is pleasant to be confirmed in the belief that many men do recant from their Platonism and turn back to things. But it cannot be exactly a *volte-face,* for there are qualifications. If pure ideas were what these men turn from, they would have had no poetry at all in the first period, and if pure things were what they turn to, they would be having not a classical poetry but a pure imagism, if such a thing is possible, in the second.

The mind does not come unscathed and virginal out of Platonism. Ontological interest would have to develop curiously, or wastefully and discontinuously, if men through their youth must cultivate the ideas so passionately that upon its expiration they are done with ideas forever and ready to become as little (and pre-logical) children. Because of the foolishness of idealists are ideas to be taboo for the adult mind? And, as critics, what are we to do with those poems (like *The Canonization* and *Lycidas*) which could not obtain admission by Moore into the anthology but which very likely are the poems we cherish beyond others?

The reputed "innocence" of the æsthetic moment, the "knowledge without desire" which Schopenhauer praises, must submit to a little scrutiny, like anything else that looks too good to be true. We come into this world as aliens come into a land which they must conquer if they are to live. For native endowment we have an exacting "biological" constitution which knows precisely what it needs and determines for us our inevitable desires. There can be no certainty that any other impulses are there, for why should they be? They scarcely belong in the biological picture. Perhaps we are simply an efficient animal species, running smoothly, working fast, finding the formula of life only too easy, and after a certain apprenticeship piling up power and wealth far beyond the capacity of our appetites to use. What will come next? Perhaps poetry, if the gigantic effort of science begins to seem disproportionate to the reward, according to a sense of diminishing returns. But before this pretty event can come to pass, it is possible that every act of attention which is allowed us is conditioned by a gross and selfish interest.

Where is innocence then? The æsthetic moment appears as a curious moment of suspension; between the Platonism in us, which is militant, always sciencing and devouring, and a starved inhibited aspiration towards innocence which, if it could only be free, would like to respect and know the object as it might of its own accord reveal itself.

The poetic impulse is not free, yet it holds out stubbornly against science for the enjoyment of its images. It means to reconstitute the world of perceptions. Finally there is suggested some such formula as the following:

Science gratifies a rational or practical impulse and exhibits the minimum of perception. Art gratifies a perceptual impulse and exhibits the minimum of reason.

Now it would be strange if poets did not develop many technical devices for the sake of increasing the volume of the percipienda or sensibilia. I will name some of them.

First Device: metre. Metre is the most obvious device. A formal metre impresses us as a way of regulating very drastically the material, and we do not stop to remark (that is, as readers) that it has no particular aim except some nominal sort of regimentation. It symbolizes the predatory method, like a sawmill which intends to reduce all the trees to fixed unit timbers, and as business men we require some sign of our business. But to the Platonic censor in us it gives a false security, for so long as the poet appears to be working faithfully at his metrical engine he is left comparatively free to attend lovingly to the things that are being metered, and metering them need not really hurt them. Metre is the gentlest violence he can do them, if he is expected to do some violence.

Second Device: fiction. The device of the fiction is probably no less important and universal in poetry. Over every poem which looks like a poem is a sign which reads: This road does not go through to action; fictitious. Art always sets out to create an "æsthetic distance" between the object and the subject, and art takes pains to announce that it is not history. The situation treated is not quite an actual situation, for science is likely to have claimed that field, and exiled art; but a fictive or hypothetical one, so that science is less greedy and perception may take hold of it. Kant asserted that the æsthetic judgment is not concerned with the existence or non-existence of the object, and may be interpreted as asserting that it is so far from depending on the object's existence that it really depends on the object's non-existence. Sometimes we have a certain melancholy experience. We enjoy a scene which we receive by report only, or dream, or meet with in art; but subsequently find ourselves in the presence of an actual one that seems the very same scene; only to discover that we have not now the power to enjoy it, or to receive it æsthetically, because the economic tension is upon us and will not indulge us in the proper mood. And it is generally easier to obtain our æsthetic experience from art than from nature, because nature is actual, and communication is forbidden. But in being called fictive or hypothetical the art-object suffers no disparagement. It cannot be true in the sense of being actual, and therefore it may be despised by science. But it is true in the sense of being fair or representative, in permitting the "illusion of reality"; just as Schopenhauer discovered that music may symbolize all the modes of existence in the world; and in keeping with the customary demand of the readers of fiction proper, that it shall be "true to life." The defenders of art must require for it from its practitioners this sort of truth, and must assert of it before the world this dignity. If jealous science succeeds in keeping the field of history for its own exclusive use, it does not therefore annihilate the arts, for they reappear in a field which may be called real though one degree removed from actuality. There the arts perform their function with much less interference, and at the same time with about as much fidelity to the phenomenal world as history has.

Third Device: tropes. I have named two important devices; I am not prepared to offer the exhaustive list. I mention but one other kind, the device which comprises the figures of speech. A proper scientific discourse has no intention of employing figurative language for its definitive sort of utterance. Figures of speech twist accidence away from the straight course, as if to intimate astonishing lapses of rationality beneath the smooth surface of discourse, inviting perceptual attention, and weakening the tyranny of science over the senses. But I skip the several easier and earlier figures, which are timid, and stop on the climactic figure, which is the metaphor; with special reference to its consequence, a poetry which once in our history it produced in a beautiful and abundant exhibit, called Metaphysical Poetry.

And what is Metaphysical Poetry? The term was added to the official vocabulary of criticism by Johnson, who probably took it from Pope, who probably took it from Dryden, who used it to describe the poetry of a certain school of poets, thus: "He [John Donne] affects the metaphysics, not only in his satires, but in his amorous verses, where nature only should reign. . . . In this Mr. Cowley has copied him to a fault." But the meaning of metaphysical which was common in Dryden's time, having come down from the Middle Ages through Shakespeare, was simply: supernatural; *miraculous*. The context of the Dryden passage indicates it.

Dryden, then, noted a miraculism in poetry and repudiated it; except where it was employed for satire, where it was not seriously intended and had the effect of wit. Dryden himself employs miraculism wittily, but seems rather to avoid it if he will be really committed by it; he may employ it in his translations of Ovid, where the responsibility is Ovid's and not Dryden's, and in an occasional classical piece where he is making polite use of myths well known to be pagan errors. In his "amorous" pieces he finds the reign of nature sufficient, and it is often the worse for his amorous pieces. He is not many removes from a naturalist. (A naturalist is a person who studies nature not because he loves it but because he wants to use it, approaches it from the standpoint of common sense, and sees it thin and not thick.) Dryden might have remarked that Donne himself had a change of heart and confined his miraculism at last to the privileged field of a more or less scriptural revelation. Perhaps Dryden found his way to accepting Milton because Milton's miraculism was mostly not a contemporary sort but classical and scriptural, pitched in a time when the age of miracles had not given way to the age of science. He knew too that Cowley had shamefully recanted from his petty miraculism, which formed the conceits, and turned to the scriptural or large order of miraculism to write his heroic (but empty) verses about David; and had written a Pindaric ode in extravagant praise of "Mr. Hobs," whose naturalistic account of nature seemed to render any other account fantastic if not contrary to the social welfare.

Incidentally, we know how much Mr. Hobbes affected Dryden too, and the whole of Restoration literature. What Bacon with his disparagement of poetry had begun, in the cause of science and protestantism, Hobbes completed. The name of Hobbes is critical in any history that would account for the chill which settled upon the poets at the very moment that English poetry was attaining magnificently to the fullness of its powers. The name stood for common sense and naturalism, and the monopoly of the scientific spirit over the mind. Hobbes was the adversary, the Satan, when the latter first intimidated the English poets. After Hobbes his name is legion.

"Metaphysics," or miraculism, informs a poetry which is the most original and exciting, and intellectually perhaps the most seasoned, that we know in our literature, and very probably it has few equivalents in other literatures. But it is evident that the metaphysical effects may be large-scale or they may be small-scale. (I believe that generically, or ontologically, no distinction is to be made between them.) If Donne and Cowley illustrate the small-scale effects, Milton will illustrate the large-scale ones, probably as a consequence of the fact that he wrote major poems. Milton, in the *Paradise Lost,* told a story which was heroic and miraculous in the first place. In telling it he dramatized it, and allowed the scenes and characters to develop of their own native energy. The virtue of a long poem on a "metaphysical" subject will consist in the dramatization or substantiation of all the parts, the poet not being required to devise fresh miracles on every page so much as to establish the perfect "naturalism" of the material upon which the grand miracle is imposed. The *Paradise Lost* possesses this virtue nearly everywhere:

> Thus *Adam* to himself lamented loud
> Through the still Night, not now, as ere man fell,
> Wholsom and cool, and mild, but with black Air
> Accompanied, with damps and dreadful gloom,
> Which to his evil Conscience represented
> All things with double terror: On the ground
> Outstretcht he lay, on the cold ground, and oft
> Curs'd his Creation, Death as oft accus'd
> Of tardie execution, since denounc't
> The day of his offence. Why comes not Death,
> Said hee, with one thrice acceptable stroke
> To end me?

This is exactly the sort of detail for a large-scale metaphysical work, but it would hardly serve the purpose with a slighter and more naturalistic subject; with "amorous" verses. For the critical mind Metaphysical Poetry refers perhaps almost entirely to the so-called "conceits" that constitute its staple. To define the conceit is to define small-scale Metaphysical Poetry.

It is easily defined, upon a little citation. Donne exhibits two conceits, or two branches of one conceit in the familiar lines:

> **Our hands were firmly cemented**
> **By a fast balm which thence did spring;**
> **Our eye-beams twisted, and did thread**
> **Our eyes upon one double string.**

The poem which follows sticks to the topic; it represents the lovers in precisely that mode of union and no other. Cowley is more conventional yet still bold in the lines:

> **Oh take my Heart, and by that means you'll prove**
> **Within, too stor'd enough of love:**
> **Give me but yours, I'll by that change so thrive**
> **That Love in all my parts shall live.**
> **So powerful is this my change, it render can,**
> **My outside Woman, and your inside Man.**

A conceit originates in a metaphor; and in fact the conceit is but a metaphor if the metaphor is meant; that is, if it is developed so literally that it must be meant, or predicated so baldly that nothing else can be meant. Perhaps this will do for a definition.

Clearly the seventeenth century had the courage of its metaphors, and imposed them imperially on the nearest things, and just as clearly the nineteenth century lacked this courage, and was half-heartedly metaphorical, or content with similes. The difference between the literary qualities of the two periods is the difference between the metaphor and the simile. (It must be admitted that this like other generalizations will not hold without its exceptions.) One period was pithy and original in its poetic utterance, the other was prolix and predictable. It would not quite commit itself to the metaphor even if it came upon one. Shelley is about as vigorous as usual when he says in *Adonais:*

> **Thou young Dawn,**
> **Turn all thy dew to splendour. . . .**

But splendor is not the correlative of dew, it has the flat tone of a

Platonic idea, while physically it scarcely means more than dew with sunshine upon it. The seventeenth century would have said: "Turn thy dew, which is water, into fire, and accomplish the transmutation of the elements." Tennyson in his boldest lyric sings:

> **Come into the garden, Maud,**
> **For the black bat, night, has flown,**

and leaves us unpersuaded of the bat. The predication would be complete without the bat, "The black night has flown," and a flying night is not very remarkable. Tennyson is only affecting a metaphor. But later in the same poem he writes:

> **The red rose cries, "She is near, she is near";**
> **And the white rose weeps, "She is late";**
> **The larkspur listens, "I hear, I hear";**
> **And the lily whispers, "I wait."**

And this is a technical conceit. But it is too complicated for this author, having a plurality of images which do not sustain themselves individually. The flowers stand for the lover's thoughts, and have been prepared for carefully in an earlier stanza, but their distinctness is too arbitrary, and these are like a schoolgirl's made-up metaphors. The passage will not compare with one on a very similar situation in *Green Candles,* by Mr. Humbert Wolfe:

> **"I know her little foot," gray carpet said:**
> **"Who but I should know her light tread?"**
> **"She shall come in," answered the open door,**
> **"And not," said the room, "go out any more."**

Wolfe's conceit works and Tennyson's does not, and though Wolfe's performance seems not very daring or important, and only pleasant, he employs the technique of the conceit correctly: he knows that the miracle must have a basis of verisimilitude.

Such is Metaphysical Poetry; the extension of a rhetorical device; as one of the most brilliant successes in our poetry, entitled to long and thorough examination; and even here demanding somewhat by way of a more ontological criticism. I conclude with it.

We may consult the dictionary, and discover that there is a miraculism or supernaturalism in a metaphorical assertion if we are ready to mean what we say, or believe what we hear. Or we may read Mr. Hobbes, the naturalist, who was very clear upon it: "II. The second cause of absurd assertions I ascribe to the giving of names of 'bodies' to 'accidents,' or of 'accidents' to 'bodies,' as they do that say 'faith is infused' or 'inspired,' when nothing can be 'poured' or 'breathed' into anything but body . . . and that 'phantasms' are 'spirits,' etc." Translated into our present terms, Hobbes is condemning the confusion of single qualities with whole things; or the substitution of concrete images for simple ideas.

Specifically, the miraculism arises when the poet discovers by analogy an identity between objects which is partial, though it should be considerable, and proceeds to an identification which is complete. It is to be contrasted with the simile, which says "as if" or "like," and is scrupulous to keep the identification partial. In Cowley's passage above, the lover is saying, not for the first time in this literature: "She and I have exchanged our hearts." What has actually been exchanged is affections, and affections are only in a limited sense the same as hearts. Hearts are unlike affections in being engines that pump blood and form body; and it is a miracle if the poet represents the lady's affection as rendering her inside into man. But he succeeds, with this mixture, in depositing with us the image of a very powerful affection.

From the strict point of view of literary criticism it must be insisted that the miraculism which produces the humblest conceit is the same miraculism which supplies to religions their substantive content. (This is said to assert the dignity not of the conceits but of the religions.) It is the poet and nobody else who gives to the God a nature, a form, faculties, and a history; to the God, most comprehensive of all terms, which, if there were no poetic impulse to actualize or "find" Him, would remain the driest and deadest among Platonic ideas, with all intension sacrificed to infinite extension. The myths are conceits, born of metaphors. Religions are periodically produced by poets and destroyed by naturalists. Religion depends for its ontological validity upon a literary understanding, and that is why it is frequently misunderstood. The metaphysical poets, perhaps like their spiritual fathers the mediæval Schoolmen, were under no illusions about this. They recognized myth, as they recognized the conceits, as a device of expression; its sanctity as the consequence of its public or social importance.

But whether the topics be Gods or amorous experiences, why do poets resort to miraculism? Hardly for the purpose of controverting natural fact or scientific theory. Religion pronounces about

God only where science is silent and philosophy is negative; for a positive is wanted, that is, a God who has his being in the physical world as well as in the world of principles and abstractions. Likewise with the little secular enterprises of poetry too. Not now are the poets so brave, not for a very long time have they been so brave, as to dispute the scientists on what they call their "truth"; though it is a pity that the statement cannot be turned round. Poets will concede that every act of science is legitimate, and has its efficacy. The metaphysical poets of the seventeenth century particularly admired the methodology of science, and in fact they copied it, and their phrasing is often technical, spare, and polysyllabic, though they are not repeating actual science but making those metaphorical substitutions that are so arresting.

The intention of Metaphysical Poetry is to complement science, and improve discourse. Naturalistic discourse is incomplete, for either of two reasons. It has the minimum of physical content and starves the sensibility, or it has the maximum, as if to avoid the appearance of evil, but is laborious and pointless. Platonic Poetry is too idealistic, but Physical Poetry is too realistic, and realism is tedious and does not maintain interest. The poets therefore introduce the psychological device of the miracle. The predication which it permits is clean and quick but it is not a scientific predication. For scientific predication concludes an act of attention but miraculism initiates one. It leaves us looking, marvelling, and revelling in the thick *dinglich* substance that has just received its strange representation.

Let me suggest as a last word, in deference to a common Puritan scruple, that the predication of Metaphysical Poetry is true enough. It is not true like history, but no poetry is true in that sense, and only a part of science. It is true in the pragmatic sense in which some of the generalizations of science are true: it accomplishes precisely the sort of representation that it means to. It suggests to us that the object is perceptually or physically remarkable, and we had better attend to it.

Marianne Moore

"The test of sanity," Shaw *wrote in his preface to* Saint Joan, *"is not the normality of the method but the reasonableness of the discovery." Both the criterion and its context are felicitous: as Marianne Moore's righteousness is luminous, so her oddly-moving poems arrive at right ends. Yet the actual state of affairs is less simple, for method makes up a greater part of her discovery. The lines are scanned syllabically, but the ostensibly arbitrary line breaks have definite functions, possibly purposes. When, commencing "The Steeple-Jack," Miss Moore writes that "Dürer would have seen a reason for living," her reader might be thrilled to the point of confusion—until he shifts to the second line, which adds, "in a town like this." Nevertheless, that momentary misapprehension comes into its own, unsanctioned by syntax; "a reason for living in a town like this" turns out to be, precisely, "a reason for living."*

Again, she may write of Irish fauna, that "discommodity makes/ them invisible; they've dis-/ appeared. The Irish say your trouble is their/ trouble and your/ joy their joy? I wish/ I could

103

believe it;" and each line is a posing of possibilities, the bulk of the passage having been "governed by the pull of the sentence as the pull of a fabric is governed by gravity." The whimsy is artful, after all; "unconfusion submits/ its confusion to proof." She regards the stanza as a unit, rather than the line, and the stanza is what formulates the fragmentary gestures, preventing them from going astray.

Miss Moore attends almost indefatigably to insoluble particulars. Poems "are what/ they're talking about," not ciphers to be decoded; and the illustrations are the lesson. A mélange of quotations, conclusions, and vivid observations, any single poem may resemble a commonplace book, but one endowed with intelligence and possessed of an extraordinarily civilized sensibility. She feels that poetic form, far from being a mere public convention, is the personal and the organic made objective and accessible, that it "is the outward equivalent of a determining inner conviction, and that the rhythm is the person." Or, noting elsewhere that "the power of the visible/ is the invisible," with engaging dissatisfaction she advances beyond externals, so as to consolidate them. And in this enterprise she is sustained by discriminatory powers so passionate that they constitute another species of morality: their very own.

A former editor of The Dial, *Marianne Moore was born on November 15, 1887, in St. Louis, Missouri.*

Idiosyncrasy and Technique*

I. TECHNIQUE

In his inaugural lecture as Professor of Poetry at Oxford,[1] Mr. Auden said, "There is only one thing that all poetry must do; it must praise all it can for being as for happening." He also said, "Every poem is rooted in imaginative awe." These statements answer, or imply an answer, to the question: Why does one write?

I was startled, indeed horrified, when a writing class in which I have an interest was asked, "Is it for money or fame?" as though it must be one or the other—and writing were not for some a felicity, if not a species of intellectual self-preservation. Gorgeously remunerated as I am for being here, it would seem both hypocriti-

---

* **From** A *Marianne Moore Reader* **by Marianne Moore.**

[1] *Making, Knowing and Judging: An Inaugural Lecture by W. H. Auden Delivered before the University of Oxford on 11 June 1956* (Oxford at the Clarendon Press).

cal and inappropriate to feign that a love of letters renders money irrelevant. Still, may I say, and with emphasis, that I do not write for money or fame. To earn a living is needful, but it can be done in routine ways. One writes because one has a burning desire to objectify what it is indispensable to one's happiness to express; a statement which is not at variance with the fact that Sir Walter Scott, driven by a fanatically sensitive conscience, shortened his life writing to pay what was not a personal debt. And Anthony Trollope, while writing to earn a living, at the same time was writing what he very much loved to write.

Amplifying the impression which Bernard Shaw, as music critic, himself gives of his "veracity, catholicity, and pugnacity," [2] Hesketh Pearson says of him as stage manager of his plays, "No author could be more modest than Shaw. He did not regard his text as sacrosanct. He laughed over his own lines as if they were jokes by somebody else and never could repeat them accurately. Once, when an actor apologized for misquoting a passage, he remarked, 'What you said is better than what I wrote. If you can always misquote so well, keep on misquoting—but remember to give the right cues!' " [3] Writing was resilience. Resilience was an adventure. Is it part of the adventure to revise what one wrote? Professor Ewing has suggested that something be said about this. My own revisions are usually the result of impatience with unkempt diction and lapses in logic; together with an awareness that for most defects, to delete is the instantaneous cure.

The rhythms of the King James Version of the Bible stand forever as writing, although certain emendations as to meaning seem obligatory. The King James Epistle of Paul to the Philippians, 3:20, reads: "For our conversation is in heaven"; the Revised Standard Version reads: "We are a heavenly body"; each a mistranslation, according to Dr. Alvin E. Magary, who feels that Dr. Moffat got it right: " 'We are a colony of heaven'—a Roman outpost as it were, in which people conformed their lives to the life of Rome—an interpretation which makes sense as applied to Christianity"; Dr. Magary also emphasizes that the beatitude, blessed are the meek, should have no connotation of subservience, since if rendered more strictly, the word would be, not the meek, but the "begging."

2 Michael Tippett, "An Irish Basset-Horn," *The Listener,* July 26, 1956.

3 Hesketh Pearson, "Bernard Shaw as Producer," *The Listener,* August 16, 1956.

The revisions by Henry James of his novels, are evidently in part the result of an insistent desire to do justice to first intention. Reverting to pronouncements on Milton and Goethe made previously, T. S. Eliot seems to feel that after-judgment can not merely be taken for granted, and when accepting the Goethe Prize in 1954 he said, "As one's reading is extended [one begins] to develop that critical ability, that power of self-criticism without which the poet will do no more than repeat himself . . ."; then further on: "To understand what Wisdom is, is to be wise oneself: and I have only the degree of understanding that can be attained by a man who knows that he is not wise, yet has some faith that he is wiser than he was twenty years ago. I say twenty years ago, because I am under the distressing necessity of quoting a sentence I printed in 1933. It is this:

> **Of Goethe perhaps it is truer to say that he dabbled in both philosophy and poetry and made no great success at either; his true role was that of a man of the world and sage, a La Rochefoucauld, a La Bruyere, a Vauvenargues.**

Mr. Eliot says he ". . . never re-read the passage in which this sentence is buried [and had] discovered it not so very long ago in Mr. Michael Hamburger's introduction to his edition and translation of the text of Holderlin's poems." He then goes on to say of Goethe, "It may be that there are areas of wisdom that he did not penetrate: but I am more interested in trying to understand the wisdom he possessed than to define its limitations. When a man is a good deal wiser than oneself, one does not complain that he is no wiser than he is." [4]

Since writing is not only an art but a trade embodying principles attested by experience, we would do well not to forget that it is an expedient for making one's self understood and that what is said should at least have the air of having meant something to the person who wrote it—as is the case with Gertrude Stein and James Joyce. Stewart Sherman one time devised a piece of jargon which he offered as indistinguishable from work by Gertrude Stein, which gave itself away at once as lacking any private air of interest. If I may venture to say again what I have already said when obscurity was deplored, one should be as clear as one's natural reticence allows one to be. Laurence Binyon, reflecting on the state

---

[4] "Discourse in Praise of Wisdom," reëntitled "Goethe as the Sage."

of letters after completing his Dante, said: "How indulgent we are
to infirmity of structure . . ." [5] and structural infirmity truly has,
under surrealism, become a kind of horticultural verbal blight
threatening firmness at the core; a situation met long ago in *The
Classic Anthology Defined by Confucius:*

> **Enjoy the good yet sink not in excess.**
> **True scholar stands by his steadfastness.** [6]
>
> **. . . . . .**
>
> **Lamb-skin for suavity, trimmed and ornate,**
> **But a good soldier who will get things straight.** [7]

In attaining this noble firmness, one must have clarity, and clarity
depends on precision; not that intentional ambiguity cannot be
an art. Reinhold Niebuhr is not famed as easy reading, but is at
times a study in precision as when he says, "The self does not
realize itself most fully when self-realization is its conscious aim";
and of conscience, says, "We will define it provisionally at least
as capacity to view itself and judge obligation in contrast with
inclination." [8] It is not "the purpose [but] the function of roots to
absorb water," Dr. Edmund Sinnott notes in his book *The Biology
of the Spirit,* in which he discusses the self-regulating properties of
protoplasm—digressing, with a shade of outrage, to deplore untidi-
ness in the use of terms. One is corrected when referring to certain
African tribes for saying they worship the devil; they propitiate
the devil; and if precise, one weeds text of adjective, adverbs and
unnecessary punctuation. As an instance of such concision, we have
Mr. Francis Watson's account of Edwin Arnold, "the traveller,
linguist, and semi-mystic, with whom Matthew Arnold did not like
to be confused." [9] Informing us that Edwin Arnold had been mar-
ried three times and that two of his wives had died—a lack-luster
kind of statement which few of us perhaps would avoid—Mr.
Watson says, "after being twice bereaved, he found a third wife
from Japan, a land whose culture he extolled in articles. . . ."
Paramount as a rule for any kind of writing—scientific, com-

---

5 *The Dalhousie Review,* January 1943.
6 Translated by Ezra Pound (Cambridge: Harvard University Press, 1954),
p. 55.
7 *Ibid.,* p. 80.
8 *The Self and the Dramas of History* (New York: Scribner, 1955).
9 "Edwin Arnold and 'The Light of Asia,' " *The Listener,* June 14, 1956.

mercial, informal, prose or verse—we dare not be dull. Finding Akira Kurosawa's film *The Magnificent Seven* too reiterative, Bosley Crowther says that "the director shows so many shots of horses' feet tromping in the mud that we wonder if those horses have heads." [10]

In his "Advice to a Young Critic" (Golding Bright),[11] Bernard Shaw says, "Never strike an attitude, national, moral, or critical"— an axiom he did not observe too fanatically if judged by the telegram he is said to have sent to an actress with a leading part in one of his plays: ". . . wonderful, marvelous, superb . . ." to which the actress replied, "Undeserving such praise"; and he: "I meant the play"; and she: "So did I."

I have a mania for straight writing—however circuitous I may be in what I myself say of plants, animals, or places; and although one may reverse the order of words for emphasis, it should not be to rescue a rhyme. There are exceptions, of course, as when Mr. Oliver Warner, speaking of Captain Cook, the explorer, in commending the remarkable drawings made by members of the Captain's staff, says: "None of Cook's artists worked to preconceived notions. They drew what they saw and wonderful it was." [12] To say "and it was wonderful" would have been very flat. We have literature, William Archer said, when we impart distinctiveness to ordinary talk and make it still seem ordinary.

Like dullness, implausibility obscures the point; so, familiar though we are with "Fenimore Cooper's Literary Offenses," by Mark Twain,[13] allow me to quote a line or two. "It is a rule of literary art in the domain of fiction," Mark Twain says, "that always the reader shall be able to tell the corpses from the others. But this detail often has been overlooked in the *Deerslayer* tale. [Cooper] bends 'a sapling' to the form of an arch over [a] narrow passage, and conceals six Indians in its foliage." Then, ". . . one of his acute Indian experts, Chingachgook (pronounced Chicago, I think), has lost the trail of a person he is tracking . . . turned a running stream out of its course, and there, in the slush of its old bed, were that person's moccasin-tracks. . . ." Even the laws of nature take a vacation when Cooper is practicing "the delicate art of the forest."

[10] *The New York Times,* November 20, 1957.
[11] *The Listener, June 14, 1956.*
[12] "In Honour of James Cook," *The Listener,* June 14, 1956.
[13] *The Shock of Recognition,* edited by Edmund Wilson (New York: Doubleday, 1943).

What has been said pertains to technique (*teknikos* from the Greek, akin to *tekto:* to produce or bring forth—as art, especially the useful arts). And, indeed if technique is of no interest to a writer, I doubt that the writer is an artist. What do I mean by straight writing, I have been asked. I mean, in part, writing that is not mannered, overconscious, or at war with common sense, as when a reviewer of *The Evolution of Cambridge Publishing,* by S. C. Roberts, refers to "a demure account of Cambridge's flirtation with the *Encyclopædia Britannica.*" [14] At the risk of seeming to find every virtue in certain authors and these authors in a certain few books or critiques, let me contrast with the unreal manner, W. D. Howells' *My Mark Twain* and a similar uninfected retrospect by the Duke of Windsor. "Of all the literary men I have known," Howells says of Mark Twain, "he was the most unliterary in his make and manner. . . . His style was what we know, for good or for bad, but his manner, if I may difference the two, was as entirely his own as if no one had ever written before. [He] despised the avoidance of repetitions out of fear of tautology. If a word served his turn better than a substitute, he would use it as many times on a page as he chose. . . . [There] never was a more biddable man in things you could show him a reason for. . . . If you wanted a thing changed, very good, he changed it; if you suggested that a word or a sentence or a paragraph had better be struck out, very good, he struck it out. His proof sheets came back each a veritable 'mush of concession,' as Emerson says." "He was always reading some vital book . . . which gave him life at first hand," Howells continues. "It is in vain that I try to give a notion of the intensity with which he compassed the whole world. . . ."

The other instance of straight writing to which I referred is "My Garden," by the Duke of Windsor.[15] Prosperity and royalty are always under suspicion. "Of course they had help," people say. "Someone must have written it for them"; as they said of the shepherd made judge, in the fable of the shepherd and the King, ". . . *he* is given the credit; we did the work; he has amassed riches; we are poor."[16] So let me say, I have in the following narra-

---

[14] Unsigned review in *The Times Literary Supplement,* London, March 2, 1956.

[15] *Life,* July 16, 1956.

[16] *The Fables of La Fontaine,* translated by Marianne Moore (New York: Viking, 1954), Book Ten, IX.

tive an impression of individuality, conviction, and verbal selectiveness.

"I think my deep enjoyment of gardening must be latent," the Duke begins. "At least it was not inherited. . . . The gardens at Sandringham and Windsor . . . made a fine show in summertime [a word with flavor, for me], but people did not really live with them. A garden is a mood, as Rousseau said, and my mood was one of intimacy, not splendor." Of his present gardening at The Mill, not far from Paris, he says, ". . . French gardens can be remarkably beautiful things. They look like continuations of the Savonnerie of Aubusson carpets in the great chateaus rolled outside the windows onto the lawns, perfectly patterned and mathematically precise. . . . I wanted an English type of garden, which means green grass and seemingly casual arrangement of flowers, and here I had the perfect framework." Commenting on one of the color photographs which supplement the account, he says, "The main entrance to the property has an old covered gateway with ancient oak doors and a cobbled drive which leads to the main building. There is a big sundial above the front door, put there when The Mill was restored about 1732. In the foreground is Trooper, one of our four pugs." Technically an oversight, perhaps —the f-o-r-e ground and f-o-u-r pugs in close proximity—this clash lends authenticity, has the charm of not too conscious writing. Unmistakably all along, the article embodies a zeal for the subject, a deep affection for flowers as seen in the complaint, "The mildest stone-mason turns scourge when it comes to plant life." The piece smiles, whereas saturninity is a bad omen. "We do not praise God by dispraising man." [17]

II. IDIOSYNCRASY

In considering technique, I tried to say that writing can be affirmative and that we must, as Dr. Nathan Scott says, "reject the attitude of philosophic distrust." The writer should have "a sense of upthrusting vitality and self-discovery" [18] without thinking about the impression made, except as one needs to make oneself understood.

We are suffering from too much sarcasm, I feel. Any touch of unfeigned gusto in our smart press is accompanied by an arch

[17] Dr. Alvin E. Magary.
[18] Maxwell Geismar, *The Nation,* April 14, 1956.

word implying, "Now to me, of course, this is a bit asinine." Denigration, indeed, is to me so disaffecting that when I was asked to write something for the Columbia Chapter of Phi Beta Kappa Class Day exercises, I felt that I should not let my sense of incapacity as an orator hinder me from saying what I feel about the mildew of disrespect and leave appreciation to Mr. Auden, to salute "literary marines landing in little magazines." I then realized that what I was so urgent to emphasize is reduced in the First Psalm to a sentence: Blessed is the man who does not sit in the seat of the scoffer.

Odd as it may seem that a few words of overwhelming urgency should be a mosaic of quotations, why paraphrase what for maximum impact should be quoted verbatim? I borrowed, at all events, Ambassador Conant's title *The Citadel of Learning,* taken for his book from Stalin: "[Facing us] stands the citadel of learning. This citadel we must capture at any price. This citadel must be taken by our youth, if they wish to be the builders of a new life, if they wish, in fact, to take the place of the old guard."[19]

Blessed is the man

who does not sit in the seat of the scoffer—
    the man who does not denigrate, depreciate, denunciate;
      who is not "characteristically intemperate,"
who does not "excuse, retreat, equivocate; and will be heard."
(Ah, Giorgione! there are those who mongrelize
    and those who heighten anything they touch; although it
                           may well be
      that if Giorgione's self-portrait were not said to be he,
it might not take my fancy. Blessed the geniuses who know

that egomania is not a duty.)
    "Diversity, controversy; tolerance"—in that "citadel
      of learning" we have a fort that ought to armor us well.
Blessed is the man who "takes the risk of a decision"—asks

himself the question: "Would it solve the problem?
    Is it right as I see it? Is it in the best interests of all?"
      Alas. Ulysses' companions are now political—
living self-indulgently until the moral sense is drowned,

---

[19] As "freely translated" by Charles Poore, reviewing James B. Conant, *The Citadel of Learning* (New Haven: Yale University Press, 1956), in the *New York Times,* April 7, 1956.

having lost all power of comparison,
   thinking license emancipates one, "slaves whom they
                            themselves have bound."
   Brazen authors, downright soiled and downright spoiled,
                                                as if sound
and exceptional, are the old quasi-modish counterfeit,

mitin-proofing conscience against character.
Affronted by "private lies and public shame," blessed is the author
   who favors what the supercilious do not favor—
who will not comply. Blessed, the unaccommodating man.

Blessed the man whose faith is different
   from possessiveness—of a kind not framed by "things which do
                                                          appear"—
      who will not visualize defeat, too intent to cower;
whose illumined eye has seen the shaft that gilds the sultan's tower.

I had written these lines about denigration as treason, and was
assembling advice for some students of verse, when I found that
Rolfe Humphries, in his little treatise entitled "Writing the
Lyric," [20] has thrown light on the use of consonants. "Take the
letter *s*," he says, "one of the most insidious sounds in the lan-
guage, one which will creep in, in a sibilant reptilian fashion like
the original serpent in the garden, and if you are not careful, not
only drive you out of Paradise, but hiss you off the stage; . . . see
if you cannot write a quatrain without using it at all." Pondering
my "Blessed is the man who does not sit in the seat of the scoffer,"
I could only say that another's expertise might save one consider-
able awkwardness. Initiate John Barry came to my rescue by citing
the *Aeneid* (II, 8):

                   Et iam nox umida caelo
            praecipitat suadentque cadentia somnos.

Convinced that denigration is baneful, one readily sanctions the
attack prompted by affection. In fact nothing is more entertaining
than the fraternal accolade in reverse; as when *The London News
Chronicle* of November 16, 1954, published a cartoon, and lines
entitled "Winniehaha," [21] concerning Mr. Churchill—Prime Min-

---

[20] In *Writers on Writing,* edited by Herschel Brickell (New York: Double-
day, 1949).
[21] Anonymous. Reprinted in the *New York Times,* November 17, 1954.

ister then—after a cousin of his, Captain Lionel Leslie, had referred to the drop of Indian blood inherited by Sir Winston through his grandmother, Clara Jerome. The complimentary cast of the sally— a parody of Longfellow's *Hiawatha*—which was written before Mr. Churchill had been knighted, when the date of his retirement was a subject of speculation, is apparent from even a line or two:

> **In the center of the village,**
> **In the wigwam of the wise ones,**
> **Where the head men of the nation**
> **Come to talk in solemn council,**
> **Squats the old chief, Winniehaha,**
> **Also known as Sitting Bulldog; . . .**
>
> **Some there are with minds that wander**
> **From the purpose of the powwow;**
> **Minds that wonder will he give us**
> **Just an inkling, to be candid,**
> **Of the date of his retirement?**
> **Not that we would wish to rush him,**
> **Wish to rush old Winniehaha,**
> **Rush our splendid Sitting Bulldog**
> **From the headship of the head men**
> **In the center of the village,**
> **In the wigwam of the wise ones.**
> **Still, it's just a bit unsettling**
> **Not to know when Winniehaha**
> **Will give place to handsome Pinstripe.**
> **Will he tell us? Will he tell us?**

In connection with personality, it is a curiosity of literature how often what one says of another seems descriptive of one's self. Would-be statesmen who spike their utterances with malice should bear this in mind and take fright as they drive home the moral of The Lion, The Wolf, and The Fox: "Slander flies home faster than rumor of good one has done." [22] In any case, Sir Winston Churchill's pronouncement on Alfred the Great does seem appropriate to himself—his own defeats, triumphs, and hardihood: "This sublime power to rise above the whole force of circumstances, to remain unbiased by the extremes of victory or defeat, to greet returning fortune with a cool eye, to have faith in men after

---

[22] *The Fables of La Fontaine,* Book Eight, III.

repeated betrayals, raises Alfred far above the turmoil of barbaric wars to his pinnacle of deathless glory." [23]

Walter de la Mare found "prose worthy of the name of literature . . . tinged with that erratic and unique factor, the personal . . ." reminding one of the statement by Mr. F. O. Matthiessen, in his study of Sarah Orne Jewett, that "style means that the author has fused his material and his technique with the distinctive quality of his personality . . ." and of the word "idiolect" used by Professor Harry Levin as meaning "the language of a speaker or writer who has an inflection of his own." In saying there is no substitute for content, one is partly saying there is no substitute for individuality —that which is peculiar to the person (the Greek: *idioma*). One also recalls the remark by Henry James: "a thing's being one's own will double the use of it." Discoveries in art, certainly, are personal before they are general.

Goya—in *The Taste of Our Time* series,[24] reviewed by Pierre Gassier somewhat as follows—should afford us creative impetus. After surviving a lethal threat, severe illness at Cádiz in 1792, Goya was left with his right side paralyzed, with dizzy spells, a buzzing in his head, and partial blindness. He recovered, only to find himself irremediably deaf. On returning to Madrid, he began work at once, painted eleven pictures for the Academy of San Fernando, and sent them with a letter to the director, Don Berbardo Iriarte. "In order to occupy an imagination mortified by the contemplation of my sufferings," he said, "and recover, partially at all events, the expenses incurred by illness, I fell to painting a set of pictures in which I have given observation a place usually denied it in works made to order, in which little scope is left for fancy and invention." Fancy and invention—not made to order— perfectly describe the work; the *Burial of the Sardine,* say: a careening throng in which one can identify a bear's mask and paws, a black monster wearing a horned hood, a huge turquoise quadracorne, a goblin mouth on a sepia fish-tailed banner, and twin dancers in filmy gowns with pink satin bows in their hair. Pieter Bruegel, the Elder, an observer as careful and as populous as Goya, "crossed the Alps and travelled the length of Italy, returning in 1555 to paint as though Michelangelo had never existed," so

23 *A History of the English-Speaking Peoples,* Vol. I: *The Birth of Britain* (New York: Dodd, Mead, 1956).

24 "Essay on Prose," *The National and English Review* (in three sections, concluded in March 1955), quoted by *Arts* (New York).

powerful was predilective intention.[25] In a television interview after receiving the National Book Award for *Ten North Frederick,* John O'Hara was asked if he might not have to find, as a background for fiction, something different from small-town life in Pennsylvania, to which he replied, "There is in one room in one day of one man's life, material for a lifetime." The artist does not—as we sometimes hear—"seek fresh sources of inspiration." A subject to which he is susceptible entices him to it; as we see in the epics of Marko Marulíc (1450-1524), the fifth centenary of whose birth Yugoslavia has celebrated, in honor largely of his Latin epic *Judita* (1501), enhanced by woodcuts such as *The Muster at Dubrovnic:* trumpeters, men at arms in an elephant-castle; dog; king, queen, and attendants. The New York Yugoslav Information Center says, "What is important is that in following the classics, Marulíc did not transplant . . . mechanically . . . but depended on his own poetic abilities," his novelty consisting in "comparisons taken from his own field of experience, in language abounding in speech forms of the people." An author, that is to say, is a fashioner of words, stamps them with his own personality, and wears the raiment he has made, in his own way.

Psychoanalysis can do some harm "taking things to pieces that it cannot put together again," as Mr. Whit Burnett said in a discourse entitled "Secrets of Creativeness." It has also been of true service, sharpening our faculties and combating complacence. Mr. Burnett drew attention to the biography of Dr. Freud by Ernest Jones, and to what is said there of genius as being not a quality but qualitative—a combination of attributes which differs with the person—three of which are honesty, a sense of the really significant, and the power of concentration.

Curiosity seems to me connected with this sense of significance. Thoreau, you may recall, demurred when commended for originality and said that it was curiosity: "I am curiosity from top to toe." I think I detect curiosity in the work of Sybille Bedford—in her novel *A Legacy*—in the statement, ". . . no one in the house was supposed to handle *used* notes [banknotes]. Everybody was paid straight off the press. The problem of change was not envisaged"; sententiousness in the writing, being offset by the unstereotyped juxtaposing of a word or two such as querulous and placid. Grandma Merz, for instance, "was a short bundle of a

25 Fritz Grossmann, *The Paintings of Bruegel* (New York: Phaidon Press, 1955).

woman swaddled in stuffs and folds . . . stuck with brooches of
rather gray diamonds. Her face was a round, large, indeterminate
expanse . . . with features that escaped attention and an expression
that was at once querulous and placid." [26]
In Marguerite Yourcenar's "Author's Note" to her *Memoirs
of Hadrian* [27]— a study which does "border on the domain of
fiction and sometimes of poetry," as has been said—one sees what
concentration editorially can be. And Paul Delarue's "Sources and
Commentary" appended to the *Borzoi Book of French Folk Tales*[28]
are similarly impressive—besides affording an exciting knowledge
of variants. In "The White Dove" (the story of Bluebeard,
abridged by Perrault), the ninth victim's pretexts for delay be-
come specific—in this early version—"to put on my petticoat, my
wedding-gown, my cap, my bouquet." And we learn that "The
Ass's Skin," enshrined for us by La Fontaine in "The Power of
Fable," [29] is the "Story of Goldilocks," and of Madame d'Aulnoy's
"Beauty and the Beast" (1698). The presentment here of obscure
minutiae, demonstrating that tales of all nations have a common
fabric, makes the most artful of detective stories seem tame.

Creative secrets, are they secrets? Impassioned interest in life,
that burns its bridges behind it and will not contemplate defeat,
is one, I would say. Discouragement is a form of temptation; but
paranoia is not optimism. In an essay entitled "Solitude" (the
theme chosen by the *Figaro* for an essay contest), Maxime Benne-
bon, a boy seventeen, visualizes "Michelangelo's *Moses*, head in
hands, the attitude of the child who prays with eyes closed; of the
pianist—his back to the audience; they must be alone that they
may offer what is most treasurable, themselves."

The master secret may be steadfastness, that of Nehemiah,
Artaxerxes' cupbearer, as it was of the three youths in the fiery
furnace, who would not bow down to the image which the King
had set up, "Why is thy countenance sad, seeing that thou art not
sick?" the King asked. Nehemiah requested that he be allowed to
rebuild the wall of Jerusalem and the King granted his request;
gave him leave of absence and a letter to the keeper of the forest

[26] Sybille Bedford, *A Legacy* (New York: Simon and Schuster, 1957).
[27] Translated from the French by Grace Frick (New York: Farrar, Strauss
and Young, 1954).
[28] Translated by Austin E. Fife (New York: Knopf, 1956).
[29] *The Fables of La Fontaine*, Book Eight, IV: "The moment The Ass's
Skin commences, Away with appearances; I am enraptured, really am."

that he might have timber for the gates of the palace—subject to sarcasm while building, such as Sanballet's, "If a fox go up, he shall break down their wall." Summoned four times to a colloquy, Nehemiah sent word: "I am doing a great work and I cannot come down." Then when warned that he would be slain, he said, "Should such a man as I flee?" "So the wall was finished." [30] A result which is sensational is implemented by what to the craftsman was private and unsensational. Tyrone Guthrie, in connection with the theater, made a statement which sums up what I have been trying to say about idiosyncrasy and technique: "It is one of the paradoxes of art that a work can only be universal if it is rooted in a part of its creator which is most privately and particularly himself."[31]

Thomas Mann, fending off eulogy, rendered a service when he said, "Praise will never subdue skepticism." We fail in some degree—and know that we do, if we are competent; but can prevail; and the following attributes, applied by a London journal to Victor Gollancz, the author and publisher, I adopt as a prescription: we can in the end prevail, if our attachment to art is sufficiently deep; "unpriggish, subtle, perceptive, and consuming."[32]

---

[30] Nehemiah 2, 4, and 6.
[31] *The New York Times Magazine,* November 27, 1955.
[32] *The Observer,* March 11, 1956.

e e cummings

e e cummings was born into a Harvard family on October 14, 1894, in Cambridge, Massachusetts. Although many of his finer poems are set in traditional forms, cummings's poetry has been famed for its eccentric manners: a punctuation which, coming from a poet who is also a painter, is always unorthodox and frequently nonexistent; an insistence on lowercase type, whether in the printing of his own name or of the first person singular pronoun; a way of typographically deploying lines and individual words so that they yield meanings which are apprehensible if unpronounceable; the use of phonetic spellings to indicate dialect or illbreeding, discover a pun, or transparently conceal an obscenity; and a predilection for grammatical shifts whereby a verb or adverb functions as another part of speech—as a noun, for example.

For all his modernist trappings and satiric forays, cummings is a lyric, affirmative romancer—very nearly a self-assured sheep in wolf's clothing. In a vendetta against abstraction, intellectualization, or whatever seems "artificial" and static, he brandishes his senti-

ment. But if, as one might gather, cummings's universe is vastly simplified, the lyrical intensity of his superbly crafted poems serves to compensate for the narrow moral range of their accommodations and discriminations.

cummings died in 1962, in the summer.

An Introduction*

The poems to come are for you and for me and are not for most-people
　　　—it's no use trying to pretend that mostpeople and ourselves are alike. Mostpeople have less in common with ourselves than the squarerootofminusone. You and I are human beings;mostpeople are snobs. Take the matter of being born. What does being born mean to mostpeople? Catastrophe unmitigated. Socialrevolution. The cultured aristocrat yanked out of his hyperexclusively ultravoluptuous superpalazzo,and dumped into an incredibly vulgar detentioncamp swarming with every conceivable species of undesirable organism. Mostpeople fancy a guaranteed birthproof safetysuit of nondestructible selflessness. If mostpeople were to be born twice they'd improbably call it dying—
　　　you and I are not snobs. We can never be born enough. We are human beings;for whom birth is a supremely welcome mystery,the mystery of growing: the mystery which happens only and whenever we are faithful to ourselves. You and I wear the dangerous looseness of doom and find it becoming. Life, for eternal us, is now;

---

* **Reprinted from** *Poems* **1923-1954.**

121

and now is much too busy being a little more than everything to seem anything,catastrophic included.

Life,for mostpeople,simply isn't. Take the socalled standardof-living. What do mostpeople mean by "living"? They don't mean living. They mean the latest and closest plural approximation to singular prenatal passivity which science,in its finite but unbounded wisdom,has succeeded in selling their wives. If science could fail,a mountain's a mammal. Mostpeople's wives can spot a genuine delusion of embryonic omnipotence ,immediately and will accept no substitutes

—luckily for us,a mountain is a mammal. The plusorminus movie to end moving,the strictly scientific parlourgame of real unreality,the tyranny conceived in misconception and dedicated to the proposition that every man is a woman and any woman a king,hasn't a wheel to stand on. What their most synthetic not to mention transparent majesty,mrsandmr collective foetus,would improbably call a ghost is walking. He isn't an undream of anaesthetized impersons, or a cosmic comfortstation,or a transcendentally sterilized lookie-soundiefeelietastiesmellie. He is a healthily complex,a naturally homogeneous,citizen of immortality. The now of his each pitying free imperfect gesture,his any birth or breathing,insults perfected inframortally millenniums of slavishness. He is a little more than everything,he is democracy;he is alive:he is ourselves.

Miracles are to come. With you I leave a remembrance of miracles:they are by somebody who can love and who shall be continually reborn,a human being;somebody who said to those near him, when his fingers would not hold a brush "tie it into my hand"—

nothing proving or sick or partial. Nothing false,nothing difficult or easy or small or colossal. Nothing ordinary or extraordinary, nothing emptied or filled,real or unreal;nothing feeble and known or clumsy and guessed. Everywhere tints childrening,innocent spontaneous,true. Nowhere possibly what flesh and impossibly such a garden,but actually flowers which breasts are among the very mouths of light. Nothing believed or doubted;brain over heart, surface:nowhere hating or to fear;shadow,mind without soul. Only how measureless cool flames of making;only each other building always distinct selves of mutual entirely opening;only alive. Never the murdered finalities of wherewhen and yesno,impotent nongames of wrongright and rightwrong;never to gain or pause,never the soft adventure of undoom,greedy anguishes and cringing ecstasies of inexistence;never to rest and never to have:only to grow.

Always the beautiful answer who asks a more beautiful question

Wallace Stevens

Profoundly aware that "an isolated fact, cut loose from the universe, has no significance" in itself, but derives significance from the reality to which it belongs—or, to turn the image slightly, "reality is not the thing but the aspect of the thing"—Wallace Stevens materializes as one of the great poets of the imagination. This does not mean that his province is the implausible, however, for what concerns him is the belief of credible people in credible things. The unfamiliar must be approached through the familiar, the unreal drawn from the real. Nothing is too mundane to provide a base for poetic construction. By divining resemblances or analogies "one may find intimations of immortality in an object on the mantelpiece; and these intimations are as real in the mind in which they occur as the mantelpiece itself."

True imagination, "the sum of our faculties," is a power that enables us to perceive "the normal in the abnormal, the opposite of chaos in chaos." "Piece the world together, boys," Stevens remarks in one poem, "but not with your hands." The imagination colors, ripens, or suffuses things without violating them; "like light, it adds

*nothing, except itself." And, as in some respects the imagination is
a function of the poet's personality, a poem may be defined as "a
particular of life thought of for so long that one's thought has
become an inseparable part of it or a particular of life so intensely
felt that the feeling has entered into it." The poem is neither bleak
fact nor moon-madness but a new nature created by the poet, a
fresh "mundo" which smacks of mortality while it resists disinte-
gration, and which would incorporate ideas rather than submit to
their strictures. "It is the mundo of the imagination in which the
imaginative man delights and not the gaunt world of reason. The
pleasure is the pleasure of powers that create a truth that cannot be
arrived at by reason alone, a truth that the poet recognizes by
sensation. The morality of the poet's radiant and productive atmos-
phere is the morality of the right sensation."*

*Stevens's poetry is sometimes reputed to be inordinately florid
or whimsical, but the flourishes are ruddy. Although equally capa-
ble of stateliness or barbarous austerity, he questioned whether
"what is called Anglo-Saxon should have the right to higgle and
haggle all over the page, contesting the right of other words. If a
poem seems to require a hierophantic phrase, the phrase should
pass. . . . One of the consequences of the ordination of style is not
to limit it, but to enlarge it, not to impoverish it, but to enrich and
liberate it." Precision is inevitably elegant, whether in the gestures
of poets or grocery clerks.*

*Wallace Stevens was born October 2, 1879, in Reading, Penn-
sylvania. He died on August 2, 1955, in Hartford, Connecticut,
where for many years he had been an insurance executive.*

The Noble Rider and the Sound of Words*

In the *Phaedrus,* Plato speaks of the soul in a figure. He says:

> Let our figure be of a composite nature—a pair of winged
> horses and a charioteer. Now the winged horses and the
> charioteer of the gods are all of them noble, and of noble breed,
> while ours are mixed; and we have a charioteer who drives
> them in a pair, and one of them is noble and of noble origin,
> and the other is ignoble and of ignoble origin; and, as might be
> expected, there is a great deal of trouble in managing them.
> I will endeavor to explain to you in what way the mortal differs
> from the immortal creature. The soul or animate being has the
> care of the inanimate, and traverses the whole heaven in divers
> forms appearing;—when perfect and fully winged she soars
> upward, and is the ruler of the universe; while the imperfect

* **From *The Necessary Angel*:** *Essays on Reality & the Imagination*
by Wallace Stevens.

soul loses her feathers, and drooping in her flight at last settles on the solid ground.

We recognize at once, in this figure, Plato's pure poetry; and at the same time we recognize what Coleridge called Plato's dear, gorgeous nonsense. The truth is that we have scarcely read the passage before we have identified ourselves with the charioteer, have, in fact, taken his place and, driving his winged horses, are traversing the whole heaven. Then suddenly we remember, it may be, that the soul no longer exists and we droop in our flight and at last settle on the solid ground. The figure becomes antiquated and rustic.

1

What really happens in this brief experience? Why does this figure, potent for so long, become merely the emblem of a mythology, the rustic memorial of a belief in the soul and in a distinction between good and evil? The answer to these questions is, I think, a simple one.

I said that suddenly we remember that the soul no longer exists and we droop in our flight. For that matter, neither charioteers nor chariots any longer exist. Consequently, the figure does not become unreal because we are troubled about the soul. Besides, unreal things have a reality of their own, in poetry as elsewhere. We do not hesitate, in poetry, to yield ourselves to the unreal, when it is possible to yield ourselves. The existence of the soul, of charioteers and chariots and of winged horses is immaterial. They did not exist for Plato, not even the charioteer and chariot; for certainly a charioteer driving his chariot across the whole heaven was for Plato precisely what he is for us. He was unreal for Plato as he is for us. Plato, however, could yield himself, was free to yield himself, to this gorgeous nonsense. We cannot yield ourselves. We are not free to yield ourselves.

Just as the difficulty is not a difficulty about unreal things, since the imagination accepts them, and since the poetry of the passage is, for us, wholly the poetry of the unreal, so it is not an emotional difficulty. Something else than the imagination is moved by the statement that the horses of the gods are all of them noble, and of noble breed or origin. The statement is a moving statement and is intended to be so. It is insistent and its insistence moves us. Its insistence is the insistence of a speaker, in this case Socrates, who, for the moment, feels delight, even if a casual delight, in the nobility and noble breed. Those images of nobility instantly become nobility itself and determine the emotional level at which the next page or two are to be read. The figure does not lose its vitality because of any failure of feeling on Plato's part. He does not communicate nobility coldly. His horses are not marble horses, the reference to their breed saves them from being that. The fact that the horses are not marble horses helps, moreover, to save the charioteer from being, say, a creature of cloud. The result is that we recognize, even if we cannot realize, the feelings of the robust poet clearly and fluently noting the images in his mind and by means of his robustness, clearness and fluency communicating much more than the images themselves. Yet we do not quite yield. We cannot. We do not feel free.

In trying to find out what it is that stands between Plato's figure and ourselves, we have to accept the idea that, however legendary it appears to be, it has had its vicissitudes. The history of a figure of speech or the history of an idea, such as the idea of nobility, cannot be very different from the history of anything else. It is the episodes that are of interest, and here the episode is that of our diffidence. By us and ourselves, I mean you and me; and yet not you and me as individuals but as representatives of a state of mind. Adams in his work on Vico makes the remark that the true history of the human race is a history of its progressive mental states. It is a remark of interest in this relation. We may assume that in the history of Plato's figure there have been incessant changes of response; that these changes have been psychological changes, and that our own diffidence is simply one more state of mind due to such a change.

The specific question is partly as to the nature of the change and partly as to the cause of it. In nature, the change is as follows: The imagination loses vitality as it ceases to adhere to what is real. When it adheres to the unreal and intensifies what is unreal, while its first effect may be extraordinary, that effect is the maximum effect that it will ever have. In Plato's figure, his imagination does not adhere to what is real. On the contrary, having created something unreal, it adheres to it and intensifies its unreality. Its first effect, its effect at first reading, is its maximum effect, when the imagination, being moved, puts us in the place of the charioteer, before the reason checks us. The case is, then, that we concede that the figure is all imagination. At the same time, we say that it has not the slightest meaning for us, except for its nobility. As to that, while we are moved by it, we are moved as observers. We recognize it perfectly. We do not realize it. We understand the feeling of it, the robust feeling, clearly and fluently communicated. Yet we understand it rather than participate in it.

As to the cause of the change, it is the loss of the figure's vitality. The reason why this particular figure has lost its vitality is that, in it, the imagination adheres to what is unreal. What happened, as we were traversing the whole heaven, is that the imagination lost its power to sustain us. It has the strength of reality or none at all.

2

What has just been said demonstrates that there are degrees of the imagination, as, for example, degrees of vitality and, therefore, of intensity. It is an implication that there are degrees of reality. The discourse about the two elements seems endless. For my own part, I intend merely to follow, in a very hasty way, the fortunes of the idea of nobility as a characteristic of the imagination, and even as its symbol or alter ego, through several of the episodes in its history, in order to determine, if possible, what its fate has been and what has determined its fate. This can be done only on the basis of the relation between the imagination and reality. What has been said in respect to the figure of the charioteer illustrates this.

I should like now to go on to other illustrations of the relation between the imagination and reality and particularly to illustrations that constitute episodes in the history of the idea of nobility. It would be agreeable to pass directly from the charioteer and his winged horses to Don Quixote. It would be like a return from what Plato calls "the back of heaven" to one's own spot. Nevertheless, there is Verrocchio (as one among others) with his statue of Bartolommeo Colleoni, in Venice, standing in the way. I have not selected him as a Neo-Platonist to relate us back from a modern time to Plato's time, although he does in fact so relate us, just as through Leonardo, his pupil, he strengthens the relationship. I have selected him because there, on the edge of the world in which we live today, he established a form of such nobility that it has never ceased to magnify us in our own eyes. It is like the form of an invincible man, who has come, slowly and boldly, through every warlike opposition of the past and who moves in our midst without dropping the bridle of the powerful horse from his hand, without taking off his helmet and without relaxing the attitude of a warrior of noble origin. What man on whose side the horseman fought could ever be anything but fearless, anything but indomitable? One feels the passion of rhetoric begin to stir and even to grow furious; and one thinks that, after all, the noble style, in whatever it creates, merely perpetuates the noble style. In this statue, the apposition between the imagination and reality is too favorable to the imagination. Our difficulty is not primarily with any detail. It is primarily with the whole. The point is not so much to analyze the difficulty as to determine whether we share it, to find out whether it exists, whether we regard this specimen of the genius of Verrocchio and of the Renaissance as a bit of uncommon panache, no longer quite the appropriate thing outdoors, or whether we regard it, in the language of Dr. Richards, as something inexhaustible to meditation or, to speak for myself, as a thing of a nobility responsive to the most minute demand. It seems, nowadays, what it may very well not have seemed a few years ago, a little overpowering, a little magnificent.

Undoubtedly, Don Quixote could be Bartolommeo Colleoni in Spain. The tradition of Italy is the tradition of the imagination. The tradition of Spain is the tradition of reality. There is no apparent reason why the reverse should not be true. If this is a just observation, it indicates that the relation between the imagination and reality is a question, more or less, of precise equilibrium. Thus it is not a question of the difference between grotesque extremes. My purpose is not to contrast Colleoni with Don Quixote. It is to say that one passed into the other, that one became and was the other. The difference between them is that Verrocchio believed in one kind of nobility and Cervantes, if he believed in any, believed in another kind. With Verrocchio it was an affair of the noble style, whatever his prepossession respecting the nobility of man as a real animal may have been. With Cervantes, nobility was not a thing of the imagination. It was a part of reality, it was something that exists in life, something so true to us that it is in danger of ceasing to exist, if we isolate it, something in the mind of a precarious tenure. These may be words. Certainly, however, Cervantes sought to set right the balance between the imagination and reality. As we come closer to our own times in Don Quixote and as we are drawn together by the intelligence common to the two periods, we may derive so much satisfaction from the restoration of reality as to become wholly prejudiced against the imagination. This is to reach a conclusion prematurely, let alone that it may be to reach a conclusion in respect to something as to which no conclusion is possible or desirable.

There is in Washington, in Lafayette Square, which is the square on which the White House faces, a statue of Andrew Jackson, riding a horse with one of the most beautiful tails in the world. General Jackson is raising his hat in a gay gesture, saluting the ladies of his generation. One looks at this work of Clark Mills and thinks of the remark of Bertrand Russell that to acquire immunity to eloquence is of the utmost importance to the citizens of a democracy. We are bound to think that Colleoni, as a mercenary, was a much less formidable man than General Jackson, that he meant less to fewer people and that, if Verrocchio could have applied his prodigious poetry to Jackson, the whole American outlook today might be imperial. This work is a work of fancy. Dr. Richards cites Coleridge's theory of fancy as opposed to imagination. Fancy is an activity of the mind which puts things together of choice, *not* the will, as a principle of the mind's being, striving to realize itself in knowing itself. Fancy, then, is an exercise of selection from among objects already supplied by association, a selection made for purposes which are not then and therein being shaped but have been already fixed. We are concerned then with an object occupying a position as remarkable as any that can be found in the United States in which there is not the slightest trace of the imagination. Treating this work as typical, it is obvious that the American will as a principle of the mind's being is easily satisfied in its efforts to realize itself in knowing itself. The statue may be dismissed, not without speaking of it again as a thing that at least makes us conscious of ourselves as we were, if not as we are. To that extent, it helps us to know ourselves. It helps us to know ourselves as we were and that helps us to know ourselves as we are. The statue is neither of the imagination nor of reality. That it is a work of fancy precludes it from being a work of the imagination. A glance at it shows it to be unreal. The bearing of this is that there can be works, and this includes poems, in which neither the imagination nor reality is present.

The other day I was reading a note about an American artist who was said to have "turned his back on the aesthetic whims and theories of the day, and established headquarters in lower Manhattan." Accompanying this note was a reproduction of a painting called *Wooden Horses*. It is a painting of a merry-go-round, possibly of several of them. One of the horses seems to be prancing. The others are going lickety-split, each one struggling to get the bit in his teeth. The horse in the center of the picture, painted yellow, has two riders, one a man, dressed in a carnival costume, who is seated in the saddle, the other a blonde, who is seated well up the horse's neck. The man has his arms under the girl's arms. He holds himself stiffly in order to keep his cigar out of the girl's hair. Her feet are in a second and shorter set of stirrups. She has the legs of a hammer-thrower. It is clear that the couple are accustomed to wooden horses and like them. A little behind them is a younger girl riding alone. She has a strong body and streaming hair. She wears a short-sleeved, red waist, a white skirt and an emphatic bracelet of pink coral. She has her eyes on the man's arms. Still farther behind, there is another girl. One does not see much more of her than her head. Her lips are painted bright red. It seems that it would be better if someone were to hold her on her horse. We, here, are not interested in any aspect of this picture except that it is a picture of ribald and hilarious reality. It is a picture wholly favorable to what is real. It is not without imagination and it is far from being without aesthetic theory.

3

These illustrations of the relation between the imagination and reality are an outline on the basis of which to indicate a tendency. Their usefulness is this: that they help to make clear, what no one may ever have doubted, that just as in this or that work the degrees of imagination and of reality may vary, so this variation may exist as between the works of one age and the works of another. What I have said up to this point amounts to this: that the idea of nobility exists in art today only in degenerate forms or in a much diminished state, if, in fact, it exists at all or otherwise than on sufferance; that this is due to failure in the relation between the imagination and reality. I should now like to add that this failure is due, in turn, to the pressure of reality.

A variation between the sound of words in one age and the sound of words in another age is an instance of the pressure of reality. Take the statement by Bateson that a language, considered semantically, evolves through a series of conflicts between the denotative and the connotative forces in words; between an asceticism tending to kill language by stripping words of all association and a hedonism tending to kill language by dissipating their sense in a multiplicity of associations. These conflicts are nothing more than changes in the relation between the imagination and reality. Bateson describes the seventeenth century in England as predominantly a connotative period. The use of words in connotative senses was denounced by Locke and Hobbes, who desired a mathematical plainness; in short, perspicuous words. There followed in the eighteenth century an era of poetic diction. This was not the language of the age but a language of poetry peculiar to itself. In time, Wordsworth came to write the preface to the second edition of the *Lyrical Ballads* (1800), in which he said that the first volume had been published, "as an experiment, which, I hoped, might be of some use to ascertain how far, by fitting to metrical arrangement a selection of the real language of man in a state of vivid sensation, that sort of pleasure and that quantity of pleasure may be imparted, which a Poet may rationally endeavour to impart."

As the nineteenth century progressed, language once more became connotative. While there have been intermediate reactions, this tendency toward the connotative is the tendency today. The interest in semantics is evidence of this. In the case of some of our prose writers, as, for example, Joyce, the language, in quite different ways, is wholly connotative. When we say that Locke and Hobbes denounced the connotative use of words as an abuse, and when we speak of reactions and reforms, we are speaking, on the one hand, of a failure of the imagination to adhere to reality, and, on the other, of a use of language favorable to reality. The statement that the tendency toward the connotative is the tendency today is disputable. The general movement in the arts, that is to say, in painting and in music, has been the other way. It is hard to say that the tendency is toward the connotative in the use of words without also saying that the tendency is toward the imagination in other directions. The interest in the subconscious and in surrealism shows the tendency toward the imaginative. Boileau's remark that Descartes had cut poetry's throat is a remark that could have been made respecting a great many people during the last hundred years, and of no one more aptly than of Freud, who, as it happens, was familiar with it and repeats it in his *Future of an Illusion*. The object of that essay was to suggest a surrender to reality. His premise was that it is the unmistakable character of the present situation not that the promises of religion have become smaller but that they appear less credible to people. He notes the decline of religious belief and disagrees with the argument that man cannot in general do without the consolation of what he calls the religious illusion and that without it he would not endure the cruelty of reality. His conclusion is that man must venture at last into the hostile world and that this may be called education to reality. There is much more in that essay inimical to poetry and not least the observation in one of the final pages that "The voice of the intellect is a soft one, but it does not rest until it has gained a hearing." This, I fear, is intended to be the voice of the realist.

A tendency in language toward the connotative might very well parallel a tendency in other arts toward the denotative. We have just seen that that is in fact the situation. I suppose that the present always appears to be an illogical complication. The language of Joyce goes along with the dilapidations of Braque and Picasso and the music of the Austrians. To the extent that this painting and this music are the work of men who regard it as part of the science of painting and the science of music it is the work of realists. Actually its effect is that of the imagination, just as the effect of abstract painting is so often that of the imagination, although that may be different. Busoni said, in a letter to his wife, "I have made the painful discovery that nobody loves and feels music." Very likely, the reason there is a tendency in language toward the connotative today is that there are many who love it and feel it. It may be that Braque and Picasso love and feel painting and that Schönberg loves and feels music, although it seems that what they love and feel is something else.

A tendency toward the connotative, whether in language or elsewhere, cannot continue against the pressure of reality. If it is the pressure of reality that controls poetry, then the immediacy of various theories of poetry is not what it was. For instance, when Rostrevor Hamilton says, "The object of contemplation is the highly complex and unified content of consciousness, which comes into being through the developing subjective attitude of the percipient," he has in mind no such "content of consciousness" as every newspaper reader experiences today.

By way of further illustration, let me quote from Croce's Oxford lecture of 1933. He said: "If . . . poetry is intuition and expression, the fusion of sound and imagery, what is the material which takes on the form of sound and imagery? It is the whole man:

the man who thinks and wills, and loves, and hates; who is strong and weak, sublime and pathetic, good and wicked; man in the exultation and agony of living; and together with the man, integral with him, it is all nature in its perpetual labour of evolution. . . . Poetry . . . is the triumph of contemplation. . . . Poetic genius chooses a strait path in which passion is calmed and calm is passionate."

Croce cannot have been thinking of a world in which all normal life is at least in suspense, or, if you like, under blockage. He was thinking of normal human experience.

Quite apart from the abnormal aspect of everyday life today, there is the normal aspect of it. The spirit ·of negation has been so active, so confident and so intolerant that the commonplaces about the romantic provoke us to wonder if our salvation, if the way out, is not the romantic. All the great things have been denied and we live in an intricacy of new and local mythologies, political, economic, poetic, which are asserted with an ever-enlarging incoherence. This is accompanied by an absence of any authority except force, operative or imminent. What has been called the disparagement of reason is an instance of the absence of authority. We pick up the radio and find that comedians regard the public use of words of more than two syllables as funny. We read of the opening of the National Gallery at Washington and we are convinced, in the end, that the pictures are counterfeit, that museums are impositions and that Mr. Mellon was a monster. We turn to a recent translation of Kierkegaard and we find him saying: "A great deal has been said about poetry reconciling one with existence; rather it might be said that it arouses one against existence; for poetry is unjust to men . . . it has use only for the elect, but that is a poor sort of reconciliation. I will take the case of sickness. Aesthetics replies proudly and quite consistently, 'That cannot be employed, poetry must not become a hospital.' Aesthetics culminates . . . by regarding sickness in accordance with the principle enunciated by Friedrich Schlegel: 'Nur Gesundheit ist liebenswürdig.' (Health alone is lovable.)"

The enormous influence of education in giving everyone a little learning, and in giving large groups considerably more: something of history, something of philosophy, something of literature; the expansion of the middle class with its common preference for realistic satisfactions; the penetration of the masses of people by the ideas of liberal thinkers, even when that penetration is indirect, as by the reporting of the reasons why people oppose the ideas that

they oppose,—these are normal aspects of everyday life. The way
we live and the way we work alike cast us out on reality. If fifty
private houses were to be built in New York this year, it would be
a phenomenon. We no longer live in homes but in housing projects
and this is so whether the project is literally a project or a club, a
dormitory, a camp or an apartment in River House. It is not only
that there are more of us and that we are actually close together.
We are close together in every way. We lie in bed and listen to a
broadcast from Cairo, and so on. There is no distance. We are inti-
mate with people we have never seen and, unhappily, they are
intimate with us. Democritus plucked his eye out because he could
not look at a woman without thinking of her as a woman. If he
had read a few of our novels, he would have torn himself to pieces.
Dr. Richards has noted "the wide-spread increase in the aptitude
of the average mind for self-dissolving introspection, the generally
heightened awareness of the goings-on of our own minds, *merely as
goings-on.*" This is nothing to the generally heightened awareness of
the goings-on of other people's minds, *merely as goings-on.* The
way we work is a good deal more difficult for the imagination than
the highly civilized revolution that is occurring in respect to work
indicates. It is, in the main, a revolution for more pay. We have
been assured, by every visitor, that the American businessman is
absorbed in his business and there is nothing to be gained by dis-
puting it. As for the workers, it is enough to say that the word has
grown to be literary. They have become, at their work, in the face
of the machines, something approximating an abstraction, an
energy. The time must be coming when, as they leave the factories,
they will be passed through an air-chamber or a bar to revive them
for riot and reading. I am sorry to have to add that to one that
thinks, as Dr. Richards thinks, that poetry is the supreme use of
language, some of the foreign universities in relation to our own
appear to be, so far as the things of the imagination are concerned,
as Verrocchio is to the sculptor of the statue of General Jackson.

These, nevertheless, are not the things that I had in mind when
I spoke of the pressure of reality. These constitute the drift of inci-
dents, to which we accustom ourselves as to the weather. Material-
ism is an old story and an indifferent one. Robert Wolseley said:
"True genius . . . will enter into the hardest and dryest thing, enrich
the most barren Soyl, and inform the meanest and most uncomely
matter . . . the baser, the emptier, the obscurer, the fouler, and the
less susceptible of Ornament the subject appears to be, the more is

the Poet's Praise . . . who, as Horace says of Homer, can fetch
Light out of Smoak, Roses out of Dunghills, and give a kind of
Life to the Inanimate . . ." (Preface to Rochester's *Valentinian,*
1685, *English Association Essays and Studies* 1939). By the
pressure of reality, I mean the pressure of an external event or
events on the consciousness to the exclusion of any power of con-
templation. The definition ought to be exact and, as it is, may be
merely pretentious. But when one is trying to think of a whole gen-
eration and of a world at war, and trying at the same time to see
what is happening to the imagination, particularly if one believes
that that is what matters most, the plainest statement of what is
happening can easily appear to be an affectation.

For more than ten years now, there has been an extraordinary
pressure of news—let us say, news incomparably more pretentious
than any description of it, news, at first, of the collapse of our
system, or, call it, of life; then of news of a new world, but of a
new world so uncertain that one did not know anything whatever
of its nature, and does not know now, and could not tell whether
it was to be all-English, all-German, all-Russian, all-Japanese, or
all-American, and cannot tell now; and finally news of a war, which
was a renewal of what, if it was not the greatest war, became such
by this continuation. And for more than ten years, the consciousness
of the world has concentrated on events which have made the ordi-
nary movement of life seem to be the movement of people in the
intervals of a storm. The disclosures of the impermanence of the
past suggested, and suggest, an impermanence of the future. Little
of what we have believed has been true. Only the prophecies are
true. The present is an opportunity to repent. This is familiar
enough. The war is only a part of a war-like whole. It is not possi-
ble to look backward and to see that the same thing was true in
the past. It is a question of pressure, and pressure is incalculable
and eludes the historian. The Napoleonic era is regarded as having
had little or no effect on the poets and the novelists who lived in it.
But Coleridge and Wordsworth and Sir Walter Scott and Jane
Austen did not have to put up with Napoleon and Marx and
Europe, Asia and Africa all at one time. It seems possible to say
that they knew of the events of their day much as we know of the
bombings in the interior of China and not at all as we know of
the bombings of London, or, rather, as we should know of the
bombings of Toronto or Montreal. Another part of the war-like
whole to which we do not respond quite as we do to the news of

war is the income tax. The blanks are specimens of mathematical prose. They titillate the instinct of self-preservation in a class in which that instinct has been forgotten. Virginia Woolf thought that the income tax, if it continued, would benefit poets by enlarging their vocabularies and I dare say that she was right.

If it is not possible to assert that the Napoleonic era was the end of one era in the history of the imagination and the beginning of another, one comes closer to the truth by making that assertion in respect to the French Revolution. The defeat or triumph of Hitler are parts of a war-like whole but the fate of an individual is different from the fate of a society. Rightly or wrongly, we feel that the fate of a society is involved in the orderly disorders of the present time. We are confronting, therefore, a set of events, not only beyond our power to tranquillize them in the mind, beyond our power to reduce them and metamorphose them, but events that stir the emotions to violence, that engage us in what is direct and immediate and real, and events that involve the concepts and sanctions that are the order of our lives and may involve our very lives; and these events are occurring persistently with increasing omen, in what may be called our presence. These are the things that I had in mind when I spoke of the pressure of reality, a pressure great enough and prolonged enough to bring about the end of one era in the history of the imagination and, if so, then great enough to bring about the beginning of another. It is one of the peculiarities of the imagination that it is always at the end of an era. What happens is that it is always attaching itself to a new reality, and adhering to it. It is not that there is a new imagination but that there is a new reality. The pressure of reality may, of course, be less than the general pressure that I have described. It exists for individuals according to the circumstances of their lives or according to the characteristics of their minds. To sum it up, the pressure of reality is, I think, the determining factor in the artistic character of an era and, as well, the determining factor in the artistic character of an individual. The resistance to this pressure or its evasion in the case of individuals of extraordinary imagination cancels the pressure so far as those individuals are concerned.

4

Suppose we try, now, to construct the figure of a poet, a possible poet. He cannot be a charioteer traversing vacant space, however ethereal. He must have lived all of the last two thousand years, and longer, and he must have instructed himself, as best he could, as he went along. He will have thought that Virgil, Dante, Shakespeare, Milton placed themselves in remote lands and in remote ages; that their men and women were the dead—and not the dead lying in the earth, but the dead still living in their remote lands and in their remote ages, and living in the earth or under it, or in the heavens— and he will wonder at those huge imaginations, in which what is remote becomes near, and what is dead lives with an intensity beyond any experience of life. He will consider that although he has himself witnessed, during the long period of his life, a general transition to reality, his own measure as a poet, in spite of all the passions of all the lovers of the truth, is the measure of his power to abstract himself, and to withdraw with him into his abstraction the reality on which the lovers of truth insist. He must be able to abstract himself and also to abstract reality, which he does by placing it in his imagination. He knows perfectly that he cannot be too noble a rider, that he cannot rise up loftily in helmet and armor on a horse of imposing bronze. He will think again of Milton and of what was said about him: that "the necessity of writing for one's living blunts the appreciation of writing when it bears the mark of perfection. Its quality disconcerts our hasty writers; they are ready to condemn it as preciosity and affectation. And if to them the musical and creative powers of words convey little pleasure, how out of date and irrelevant they must find the . . . music of Milton's verse." Don Quixote will make it imperative for him to make a choice, to come to a decision regarding the imagina- tion and reality; and he will find that it is not a choice of one over the other and not a decision that divides them, but something subtler, a recognition that here, too, as between these poles, the universal interdependence exists, and hence his choice and his decision must be that they are equal and inseparable. To take a single instance: When Horatio says,

> **Now cracks a noble heart. Good night, sweet prince,**
> **And flights of angels sing thee to thy rest!**

are not the imagination and reality equal and inseparable? Above all, he will not forget General Jackson or the picture of the *Wooden Horses.*

I said of the picture that it was a work in which everything was favorable to reality. I hope that the use of that bare word has been enough. But without regard to its range of meaning in thought, it includes all its natural images, and its connotations are without limit. Bergson describes the visual perception of a motionless object as the most stable of internal states. He says: "The object may remain the same, I may look at it from the same side, at the same angle, in the same light; nevertheless, the vision I now have of it differs from that which I have just had, even if only because the one is an instant later than the other. My memory is there, which conveys something of the past into the present."

Dr. Joad's comment on this is: "Similarly with external things. Every body, every quality of a body resolves itself into an enormous number of vibrations, movements, changes. What is it that vibrates, moves, is changed? There is no answer. Philosophy has long dismissed the notion of substance and modern physics has endorsed the dismissal. . . . How, then, does the world come to appear to us as a collection of solid, static objects extended in space? Because of the intellect, which presents us with a false view of it."

The poet has his own meaning for reality, and the painter has, and the musician has; and besides what it means to the intelligence and to the senses, it means something to everyone, so to speak. Notwithstanding this, the word in its general sense, which is the sense in which I have used it, adapts itself instantly. The subject-matter of poetry is not that "collection of solid, static objects extended in space" but the life that is lived in the scene that it composes; and so reality is not that external scene but the life that is lived in it. Reality is things as they are. The general sense of the word proliferates its special senses. It is a jungle in itself. As in the case of a jungle, everything that makes it up is pretty much of one color. First, then, there is the reality that is taken for granted, that is latent and, on the whole, ignored. It is the comfortable American state of life of the eighties, the nineties and the first ten years of the present century. Next, there is the reality that has ceased to be indifferent, the years when the Victorians had been disposed of and intellectual minorities and social minorities began to take their place and to convert our state of life to something that might not be final. This much more vital reality made the life that had preceded it look like a volume of Ackermann's colored plates or one of Töpfer's books of sketches in Switzerland. I am trying to give the feel of it. It was the reality of twenty or thirty years ago. I say that it was a vital reality. The phrase gives a false impression. It was vital in the sense of being tense, of being instinct with the fatal or with what might be the fatal. The minorities began to convince us that the Victorians had left nothing behind. The Russians followed the Victorians, and the Germans, in their way, followed the Russians. The British Empire, directly or indirectly, was what was left and as to that one could not be sure whether it was a shield or a target. Reality then became violent and so remains. This much ought to be said to make it a little clearer that in speaking of the pressure of reality, I am thinking of life in a state of violence, not physically violent, as yet, for us in America, but physically violent for millions of our friends and for still more millions of our enemies and spiritually violent, it may be said, for everyone alive.

A possible poet must be a poet capable of resisting or evading the pressure of the reality of this last degree, with the knowledge that the degree of today may become a deadlier degree tomorrow. There is, however, no point to dramatizing the future in advance of the fact. I confine myself to the outline of a possible poet, with only the slightest sketch of his background.

5

Here I am, well-advanced in my paper, with everything of interest that I started out to say remaining to be said. I am interested in the nature of poetry and I have stated its nature, from one of the many points of view from which it is possible to state it. It is an interdependence of the imagination and reality as equals. This is not a definition, since it is incomplete. But it states the nature of poetry. Then I am interested in the role of the poet and this is paramount. In this area of my subject I might be expected to speak of the social, that is to say sociological or political, obligation of the poet. He has none. That he must be contemporaneous is as old as Longinus and I dare say older. But that he *is* contemporaneous is almost inevitable. How contemporaneous in the direct sense in which being contemporaneous is intended were the four great poets of whom I spoke a moment ago? I do not think that a poet owes any more as a social obligation than he owes as a moral obligation, and if there is anything concerning poetry about which people agree it is that the role of the poet is not to be found in morals. I cannot say what that wide agreement amounts to because the agreement (in which I do not join) that the poet is under a social obligation is equally wide. Reality is life and life is society and the imagination and reality; that is to say, the imagination and society are inseparable. That is pre-eminently true in the case of the poetic drama. The poetic drama needs a terrible genius before it is anything more than a literary relic. Besides the theater has forgotten that it could ever be terrible. It is not one of the instruments of fate, decidedly. Yes: the all-commanding subject-matter of poetry is life, the never-ceasing source. But it is not a social obligation. One does not love and go back to one's ancient mother as a social obligation. One goes back out of a suasion not to be denied. Unquestionably if a social movement moved one deeply enough, its moving poems would follow. No politician can command the imagination, directing it to do this or that. Stalin might grind his teeth the whole of a Russian winter and yet all the poets in the Soviets might remain silent the following spring. He might excite their imaginations by something he said or did. He would not command them. He is singularly free from that "cult of pomp," which is the comic side of the European disaster; and that means as much as anything to us. The truth is that the social obligation so closely urged is a phase of the pressure of reality which a poet (in the absence of dramatic poets) is bound to resist or evade today. Dante in Purgatory and Paradise was still the voice of the Middle Ages but not through fulfilling any social obligation. Since that is the role most frequently urged, if that role is eliminated, and if a possible poet is left facing life without any categorical exactions upon him, what then? What is his function? Certainly it is not to lead people out of the confusion in which they find themselves. Nor is it, I think, to comfort them while they follow their readers to and fro. I think that his function is to make his imagination theirs and that he fulfills himself only as he sees his imagination become the light in the minds of others. His role, in short, is to help people to live their lives. Time and time again it has been said that he may not address himself to an élite. I think he may. There is not a poet whom we prize living today that does not address himself to an élite. The poet will continue to do this: to address himself to an élite even in a classless society, unless, perhaps, this exposes him to imprisonment or exile. In that event he is likely not to address himself to anyone at all. He may, like Shostakovich, content himself with pretence. He will, nevertheless, still be addressing himself to an élite, for all poets address themselves to someone and it is of the essence of that instinct, and it seems to amount to an instinct, that it should be to an élite, not to a drab but to a woman with the hair of a pythoness, not to a chamber of commerce but to a gallery of one's own, if there are enough of one's own to fill a gallery. And that élite, if it responds, not out of complaisance, but because the poet has quickened it, because he has educed from it that for which it was searching in itself and in the life around it and which it had not yet quite found, will thereafter do for the poet what he cannot do for himself, that is to say, receive his poetry.

I repeat that his role is to help people to live their lives. He has had immensely to do with giving life whatever savor it possesses. He has had to do with whatever the imagination and the senses have made of the world. He has, in fact, had to do with life except as the intellect has had to do with it and, as to that, no one is needed to tell us that poetry and philosophy are akin. I want to repeat for two reasons a number of observations made by Charles Mauron. The first reason is that these observations tell us what it is that a poet does to help people to live their lives and the second is that they prepare the way for a word concerning escapism. They are: that the artist transforms us into epicures; that he has to discover the possible work of art in the real world, then to extract it, when he does not himself compose it entirely; that he is *un amoureux perpétuel* of the world that he contemplates and thereby enriches; that art sets out to express the human soul; and finally that everything like a firm grasp of reality is eliminated from the aesthetic field. With these aphorisms in mind, how is it possible to condemn escapism? The poetic process is psychologically an escapist process. The chatter about escapism is, to my way of thinking, merely common cant. My own remarks about resisting or evading the pressure of reality mean escapism, if analyzed. Escapism has a pejorative sense, which it cannot be supposed that I include in the sense in which I use the word. The pejorative sense applies where the poet is not attached to reality, where the imagination does not adhere to reality, which, for my part, I regard as fundamental. If we go back to the collection of solid, static objects extended in space, which Dr. Joad posited, and if we say that the space is blank space, nowhere, without color, and that the objects, though solid, have no shadows and, though static, exert a mournful power, and, without elaborating this complete poverty, if suddenly we hear a different and familiar description of the place:

> This City now doth, like a garment, wear
> The beauty of the morning, silent bare,
> Ships, towers, domes, theatres, and temples lie
> Open unto the fields, and to the sky;
> All bright and glittering in the smokeless air;

If we have this experience, we know how poets help people to live their lives. This illustration must serve for all the rest. There is, in fact, a world of poetry indistinguishable from the world in which we live, or, I ought to say, no doubt, from the world in which we shall come to live, since what makes the poet the potent figure that he is, or was, or ought to be, is that he creates the world to which we turn incessantly and without knowing it and that he gives to life the supreme fictions without which we are unable to conceive of it.

And what about the sound of words? What about nobility, of which the fortunes were to be a kind of test of the value of the poet? I do not know of anything that will appear to have suffered more from the passage of time than the music of poetry and that has suffered less. The deepening need for words to express our thoughts and feelings which, we are sure, are all the truth that we shall ever experience, having no illusions, makes us listen to words when we hear them, loving them and feeling them, makes us search the sound of them, for a finality, a perfection, an unalterable vibration, which it is only within the power of the acutest poet to give them. Those of us who may have been thinking of the path of poetry, those who understand that words are thoughts and not only our own thoughts but the thoughts of men and women ignorant of what it is that they are thinking, must be conscious of this: that, above everything else, poetry is words; and that words, above everything else, are, in poetry, sounds. This being so, my time and yours might have been better spent if I had been less interested in trying to give our possible poet an identity and less interested in trying to appoint him to his place. But unless I had done these things, it might have been thought that I was rhetorical, when I was speaking in the simplest way about things of such importance that nothing is more so. A poet's words are of things that do not exist without the words. Thus, the image of the charioteer and of the winged horses, which has been held to be precious for all of time that matters, was created by words of things that never existed without the words. A description of Verrocchio's statue could be the integration of an illusion equal to the statue itself. Poetry is a revelation in words by means of the words. Croce was not speaking of poetry in particular when he said that language is perpetual creation. About nobility I cannot be sure that the decline, not to say the disappearance of nobility is anything more than a maladjustment between the imagination and reality. We have been a little insane about the truth. We have had an obsession. In its ultimate extension, the truth about which we have been insane will lead us to look beyond the truth to something in which the imagination will be the dominant complement. It is not only that the imagination adheres to reality, but, also, that reality adheres to the imagination and that the interdependence is essential. We may emerge from our *bassesse* and, if we do, how would it happen if not by the intervention of some fortune of the mind? And what would that fortune of the mind happen to be? It might be only commonsense but even that, a commonsense beyond the truth, would be a nobility of long descent.

The poet refuses to allow his task to be set for him. He denies that he has a task and considers that the organization of materia poetica is a contradiction in terms. Yet the imagination gives to everything that it touches a peculiarity, and it seems to me that the peculiarity of the imagination is nobility, of which there are many degrees. This inherent nobility is the natural source of another, which our extremely headstrong generation regards as false and decadent. I mean that nobility which is our spiritual height and depth; and while I know how difficult it is to express it, nevertheless I am bound to give a sense of it. Nothing could be more evasive and inaccessible. Nothing distorts itself and seeks disguise more quickly. There is a shame of disclosing it and in its definite presentations a horror of it. But there it is. The fact that it is there is what makes it possible to invite to the reading and writing of poetry men of intelligence and desire for life. I am not thinking of the ethical or the sonorous or at all of the manner of it. The manner of it is, in fact, its difficulty, which each man must feel each day differently, for himself. I am not thinking of the solemn, the portentous or demoded. On the other hand, I am evading a definition. If it is defined, it will be fixed and it must not be fixed. As in the case of an external thing, nobility resolves itself into an enormous number of vibrations, movements, changes. To fix it is to put an end to it. Let me show it to you unfixed.

Late last year Epstein exhibited some of his flower paintings at the Leicester Galleries in London. A commentator in *Apollo* said: *"How with this rage can beauty hold a plea . . .* The quotation from Shakespeare's 65th sonnet prefaces the catalogue. . . . It would be apropos to any other flower paintings than Mr. Epstein's. His make no pretence to fragility. They shout, explode all over the picture space and generally oppose the rage of the world with such a rage of form and colour as no flower in nature or pigment has done since Van Gogh."

What ferocious beauty the line from Shakespeare puts on when used under such circumstances! While it has its modulation of despair, it holds its plea and its plea is noble. There is no element more conspicuously absent from contemporary poetry than nobility. There is no element that poets have sought after, more curiously and more piously, certain of its obscure existence. Its voice is one of the inarticulate voices which it is their business to overhear and to record. The nobility of rhetoric is, of course, a lifeless nobility. Pareto's epigram that history is a cemetery of aristocracies easily becomes another: that poetry is a cemetery of nobilities. For the sensitive poet, conscious of negations, nothing is more difficult than the affirmations of nobility and yet there is nothing that he requires of himself more persistently, since in them and in their kind, alone, are to be found those sanctions that are the reasons for his being and for that occasional ecstasy, or ecstatic freedom of the mind, which is his special privilege.

It is hard to think of a thing more out of time than nobility. Looked at plainly it seems false and dead and ugly. To look at it at all makes us realize sharply that in our present, in the presence of our reality, the past looks false and is, therefore, dead and is, therefore, ugly; and we turn away from it as from something repulsive and particularly from the characteristic that it has a way of assuming: something that was noble in its day, grandeur that was, the rhetorical once. But as a wave is a force and not the water of which it is composed, which is never the same, so nobility is a force and not the manifestations of which it is composed, which are never the same. Possibly this description of it as a force will do more than anything else I can have said about it to reconcile you to it. It is not an artifice that the mind has added to human nature. The mind has added nothing to human nature. It is a violence from within that protects us from a violence without. It is the imagination pressing back against the pressure of reality. It seems, in the last analysis, to have something to do with our self-preservation; and that, no doubt, is why the expression of it, the sound of its words, helps us to live our lives.

Selections from "Adagia"*

Progress in any aspect is a movement through changes of terminology.

•

To give a sense of the freshness or vividness of life is a valid purpose for poetry. A didactic purpose justifies itself in the mind of the teacher; a philosophical purpose justifies itself in the mind of the philosopher. It is not that one purpose is as justifiable as another but that some purposes are pure, others impure. Seek those purposes that are purely the purposes of the pure poet.

The poet makes silk dresses out of worms.

•

Authors are actors, books are theatres.

•

---

* **From** *Opus Posthumous* **by Wallace Stevens.**

146

Literature is the better part of life. To this it seems inevitably necessary to add, provided life is the better part of literature.

•

After one has abandoned a belief in God, poetry is that essence which takes its place as life's redemption.

•

Accuracy of observation is the equivalent of accuracy of thinking.

•

The relation of art to life is of the first importance especially in a skeptical age since, in the absence of a belief in God, the mind turns to its own creations and examines them, not alone from the aesthetic point of view, but for what they reveal, for what they validate and invalidate, for the support that they give.

Life is the reflection of literature.

As life grows more terrible, its literature grows more terrible.

Poetry and materia poetica are interchangeable terms.

•

The real is only the base. But it is the base.

•

The poem reveals itself only to the ignorant man.

The relation between the poetry of experience and the poetry of rhetoric is not the same thing as the relation between the poetry of reality and that of the imagination. Experience, at least in the case of a poet of any scope, is much broader than reality.

•

Not all objects are equal. The vice of imagism was that it did not recognize this.

•

All poetry is experimental poetry.

The bare image and the image as a symbol are the contrast: the image without meaning and the image as meaning. When the image is used to suggest something else, it is secondary. Poetry as an imaginative thing consists of more than lies on the surface.

•

It is the belief and not the god that counts.

What we see in the mind is as real to us as what we see by the eye.

•

There is nothing in life except what one thinks of it.

There is nothing beautiful in life except life.

There is no wing like meaning.

Consider: I. That the whole world is material for poetry; II. That there is not a specifically poetic material.

One reads poetry with one's nerves.

The poet is the intermediary between people and the world in which they live and also, between people as between themselves; but not between people and some other world.

Sentimentality is a failure of feeling.

•

The final belief is to believe in a fiction, which you know to be a fiction, there being nothing else. The exquisite truth is to know that it is a fiction and that you believe in it willingly.

All of our ideas come from the natural world: trees = umbrellas.

•

Ethics are no more a part of poetry than they are of painting.

As the reason destroys, the poet must create.

The exquisite environment of fact. The final poem will be the poem of fact in the language of fact. But it will be the poem of fact not realized before.

•

To live in the world but outside of existing conceptions of it.

•

Poetry has to be something more than a conception of the mind. It has to be a revelation of nature. Conceptions are artificial. Perceptions are essential.

•

Money is a kind of poetry.

Poetry is an effort of a dissatisfied man to find satisfaction through words, occasionally of the dissatisfied thinker to find satisfaction through his emotions.

•

The poem is a nature created by the poet.

The aesthetic order includes all other orders but is not limited to them.

Religion is dependent on faith. But æsthetics is independent of faith. The relative positions of the two might be reversed. It is possible to establish æsthetics in the individual mind as immeasurably a greater thing than religion. Its present state is the result of the difficulty of establishing it except in the individual mind.

The ultimate value is reality.

Realism is a corruption of reality.

•

The world is the only thing fit to think about.

•

Poetry is a purging of the world's poverty and change and evil and death. It is a present perfecting, a satisfaction in the irremediable poverty of life.

•

The time will come when poems like Paradise will seem like very *triste* contraptions.

•

All men are murderers.

•

There must be something of the peasant in every poet.

•

Metaphor creates a new reality from which the original appears to be unreal.

•

Description is an element, like air or water.

•

Poets acquire humanity.

Thought tends to collect in pools.

Life is not people and scene but thought and feeling.

•

God is a postulate of the ego.

•

Poetry must resist the intelligence almost successfully.

•

Literature is based not on life but on propositions about life, of which this is one.

Life is a composite of the propositions about it.

A change of style is a change of subject.

•

Poetry is a pheasant disappearing in the brush.

We never arrive intellectually. But emotionally we arrive constantly (as in poetry, happiness, high mountains, vistas).

•

The poet represents the mind in the act of defending us against itself.

•

Every poem is a poem within a poem: the poem of the idea within the poem of the words.

•

Poetry is the gaiety (joy) of language.

To be at the end of fact is not to be at the beginning of imagination but it is to be at the end of both.

•

There is a nature that absorbs the mixedness of metaphors.

•

Imagination applied to the whole world is vapid in comparison to imagination applied to a detail.

•

Poetry is a response to the daily necessity of getting the world right.

•

The essential fault of surrealism is that it invents without discovering. To make a clam play an accordion is to invent not to discover. The observation of the unconscious, so far as it can be observed, should reveal things of which we have previously been unconscious, not the familiar things of which we have been conscious plus imagination.

•

French and English constitute a single language.

•

Reality is a cliché from which we escape by metaphor. It is only *au pays de la métaphore qu'on est poète*.

The degrees of metaphor. The absolute object slightly turned is a metaphor of the object.

Some objects are less susceptible to metaphor than others. The whole world is less susceptible to metaphor than a tea-cup is.

There is no such thing as a metaphor of a metaphor. One does not progress through metaphors. Thus reality is the indispensable element of each metaphor. When I say that man is a god it is very easy to see that if I also say that a god is something else, god has become reality.

In the long run the truth does not matter.

•

Poetry creates a fictitious existence on an exquisite plane. This definition must vary as the plane varies, an exquisite plane being merely illustrative.

Hart Crane

Hart Crane was born July 21, 1899, the son of a Garretsville, Ohio, candy manufacturer. He conceived his most ambitious poem, The Bridge, *as an epic of the modern consciousness, a contemporary review of America's popular history. However, as R. P. Blackmur noted, Crane used the private lyric to write a cultural epic. The genuine achievements of* The Bridge *do not unfold from the deposit of tradition which is the poem's ostensible subject, but are the fruits of an intensely personal entrance into a common language and a common pain. It is a measure of Crane's genius that he transformed and reactivated the language; whereas the humiliation which modern America seemed to exact of him, somehow making a denizen of a native, could be neither dissipated nor put off. On April 26, 1932, en route to the United States aboard the* S. S. Orizaba, *he leapt from the stern and disappeared into the Gulf of Mexico.*

Crane conjures the histories and hidden stresses, the labyrinthine communings, of words. Or he tries to enforce new emphases, his avowed aim being "to get an 'interior' form, a form that is so thorough and intense as to dye the words themselves with a peculiarity of meaning, slightly different maybe from the ordinary definition of them separate from the poem." Not only are the words redefined, but in poetry they are reconstituted as facts which have been drenched in particular sensations and secured by an emotion. For poetry is both perception and the thing perceived, an interpenetration of phenomenon and noumenon, or synthesis of subject and object—it is, in effect, the linguistic fiat by which one may have his cake and eat it too. Such poetry would have the supralogical validity, and presumably the impact, of felt revelation. Yet, contrary to what this comparison or his style may suggest, Crane had no religious or other assurances. And his great subject was not the myth of America, nor even New York City or the tropics or the sea, but the lonely human feelings: a subject which may be evoked or exuded, but never quite said. Or else the saying, beset by the gorgeous intonings that rise before and after, predicates its own silence:

> And so it was I entered the broken world
> To trace the visionary company of love, its voice
> An instant in the wind (I know not whither hurled)
> But not for long to hold each desperate choice.

Crane's appreciation of Charlie Chaplin seems pertinent, for each "may be a sentimentalist, after all, but he carries the theme with such power and universal portent that sentimentality is made to transcend itself into a new kind of tragedy. . . ."

General Aims and Theories*

When I started writing Faustus & Helen it was my intention to embody in modern terms (words, symbols, metaphors) a contemporary approximation to an ancient human culture or mythology that seems to have been obscured rather than illumined with the frequency of poetic allusions made to it during the last century. The name of Helen, for instance, has become an all-too-easily employed crutch for evocation whenever a poet felt a stitch in his side. The real evocation of this (to me) very real and absolute conception of beauty seemed to consist in a reconstruction in these modern terms of the basic emotional attitude toward beauty that the Greeks had. And in so doing I found that I was really building a bridge between so-called classic experience and many divergent realities of our seething, confused cosmos of today, which has no formulated mythology yet for classic poetic reference or for religious exploitation.

* **From** *Hart Crane: The Life of an American Poet* by **Philip Horton.**

So I found "Helen" sitting in a street car; the Dionysian revels of her court and her seduction were transferred to a Metropolitan roof garden with a jazz orchestra; and the *katharsis* of the fall of Troy I saw approximated in the recent World War. The importance of this scaffolding may easily be exaggerated, but it gave me a series of correspondences between two widely separated worlds on which to sound some major themes of human speculation—love, beauty, death, renascence. It was a kind of grafting process that I shall doubtless not be interested in repeating, but which is consistent with subsequent theories of mine on the relation of tradition to the contemporary creating imagination.

It is a terrific problem that faces the poet today—a world that is so in transition from a decayed culture toward a reorganization of human evaluations that there are few common terms, general denominators of speech that are solid enough or that ring with any vibration or spiritual conviction. The great mythologies of the past (including the Church) are deprived of enough façade to even launch good raillery against. Yet much of their traditions are operative still—in millions of chance combinations of related and unrelated detail, psychological references, figures of speech, precepts, etc. These are all a part of our common experience and the terms, at least partially, of that very experience when it defines or extends itself.

The deliberate program, then, of a "break" with the past or tradition seems to me to be a sentimental fallacy. . . . The poet has a right to draw on whatever practical resources he finds in books or otherwise about him. He must tax his sensibility and his touchstone of experience for the proper selections of these themes and details, however,—and that is where he either stands, or falls into useless archeology.

I put no particular value on the simple objective of "modernity." The element of the temporal location of an artist's creation is of very secondary importance; it can be left to the impressionist or historian just as well. It seems to me that a poet will accidentally define his time well enough simply by reacting honestly and to the full extent of his sensibilities to the states of passion, experience and rumination that fate forces on him, first hand. He must, of course, have a sufficiently universal basis of experience to make his imagination selective and valuable. His picture of the "period," then, will simply be a by-product of his curiosity and the relation of his experience to a postulated "eternity."

I am concerned with the future of America, but not because I think that America has any so-called par value as a state or as a group of people. . . . It is only because I feel persuaded that here are destined to be discovered certain as yet undefined spiritual quantities, perhaps a new hierarchy of faith not to be developed so completely elsewhere. And in this process I like to feel myself as a potential factor; certainly I must speak in its terms and what discoveries I may make are situated in its experience.

But to fool one's self that definitions are being reached by merely referring frequently to skyscrapers, radio antennae, steam whistles, or other surface phenomena of our time is merely to paint a photograph. I think that what is interesting and significant will emerge only under the conditions of our submission to, and examination and assimilation of the organic effects on us of these and other fundamental factors of our experience. It can certainly not be an organic expression otherwise. And the expression of such values may often be as well accomplished with the vocabulary and blank verse of the Elizabethans as with the calligraphic tricks and slang used so brilliantly at times by an impressionist like Cummings.

It may not be possible to say that there is, strictly speaking, any "absolute" experience. But it seems evident that certain aesthetic experience (and this may for a time engross the total faculties of the spectator) can be called absolute, inasmuch as it approximates a formally convincing statement of a conception or apprehension of life that gains our unquestioning assent, and under the conditions of which our imagination is unable to suggest a further detail consistent with the design of the aesthetic whole.

I have been called an "absolutist" in poetry, and if I am to welcome such a label it should be under the terms of the above definition. It is really only a *modus operandi,* however, and as such has been used organically before by at least a dozen poets such as Donne, Blake, Baudelaire, Rimbaud, etc. I may succeed in defining it better by contrasting it with the impressionistic method. The impressionist is interesting as far as he goes—but his goal has been reached when he has succeeded in projecting certain selected factual details into his reader's consciousness. He is really not interested in the *causes* (metaphysical) of his materials, their emotional derivations or their utmost spiritual consequences. A kind of retinal registration is enough, along with a certain psychological stimulation. And this is also true of your realist (of the Zola type), and to a certain extent of the classicist, like Horace, Ovid, Pope, etc. Blake meant these differences when he wrote:

We are led to believe in a lie
When we see *with* not *through* the eye.

The impressionist creates only with the eye and for the readiest surface of the consciousness, at least relatively so. If the effect has been harmonious or even stimulating, he can stop there, relinquishing entirely to his audience the problematic synthesis of the details into terms of their own personal consciousness.

It is my hope to go *through* the combined materials of the poem, using our "real" world somewhat as a spring-board and to give the poem *as a whole* an orbit or predetermined direction of its own. I would like to establish it as free from my own personality as from any chance evaluation on the reader's part. (This is, of course, an impossibility, but it is a characteristic worth mentioning.) Such a poem is at least a stab at a truth, and to such an extent may be differentiated from other kinds of poetry and called "absolute." Its evocation will not be toward decoration or amusement, but rather toward a state of consciousness, an "innocence" (Blake) or absolute beauty. In this condition there may be discoverable under new forms certain spiritual illuminations, shining with a morality essentialized from experience directly, and not from previous precepts or preconceptions. It is as though a poem gave the reader as he left it a single, new *word,* never before spoken and impossible to actually enunciate, but self-evident as an active principle in the reader's consciousness henceforward.

As to technical considerations: the motivation of the poem must be derived from the implicit emotional dynamics of the materials used, and the terms of expression employed are often selected less for their logical (literal) significance than for their associational meanings. Via this and their metaphorical inter-relationships, the entire construction of the poem is raised on the organic principle of a "logic of metaphor," which antedates our so-called pure logic, and which is the genetic basis of all speech, hence consciousness and thought-extension.

These dynamics often result, I'm told, in certain initial difficulties in understanding my poems. But on the other hand I find them at times the only means possible for expressing certain concepts in any forceful or direct way whatever. To cite two examples:—when, in Voyages (II), I speak of "adagios of islands," the reference is to the motion of a boat through islands clustered thickly, the rhythm of the motion, etc. And it seems a much more direct and creative statement than any more logical employment of words such as "coasting slowly through the islands," besides ushering in a whole world of music. Similarly in Faustus and Helen (III) the speed and tense altitude of an aeroplane are much better suggested by the idea of "nimble blue plateaus"—*implying* the aeroplane and its speed against a contrast of stationary elevated earth. Although the statement is pseudo in relation to formal logic —it *is* completely logical in relation to the truth of the imagination, and there is expressed a concept of speed and space that could not be handled so well in other terms.

In manipulating the more imponderable phenomena of psychic motives, pure emotional crystallizations, etc. I have had to rely even more on these dynamics of inferential mention, and I am doubtless still very unconscious of having committed myself to what seems nothing but obscurities to some minds. A poem like Possessions really cannot be technically explained. It must rely (even to a large extent with myself) on its organic impact on the imagination to successfully imply its meaning. This seems to me to present an exceptionally difficult problem, however, considering the real clarity and consistent logic of many of the other poems.

I know that I run the risk of much criticism by defending such theories as I have, but as it is part of a poet's business to risk not only criticism—but folly—in the conquest of consciousness I can only say that I attach no intrinsic value to what means I use beyond their practical service in giving form to the living stuff of the imagination.

New conditions of life germinate new forms of spiritual articulation. And while I feel that my work includes a more consistent extension of traditional literary elements than many contemporary poets are capable of appraising, I realize that I am utilizing the gifts of the past as instruments principally; and that the voice of the present, if it is to be known, must be caught at the risk of speaking in idioms and circumlocutions sometimes shocking to the scholar and historians of logic. Language has built towers and bridges, but itself is inevitably as fluid as always.

From Mr. Crane to the Editor (Harriet Monroe)*

Your good nature and manifest interest in writing me about the obscurities apparent in my Melville poem[1] certainly prompt a wish to clarify my intentions in that poem as much as possible. But I realize that my explanations will not be very convincing. For a paraphrase is generally a poor substitute for any organized conception that one has fancied he has put into the more essentialized form of the poem itself.

At any rate, and though I imagine us to have considerable differences of opinion regarding the relationship of poetic metaphor to ordinary logic (I judge this from the angle of approach you use toward portions of the poem), I hope my answers will not be taken as a defense of merely certain faulty lines. I am really much more interested in certain theories of metaphor and technique involved generally in poetics, than I am concerned in vindicating any particular perpetrations of my own.

My poem may well be elliptical and actually obscure in the

---

* From *Hart Crane: The Life of an American Poet* by **Philip Horton. Miss Monroe was founder—October, 1912—and editor of** *Poetry: A Magazine of Verse.*

[1] ["At Melville's Tomb."]

ordering of its content, but in your criticism of this very possible deficiency you have stated your objections in terms that allow me, at least for the moment, the privilege of claiming your ideas and ideals as theoretically, at least, quite outside the issues of my own aspirations. To put it more plainly, as a poet I may very possibly be more interested in the so-called illogical impingements of the connotations of words on the consciousness (and their combinations and interplay in metaphor on this basis) than I am interested in the preservation of their logically rigid significations at the cost of limiting my subject matter and perceptions involved in the poem.

This may sound as though I merely fancied juggling words and images until I found something novel, or esoteric; but the process is much more predetermined and objectified than that. The nuances of feeling and observation in a poem may well call for certain liberties which you claim the poet has no right to take. I am simply making the claim that the poet does have that authority, and that to deny it is to limit the scope of the medium so considerably as to outlaw some of the richest genius of the past.

This argument over the dynamics of metaphor promises as active a future as has been evinced in the past. Partaking so extensively as it does of the issues involved in the propriety or nonpropriety of certain attitudes toward subject matter, etc., it enters the critical distinctions usually made between "romantic," "classic" as an organic factor. It is a problem that would require many pages to state adequately—merely from my own limited standpoint on the issues. Even this limited statement may prove onerous reading, and I hope you will pardon me if my own interest in the matter carries me to the point of presumption.

Its paradox, of course, is that its apparent illogic operates so logically in conjunction with its context in the poem as to establish its claim to another logic, quite independent of the original definition of the word or phrase or image thus employed. It implies (this *inflection* of language) a previous or prepared receptivity to its stimulus on the part of the reader. The reader's sensibility simply responds by identifying this inflection of experience with some event in his own history or perceptions—or rejects it altogether. The logic of metaphor is so organically entrenched in pure sensibility that it can't be thoroughly traced or explained outside of historical sciences, like philology and anthropology. This "pseudo-statement," as I. A. Richards calls it in an admirable essay touching our contentions in last July's *Criterion*, demands completely other faculties of recognition than the pure rationalistic associations permit. Much fine poetry may be completely rationalistic in its use of symbols, but there is much great poety of another order which will yield the reader very little when inspected under the limitation of such arbitrary concerns as are manifested in your judgment of the Melville poem, especially when you constitute such requirements of ordinary logical relationship between word and word as irreducible.

I don't wish to enter here defense of the particular symbols employed in my own poem, because, as I said, I may well have failed to supply the necessary emotional connectives to the content featured. But I would like to counter a question or so of yours with a similar question. Here the poem is less dubious in quality than my own, and as far as the abstract pertinacity of question and its immediate consequences are concerned the point I'm arguing about can be better demonstrated. Both quotations are familiar to you, I'm sure.

You ask me how a *portent* can possibly be wound in a *shell*. Without attempting to answer this for the moment, I ask you how Blake could possibly say that "a *sigh* is a *sword* of an Angel King." You ask me how *compass, quadrant and sextant "contrive"* tides. I ask you how Eliot can possibly believe that "Every street *lamp* that I pass *beats* like a fatalistic *drum!*" Both of my metaphors may fall down completely. I'm not defending their actual value in themselves; but your criticism of them in each case was leveled at an illogicality of relationship between symbols, which similar fault you must have either overlooked in case you have ever admired the Blake and Eliot lines, or have there condoned them on account of some more ultimate convictions pressed on you by the impact of the poems in their entirety.

It all comes to the recognition that emotional dynamics are not to be confused with any absolute order of rationalized definitions; ergo, in poetry the *rationale* of metaphor belongs to another order of experience than science, and is not to be limited by a scientific and arbitrary code of relationships either in verbal inflections or concepts.

There are plenty of people who have never accumulated a sufficient series of reflections (and these of a rather special nature) to perceive the relation between a *drum* and a *street lamp*—*via* the *unmentioned* throbbing of the heart and nerves in a distraught man which *tacitly* creates the reason and "logic" of the Eliot metaphor. They will always have a perfect justification for ignoring those lines and to claim them obscure, excessive, etc., until by some experience of their own the words accumulate the necessary connotations to complete their connection. It is the same with the "patient etherized upon a table," isn't it? Surely that line must lack all eloquence to many people who, for instance, would delight in agreeing that the sky was like a dome of many-colored glass.

If one can't count on some such bases in the reader now and then, I don't see how the poet has any chance to ever get beyond the simplest conceptions of emotion and thought, of sensation and lyrical sequence. If the poet is to be held completely to the already evolved and exploited sequences of imagery and logic—what field of added consciousness and increased perceptions (the actual province of poetry, if not lullabyes) can be expected when one has to relatively return to the alphabet every breath or so? In the minds of people who have sensitively read, seen and experienced a great deal, isn't there a terminology something like short-hand as compared to usual description and dialectics, which the artist ought to be right in trusting as a reasonable connective agent toward fresh concepts, more inclusive evaluations? The question is more important to me than it perhaps ought to be; but as long as poetry is written, an audience, however small, is implied, and there remains the question of an active or an inactive imagination as its characteristic.

It is of course understood that a street-lamp simply can't beat with a sound like a drum; but it often happens that images, themselves totally dissociated, when joined in the circuit of a particular emotion located with specific relation to both of them, conduce to great vividness and accuracy of statement in defining that emotion.

Not to rant on forever, I'll beg your indulgence and come at once to the explanations you requested on the Melville poem.

"The dice of drowned men's bones he saw bequeath
An embassy."

Dice bequeath an embassy, in the first place, by being ground (in this connection only, of course) in little cubes from the bones of drowned men by the action of the sea, and are finally thrown up on the sand, having "numbers" but no identification. These being the bones of dead men who never completed their voyage, it seems legitimate to refer to them as the only surviving evidence of certain messages undelivered, mute evidence of certain things, experiences that the dead mariners might have had to deliver. Dice as a symbol of chance and circumstance is also implied.

"The calyx of death's bounty giving back," etc.

This calyx refers in a double ironic sense both to a cornucopia and the vortex made by a sinking vessel. As soon as the water has closed over a ship this whirlpool sends up broken spars, wreckage, etc., which can be alluded to as livid *hieroglyphs,* making a *scattered chapter* so far as any complete record of the recent ship and her crew is concerned. In fact, about as much definite knowledge might come from all this as anyone might gain from the roar of his own veins, which is easily heard (haven't you ever done it?) by holding a shell close to one's ear.

"Frosted eyes lift altars."

Refers simply to a conviction that a man, not knowing perhaps a definite god yet being endowed with a reverence for deity—such a man naturally postulates a deity somehow, and the altar of that deity by the very *action* of the eyes *lifted* in searching.

"Compass, quadrant and sextant contrive no farther tides."

Hasn't it often occurred that instruments originally invented for record and computation have inadvertently so extended the concepts of the entity they were invented to measure (concepts of space, etc.) in the mind and imagination that employed them, that they may metaphorically be said to have extended the original boundaries of the entity measured? This little bit of "relativity" ought not to be discredited in poetry now that scientists are proceeding to measure the universe on principles of pure *ratio,* quite as metaphorical, so far as previous standards of scientific methods extended, as some of the axioms in *Job.*

I may have completely failed to provide any clear interpretation of these symbols in their context. And you will not doubt feel that I have rather heatedly explained them for anyone who professes no claims for their particular value. I hope, at any rate, that I have clarified them enough to suppress any suspicion that their obscurity derives from a lack of definite intentions in the subject-matter of the poem. The execution is another matter, and you must be accorded a superior judgment to mine in that regard.

W. H. Auden

The public once associated W. H. Auden (who was born in York, England, on February 21, 1907) with C. Day Lewis, Stephen Spender, and Louis MacNeice, all of whom had attended Oxford. Responsive to the economic collapse of the thirties and the portentous Spanish Civil War, their poetic stances inclined, in differing degrees, toward the Left. But at the end of the decade Auden emigrated to the United States, the nominal melting pot for whatever forces were settling into the modern world, and in 1946 he became a United States citizen.

Remarking that every poem he writes involves his whole past, Auden refers primarily to the emotions and sentiments of the past, not to the ideologies or terminologies that date it. His quest for order has already led through Marx and Freud, through sociology and psychology, and on to Christianity, at least for the time being; but intellectual restlessness sorts well with his technical genius, which has ranged from assimilations of Anglo-Saxon poetry through ballads and blues, and from a pithy, epigrammatic manner through the longer, continuing lines of his later work. And, in truth, an almost improvisatory air suggests that he is concerned less with affirming ideology than with wielding it for the revolutionary purpose of making poems.

As one who believes that "a suffering, a weakness, which cannot be expressed as an aphorism should not be mentioned," he has preferred the more public aspects of life. Man may indeed be an animal, but he is a political one. Images of state so permeate Auden's thought and condition his values that he has defined a poem as "an attempt to present an analogy to the paradisal state in which Freedom and Law, System and Order are united in harmony," while he has also described a good poem as, by analogy, "very nearly a Utopia."

Social and political preoccupations, however, tend to de-sex the intelligence, putting concepts in the place of senses, and substituting argument for revelation, or ethics for aesthetics. Art ceases to be enough: "the artist, the man who makes, is less important to mankind, for good or evil, than the apostle, the man with a message." Yet within Auden himself there exists a tension between the believer in beauty and the believer in truth ("art arises out of our desire for beauty and truth and our knowledge that they are not identical"); which has resulted in some of the loveliest pathetic lyrics of our time.

Perhaps Auden flourished his ultimate loyalty when he said that every poem, whatever *its actual content or overt interest, "is rooted in imaginative awe. Poetry can do a hundred and one things, delight, sadden, disturb, amuse, instruct—it may express every possible shade of emotion, and describe every conceivable kind of event, but there is only one thing that all poetry must do; it must praise all it can for being and for happening."*

The Poet & the City*

. . . Being everything, let us admit that is to be
something,
Or give ourselves the benefit of the doubt . . .

There is little or nothing to be remembered
written on the subject of getting an honest living.
Neither the New Testament nor Poor Richard
speaks to our condition. One would never think,
from looking at literature, that this question had
ever disturbed a solitary individual's musings.

H. D. THOREAU

It is astonishing how many young people of both sexes, when
asked what they want to do in life, give neither a sensible answer
like "I want to be a lawyer, an innkeeper, a farmer" nor a romantic
answer like "I want to be an explorer, a racing motorist, a mission-

---

* **Reprinted From** *The Dyer's Hand,* **by W. H. Auden.**

ary, President of the United States." A surprisingly large number say "I want to be a writer," and by writing they mean "creative" writing. Even if they say "I want to be a journalist," this is because they are under the illusion that in that profession they will be able to create; even if their genuine desire is to make money, they will select some highly paid subliterary pursuit like Advertising.

Among these would-be writers, the majority have no marked literary gift. This in itself is not surprising; a marked gift for any occupation is not very common. What is surprising is that such a high percentage of those without any marked talent for any profession should think of writing as the solution. One would have expected that a certain number would imagine that they had a talent for medicine or engineering and so on, but this is not the case. In our age, if a young person is untalented, the odds are in favor of his imagining he wants to write. (There are, no doubt, a lot without any talent for acting who dream of becoming film stars but they have at least been endowed by nature with a fairly attractive face and figure.)

In accepting and defending the social institution of slavery, the Greeks were harder-hearted than we but clearer-headed; they knew that labor as such is slavery, and that no man can feel a personal pride in being a laborer. A man can be proud of being a worker—someone, that is, who fabricates enduring objects, but in our society, the process of fabrication has been so rationalized in the interests of speed, economy and quantity that the part played by the individual factory employee has become too small for it to be meaningful to him as work, and practically all workers have been reduced to laborers. It is only natural, therefore, that the arts which cannot be rationalized in this way—the artist still remains personally responsible for what he makes—should fascinate those who, because they have no marked talent, are afraid, with good reason, that all they have to look forward to is a lifetime of meaningless labor. This fascination is not due to the nature of art itself, but to the way in which an artist works; he, and in our age, almost nobody else, is his own master. The idea of being one's own master appeals to most human beings, and this is apt to lead to the fantastic hope that the capacity for artistic creation is universal, something nearly all human beings, by virtue, not of some special talent, but of their humanity, could do if they tried.

Until quite recently a man was proud of not having to earn his own living and ashamed of being obliged to earn it, but today, would any man dare describe himself when applying for a passport as *Gentleman,* even if, as a matter of fact, he has independent means and no job? Today, the question "What do you do?" means "How do you earn your living?" On my own passport I am described as a "Writer"; this is not embarrassing for me in dealing with the authorities, because immigration and customs officials know that some kinds of writers make lots of money. But if a stranger in the train asks me my occupation I never answer "writer" for fear that he may go on to ask me what I write, and to answer "poetry" would embarrass us both, for we both know that nobody can earn a living simply by writing poetry. (The most satisfactory answer I have discovered, satisfactory because it withers curiosity, is to say *Medieval Historian.*)

Some writers, even some poets, become famous public figures, but writers as such have no social status, in the way that doctors and lawyers, whether famous or obscure, have.

There are two reasons for this. Firstly, the so-called fine arts have lost the social utility they once had. Since the invention of printing and the spread of literacy, verse no longer has a utility value as a mnemonic, a device by which knowledge and culture were handed on from one generation to the next, and, since the invention of the camera, the draughtsman and painter are no longer needed to provide visual documentation; they have, consequently, become "pure" arts, that is to say, gratuitous activities. Secondly, in a society governed by the values appropriate to Labor (capitalist America may well be more completely governed by these than communist Russia) the gratuitous is no longer regarded—most earlier cultures thought differently—as sacred, because, to Man the Laborer, leisure is not sacred but a respite from laboring, a time for relaxation and the pleasures of consumption. In so far as such a society thinks about the gratuitous at all, it is suspicious of it—artists do not labor, therefore, they are probably parasitic idlers—or, at best, regards it as trivial—to write poetry or paint pictures is a harmless private hobby.

In the purely gratuitous arts, poetry, painting, music, our century has no need, I believe, to be ashamed of its achievements, and in its fabrication of purely utile and functional articles like airplanes, dams, surgical instruments, it surpasses any previous age. But whenever it attempts to combine the gratuitous with the utile, to fabricate something which shall be both functional and beautiful, it fails utterly. No previous age has created anything so hideous as the average modern automobile, lampshade, or building, whether domestic or public. What could be more terrifying than a modern office building? It seems to be saying to the white-collar slaves who work in it: "For labor in this age, the human body is much more complicated than it need be: you would do better and be happier if it were simplified."

In the affluent countries today, thanks to the high per capita income, small houses and scarcity of domestic servants, there is one art in which we probably excel all other societies that ever existed, the art of cooking. (It is the one art which Man the Laborer regards as sacred.) If the world population continues to increase at its present rate, this cultural glory will be short-lived, and it may well be that future historians will look nostalgically back to the years 1950-1975 as The Golden Age of Cuisine. It is difficult to imagine a *haute cuisine* based on algae and chemically treated grass.

A poet, painter or musician has to accept the divorce in his art between the gratuitous and the utile as a fact for, if he rebels, he is liable to fall into error.

Had Tolstoi, when he wrote *What Is Art?*, been content with the proposition, "When the gratuitous and the utile are divorced from each other, there can be no art," one might have disagreed with him, but he would have been difficult to refute. But he was unwilling to say that, if Shakespeare and himself were not artists, there was no modern art. Instead he tried to persuade himself that utility alone, a spiritual utility maybe, but still utility without gratuity, was sufficient to produce art, and this compelled him to be dishonest and praise works which aesthetically he must have despised. The notion of *l'art engagé* and art as propaganda are extensions of this heresy, and when poets fall into it, the cause, I fear, is less their social conscience than their vanity; they are nostalgic for a past when poets had a public status. The opposite heresy is to endow the gratuitous with a magic utility of its own, so that the poet comes to think of himself as the god who creates his subjective universe out of nothing—to him the visible material universe *is* nothing. Mallarmé, who planned to write the sacred book of a new universal religion, and Rilke with his notion of *Gesang ist Dasein*, are heresiarchs of this type. Both were geniuses but, admire them as one may and must, one's final impression of their work is of something false and unreal. As Erich Heller says of Rilke:

> In the great poetry of the European tradition, the emotions do not interpret; they respond to the interpreted world: in Rilke's mature poetry the emotions do the interpreting and then respond to their own interpretation.

In all societies, educational facilities are limited to those activities and habits of behavior which a particular society considers important. In a culture like that of Wales in the Middle Ages, which regarded poets as socially important, a would-be poet, like a would-be dentist in our own culture, was systematically trained and admitted to the rank of poet only after meeting high professional standards.

In our culture a would-be poet has to educate himself: he may be in the position to go to a first-class school and university, but such places can only contribute to his poetic education by accident, not by design. This has its drawbacks; a good deal of modern poetry, even some of the best, shows just that uncertainty of taste, crankiness and egoism which self-educated people so often exhibit.

A metropolis can be a wonderful place for a mature artist to live in, but, unless his parents are very poor, it is a dangerous place for a would-be artist to grow up in; he is confronted with too much of the best in art too soon. This is like having a liaison with a wise and beautiful woman twenty years older than himself; all too often his fate is that of *Chéri*.

In my daydream College for Bards, the curriculum would be as follows:

1) In addition to English, at least one ancient language, probably Greek or Hebrew, and two modern languages would be required.

2) Thousands of lines of poetry in these languages would be learned by heart.

3) The library would contain no books of literary criticism, and the only critical exercise required of students would be the writing of parodies.

4) Courses in prosody, rhetoric and comparative philology would be required of all students, and every student would have to select three courses out of courses in mathematics, natural history, geology, meteorology, archaeology, mythology, liturgics, cooking.

5) Every student would be required to look after a domestic animal and cultivate a garden plot.

A poet has not only to educate himself as a poet, he has also to consider how he is going to earn his living. Ideally, he should have a job which does not in any way involve the manipulation of words. At one time, children training to become rabbis were also taught some skilled manual trade, and if only they knew their child was going to become a poet, the best thing parents could do would be to get him at an early age into some Craft Trades Union. Unfortunately, they cannot know this in advance, and, except in very rare cases, by the time he is twenty-one, the only nonliterary job for which a poet-to-be is qualified is unskilled manual labor. In earning his living, the average poet has to choose between being a translator, a teacher, a literary journalist or a writer of advertising copy and, of these, all but the first can be directly detrimental to his poetry, and even translation does not free him from leading a too exclusively literary life.

There are four aspects of our present *Weltanschauung* which have made an artistic vocation more difficult than it used to be.

1) The loss of belief in the eternity of the physical universe. The possibility of becoming an artist, a maker of things which shall outlast the maker's life, might never have occurred to man, had he not had before his eyes, in contrast to the transitoriness of human life, a universe of things, earth, ocean, sky, sun, moon, stars, etc., which appeared to be everlasting and unchanging.

Physics, geology and biology have now replaced this everlasting universe with a picture of nature as a process in which nothing is now what it was or what it will be. Today, Christian and Atheist alike are eschatologically minded. It is difficult for a modern artist to believe he can make an enduring object when he has no model of endurance to go by; he is more tempted than his predecessors to abandon the search for perfection as a waste of time and be content with sketches and improvisations.

2) *The loss of belief in the significance and reality of sensory phenomena.* This loss has been progressive since Luther, who denied any intelligible relation between subjective Faith and objective Works, and Descartes, with his doctrine of primary and secondary qualities. Hitherto, the traditional conception of the phenomenal world had been one of sacramental analogies; what the senses perceived was an outward and visible sign of the inward and invisible, but both were believed to be real and valuable. Modern science has destroyed our faith in the naïve observation of our senses: we cannot, it tells us, ever know what the physical universe is *really* like; we can only hold whatever subjective notion is appropriate to the particular human purpose we have in view.

This destroys the traditional conception of *art* as *mimesis,* for there is no longer a nature "out there" to be truly or falsely imitated; all an artist can be *true* to are his subjective sensations and feelings. The change in attitude is already to be seen in Blake's remark that some people see the sun as a round golden disc the size of a guinea but that he sees it as a host crying Holy, Holy, Holy. What is significant about this is that Blake, like the Newtonians he hated, accepts a division between the physical and the spiritual, but, in opposition to them, regards the material universe as the abode of Satan, and so attaches no value to what his physical eye sees.

3) *The loss of belief in a norm of human nature which will always require the same kind of man-fabricated world to be at home in.* Until the Industrial Revolution, the way in which men lived changed so slowly that any man, thinking of his great-grandchildren, could imagine them as people living the same kind of life with the same kind of needs and satisfactions as himself. Technology, with its ever-accelerating transformation of man's way of living, has made it impossible for us to imagine what life will be like even twenty years from now.

Further, until recently, men knew and cared little about

cultures far removed from their own in time or space; by human nature, they meant the kind of behavior exhibited in their own culture. Anthropology and archaeology have destroyed this provincial notion; we know that human nature is so plastic that it can exhibit varieties of behavior which, in the animal kingdom, could only be exhibited by different species.

The artist, therefore, no longer has any assurance, when he makes something, that even the next generation will find it enjoyable or comprehensible.

He cannot help desiring an immediate success, with all the danger to his integrity which that implies.

Further, the fact that we now have at our disposal the arts of all ages and cultures, has completely changed the meaning of the word tradition. It no longer means a way of working handed down from one generation to the next; a sense of tradition now means a consciousness of the whole of the past as present, yet at the same time as a structured whole the parts of which are related in terms of before and after. Originality no longer means a slight modification in the style of one's immediate predecessors; it means a capacity to find in any work of any date or place a clue to finding one's authentic voice. The burden of choice and selection is put squarely upon the shoulders of each individual poet and it is a heavy one.

4) *The disappearance of the Public Realm as the sphere of revelatory personal deeds.* To the Greeks the Private Realm was the sphere of life ruled by the necessity of sustaining life, and the Public Realm the sphere of freedom where a man could disclose himself to others. Today, the significance of the terms private and public has been reversed; public life is the necessary impersonal life, the place where a man fulfills his social function, and it is in his private life that he is free to be his personal self.

In consequence the arts, literature in particular, have lost their traditional principal human subject, the man of action, the doer of public deeds.

The advent of the machine has destroyed the direct relation between a man's intention and his deed. If St. George meets the dragon face to face and plunges a spear into its heart, he may legitimately say "I slew the dragon," but, if he drops a bomb on the dragon from an altitude of twenty thousand feet, though his intention—to slay it—is the same, his act consists in pressing a lever and it is the bomb, not St. George, that does the killing.

If, at Pharaoh's command, ten thousand of his subjects toil for five years at draining the fens, this means that Pharaoh commands the personal loyalty of enough persons to see that his orders are carried out; if his army revolts, he is powerless. But if Pharaoh can have the fens drained in six months by a hundred men with bulldozers, the situation is changed. He still needs some authority, enough to persuade a hundred men to man the bulldozers, but that is all: the rest of the work is done by machines which know nothing of loyalty or fear, and if his enemy, Nebuchadnezzar, should get hold of them, they will work just as efficiently at filling up the canals as they have just worked at digging them out. It is now possible to imagine a world in which the only human work on such projects will be done by a mere handful of persons who operate computers.

It is extremely difficult today to use public figures as themes for poetry because the good or evil they do depends less upon their characters and intentions than upon the quantity of impersonal force at their disposal.

Every British or American poet will agree that Winston Churchill is a greater figure than Charles II, but he will also know that he could not write a good poem on Churchill, while Dryden had no difficulty in writing a good poem on Charles. To write a good poem on Churchill, a poet would have to know Winston Churchill intimately, and his poem would be about the man, not about the Prime Minister. All attempts to write about persons or events, however important, to which the poet is not intimately related in a personal way are now doomed to failure. Yeats could write great poetry about the Troubles in Ireland, because most of the protagonists were known to him personally and the places where the events occurred had been familiar to him since childhood.

The true men of action in our time, those who transform the world, are not the politicians and statesmen, but the scientists. Unfortunately poetry cannot celebrate them because their deeds are concerned with things, not persons, and are, therefore, speechless.

When I find myself in the company of scientists, I feel like a shabby curate who has strayed by mistake into a drawing room full of dukes.

The growth in size of societies and the development of mass media of communication have created a social phenomenon which was unknown to the ancient world, that peculiar kind of crowd which Kierkegaard calls the Public.

A public is neither a nation nor a generation, nor a community, nor a society, nor these particular men, for all these are only what they are through the concrete; no single person who belongs to the public makes a real commitment; for some hours of the day, perhaps, he belongs to the public—at moments when he is nothing else, since when he really is what he is, he does not form part of the public. Made up of such individuals at the moments when they are nothing, a public is a kind of gigantic something, an abstract and deserted void which is everything and nothing.

The ancient world knew the phenomenon of the crowd in the sense that Shakespeare uses the word, a visible congregation of a large number of human individuals in a limited physical space, who can, on occasions, be transformed by demagogic oratory into a mob which behaves in a way of which none of its members would be capable by himself, and this phenomenon is known, of course, to us, too. But the public is something else. A student in the subway during the rush· hour whose thoughts are concentrated on a mathematical problem or his girl friend is a member of a crowd but not a member of the public. To join the public, it is not necessary for a man to go to some particular spot; he can sit at home; open a newspaper or turn on his TV set.

A man has his distinctive personal scent which his wife, his children and his dog can recognize. A crowd has a generalized stink. The public is odorless.

A mob is active: it smashes, kills and sacrifices itself. The public is passive, or, at most, curious. It neither murders nor sacrifices itself; it looks on, or looks away, while the mob beats up a Negro or the police round up Jews for the gas ovens.

The public is the least exclusive of clubs; anybody, rich or poor, educated or unlettered, nice or nasty, can join it: it even tolerates a pseudo revolt against itself, that is, the formation within itself of clique publics.

In a crowd, a passion like rage or terror is highly contagious; each member of a crowd excites all the others, so that passion increases at a geometric rate. But among members of the Public, there is no contact. If two members of the public meet and speak to each other, the function of their words is not to convey meaning or arouse passion but to conceal by noise the silence and solitude of the void in which the Public exists.

Occasionally the Public embodies itself in a crowd and so becomes visible—in the crowd, for example, which collects to watch the wrecking gang demolish the old family mansion, fascinated by yet another proof that physical force is the Prince of this world against whom no lover of the heart shall prevail.

Before the phenomenon of the Public appeared in society, there existed naive art and sophisticated art which were different from each other but only in the way that two brothers are different. The Athenian court may smile at the mechanics' play of Pyramus and Thisbe, but they recognize it as a play. Court poetry and Folk poetry were bound by the common tie that both were made by hand and both were intended to last; the crudest ballad was as custom-built as the most esoteric sonnet. The appearance of the Public and the mass media which cater to it have destroyed naïve popular art. The sophisticated "highbrow" artist survives and can still work as he did a thousand years ago, because his audience is too small to interest the mass media. But the audience of the popular artist is the majority and this the mass media must steal from him if they are not to go bankrupt. Consequently, aside from a few comedians, the only art today is "highbrow." What the mass media offer is not popular art, but entertainment which is intended to be consumed like food, forgotten, and replaced by a new dish. This is bad for everyone; the majority lose all genuine taste of their own, and the minority become cultural snobs.

The two characteristics of art which make it possible for an art historian to divide the history of art into periods, are, firstly, a common style of expression over a certain period and, secondly, a common notion, explicit or implicit, of the hero, the kind of human being who most deserves to be celebrated, remembered and, if possible, imitated. The characteristic style of "Modern" poetry is an intimate tone of voice, the speech of one person addressing one person, not a large audience; whenever a modern poet raises his voice he sounds phony. And its characteristic hero is neither the "Great Man" nor the romantic rebel, both doers of extraordinary deeds, but the man or woman in any walk of life who, despite all the impersonal pressures of modern scoiety, manages to acquire and preserve a face of his own.

Poets are, by the nature of their interests and the nature of artistic fabrication, singularly ill-equipped to understand politics or economics. Their natural interest is in singular individuals and personal relations, while politics and economics are concerned with large numbers of people, hence with the human average (the poet is bored to death by the idea of the Common Man) and with impersonal, to a great extent involuntary, relations. The poet cannot understand the function of money in modern society because for him there is no relation between subjective value and market value; he may be paid ten pounds for a poem which he believes is very good and took him months to write, and a hundred pounds for a piece of journalism which costs him but a day's work. If he is a successful poet—though few poets make enough money to be called successful in the way that a novelist or playwright can—he is a member of the Manchester school and believes in absolute *laisser-faire;* if he is unsuccessful and embittered, he is liable to combine aggressive fantasies about the annihilation of the present order with impractical daydreams of Utopia. Society has always to beware of the utopias being planned by artists *manqués* over cafeteria tables late at night.

All poets adore explosions, thunderstorms, tornadoes, conflagrations, ruins, scenes of spectacular carnage. The poetic imagination is not at all a desirable quality in a statesman.

In a war or a revolution, a poet may do very well as a guerilla fighter or a spy, but it is unlikely that he will make a good regular soldier, or, in peace time, a conscientious member of a parliamentary committee.

All political theories which, like Plato's, are based on analogies drawn from artistic fabrication are bound, if put into practice, to turn into tyrannies. The whole aim of a poet, or any other kind of artist, is to produce something which is complete and will endure without change. A poetic city would always contain exactly the same number of inhabitants doing exactly the same jobs for ever.

Moreover, in the process of arriving at the finished work, the artist has continually to employ violence. A poet writes:

The mast-high anchor dives through a cleft

changes it to

The anchor dives through closing paths

changes it again to

The anchor dives among hayricks

and finally to

The anchor dives through the floors of a church.

A *cleft* and *closing paths* have been liquidated, and hayricks deported to another stanza.

A society which was really like a good poem, embodying the aesthetic virtues of beauty, order, economy and subordination of detail to the whole, would be a nightmare of horror for, given the historical reality of actual men, such a society could only come into being through selective breeding, extermination of the physically and mentally unfit, absolute obedience to its Director, and a large slave class kept out of sight in cellars.

Vice versa, a poem which was really like a political democracy—examples, unfortunately, exist—would be formless, windy, banal and utterly boring.

There are two kinds of political issues, Party issues and Revolutionary issues. In a party issue, all parties are agreed as to the nature and justice of the social goal to be reached, but differ in their policies for reaching it. The existence of different parties is justified, firstly, because no party can offer irrefutable proof that its policy is the only one which will achieve the commonly desired goal and, secondly, because no social goal can be achieved without some sacrifice of individual or group interest and it is natural for each individual and social group to seek a policy which will keep its sacrifice to a minimum, to hope that, if sacrifices must be made, it would be more just if someone else made them. In a party issue, each party seeks to convince the members of its society, primarily by appealing to their reason; it marshals facts and arguments to convince others that its policy is more likely to achieve the desired goal than that of its opponents. On a party issue it is essential that passions be kept at a low temperature: effective oratory requires, of course, some appeal to the emotions of the audience, but in party politics orators should display the mock-passion of prosecuting and defending attorneys, not really lose their tempers. Outside the Chamber, the rival deputies should be able to dine in each other's houses; fanatics have no place in party politics.

A revolutionary issue is one in which different groups within a society hold different views as to what is just. When this is the case, argument and compromise are out of the question; each group is bound to regard the other as wicked or mad or both. Every revolutionary issue is potentially a *casus belli*. On a revolutionary issue, an orator cannot convince his audience by appealing to their reason; he may convert some of them by awakening and appealing to their conscience, but his principal function, whether he represent the revolutionary or the counterrevolutionary group, is to arouse its passion to the point where it will give all its energies to achieving total victory for itself and total defeat for its opponents. When an issue is revolutionary, fanatics are essential.

Today, there is only one genuine world-wide revolutionary issue, racial equality. The debate between capitalism, socialism and communism is really a party issue, because the goal which all seek is really the same, a goal which is summed up in Brecht's well-known line:

Erst kommt das Fressen, dann kommt die Moral.

I.e., Grub first, then Ethics. In all the technologically advanced countries today, whatever political label they give themselves, their policies have, essentially, the same goal: to guarantee to every member of society, as a psychophysical organism, the right to physical and mental health. The positive symbolic figure of this goal is a naked anonymous baby, the negative symbol, a mass of anonymous concentration camp corpses.

What is so terrifying and immeasurably depressing about most contemporary politics is the refusal—mainly but not, alas, only by the communists—to admit that this is a party issue to be settled by appeal to facts and reason, the insistence that there is a revolutionary issue between us. If an African gives his life for the cause of racial equality, his death is meaningful to him; but what is utterly absurd, is that people should be deprived every day of their liberties and their lives, and that the human race may quite possibly destroy itself over what is really a matter of practical policy like asking whether, given its particular historical circumstances, the health of a community is more or less likely to be secured by Private Practice or by Socialized Medicine.

What is peculiar and novel to our age is that the principal goal of politics in every advanced society is not, strictly speaking, a political one, that is to say, it is not concerned with human beings as persons and citizens but with human bodies, with the precultural, prepolitical human creature. It is, perhaps, inevitable that respect for the liberty of the individual should have so greatly diminished and the authoritarian powers of the State have so greatly increased from what they were fifty years ago, for the main political issue today is concerned not with human liberties but with human necessities.

As creatures we are all equally slaves to natural necessity; we are not free to vote how much food, sleep, light and air we need to keep in good health; we all need a certain quantity, and we all need the same quantity.

Every age is one-sided in its political and social preoccupation and in seeking to realize the particular value it esteems most highly, it neglects and even sacrifices other values. The relation of a poet, or any artist, to society and politics is, except in Africa or still backward semifeudal countries, more difficult than it has ever been because, while he cannot but approve of the importance of *everybody* getting enough food to eat and enough leisure, this problem has nothing whatever to do with art, which is concerned with *singular persons,* as they are alone and as they are in their personal relations. Since these interests are not the predominant ones in his society; indeed, in so far as it thinks about them at all, it is with suspicion and latent hostility—it secretly or openly thinks that the claim that one is a singular person, or a demand for privacy, is putting on airs, a claim to be superior to other folk—every artist feels himself at odds with modern civilization.

In our age, the mere making of a work of art is itself a political act. So long as artists exist, making what they please and think they ought to make, even if it is not terribly good, even if it appeals to only a handful of people, they remind the Management of something managers need to be reminded of, namely, that the managed are people with faces, not anonymous members, that *Homo Laborans* is also *Homo Ludens.*

If a poet meets an illiterate peasant, they may not be able to say much to each other, but if they both meet a public official, they share the same feeling of suspicion; neither will trust one further than he can throw a grand piano. If they enter a government building, both share the same feeling of apprehension; perhaps they will never get out again. Whatever the cultural differences between them, they both sniff in any official world the smell of an unreality in which persons are treated as statistics. The peasant may play cards in the evening while the poet writes verses, but there is one political principle to which they both subscribe, namely, that among the half dozen or so things for which a man of honor should be prepared, if necessary, to die, the right to play, the right to frivolity, is not the least.

Dylan Thomas

Dylan Thomas was born in Swansea, Wales, on October 22, 1914. He believed not only that "a poem on a page is only half a poem," but that "reading one's own poems aloud is letting the cat out of the bag." Each poem is a performance as well as a script, the performance being both a realization and a criticism of the text. Thomas, who had an extraordinary voice, often eloquent and moving, at times engagingly melodramatic, died in New York City on November 9, 1953, while on a reading tour of the United States.

In a characteristic vein, Thomas enters directly into processes as momentous as birth and death. Poetry itself is a renascence, a "movement from an overclothed blindness to a naked vision that depends in its intensity on the strength of the labour put into the creation of the poetry," so that his own poems become the record of an "individual struggle from darkness towards some measure of light." It is as though the spirit were heaving through encrustations, like a Lazarus unwinding from the piled earth and almost shaking it off. Yet there is occasional disagreement as to whether he sees with visionary freshness, or obscures, rather, through his proliferate style. Using every means conceivable—from unorthodox punctuation and words heady with connotation, through periphrases, to disassembled or mixed metaphors—Thomas attempts to freight his language with a maximum of meaning. Until the subject seems to be neither birth nor death nor even "meaning," but the infinite variety of the English language.

A poem by Thomas is a "watertight compartment," an elaborate yet strict formality, that contains a sequence of "creations recreations, destructions, contradictions." At the center of each poem seethes a host of images: "I make one image—though 'make' is not the word; I let, perhaps, an image be 'made' emotionally in me and then apply to it what intellectual and critical forces I possess—let it breed another, let that image contradict the first, make, of the third image bred out of the other two together, a fourth contradictory image, and let them all, within my imposed formal limits, conflict." Out of such a conflict of images Thomas tried to make, in his own words, "that momentary peace which is a poem."

Notes on the Art of Poetry*

You want to know why and how I just began to write poetry, and which poets or kinds of poetry I was first moved and influenced by.

To answer the first part of this question, I should say I wanted to write poetry in the beginning because I had fallen in love with words. The first poems I knew were nursery rhymes, and before I could read them for myself I had come to love just the words of them, the words alone. What the words stood for, symbolised, or meant, was of very secondary importance. What mattered was the *sound* of them as I heard them for the first time on the lips of the remote and incomprehensible grown-ups who seemed, for some reason, to be living in my world. And these words were, to me, as the notes of bells, the sounds of musical instruments, the noises of wind, sea, and rain, the rattle of milkcarts, the clopping of hooves on cobbles, the fingering of branches on a window pane, might be to someone, deaf from birth, who has miraculously found his hear-

* Written in the summer of 1951, at Laugharne, in reply to questions posed by a student.

ing. I did not care what the words said, overmuch, nor what happened to Jack and Jill and the Mother Goose rest of them; I cared for the shapes of sound that their names, and the words describing their actions, made in my ears; I cared for the colours the words cast on my eyes. I realise that I may be, as I think back all that way, romanticising my reactions to the simple and beautiful words of those pure poems; but that is all I can honestly remember, however much time might have falsified my memory. I fell in love—that is the only expression I can think of—at once, and am still at the mercy of words, though sometimes now, knowing a little of their behaviour very well, I think I can influence them slightly and have even learned to beat them now and then, which they appear to enjoy. I tumbled for words at once. And, when I began to read the nursery rhymes for myself, and, later, to read other verses and ballads, I knew that I had discovered the most important things, to me, that could be ever. There they were, seemingly lifeless, made only of black and white, but out of them, out of their own being, came love and terror and pity and pain and wonder and all the other vague abstractions that make our ephemeral lives dangerous, great, and bearable. Out of them came the gusts and grunts and hiccups and heehaws of the common fun of the earth; and though what the words meant was, in its own way, often deliciously funny enough, so much funnier seemed to me, at that almost forgotten time, the shape and shade and size and noise of the words as they hummed, strummed, jugged and galloped along. That was the time of innocence; words burst upon me, unencumbered by trivial or portentous association; words were their spring-like selves, fresh with Eden's dew, as they flew out of the air. They made their own original associations as they sprang and shone. The words, "Ride a cock-horse to Banbury Cross," were as haunting to me, who did not know then what a cock-horse was nor cared a damn where Banbury Cross might be, as, much later, were such lines as John Donne's, "Go and catch a falling star, Get with child a mandrake root," which also I could not understand when I first read them. And as I read more and more, and it was not all verse, by any means, my love for the real life of words increased until I knew that I must live *with* them and *in* them always. I knew, in fact, that I must be a writer of words, and nothing else. The first thing was to feel and know their sound and substance; what I was going to do with those words, what use I was going to make of them, what I was going to *say* through them, would come later. I knew I had to know them most intimately in all their forms and moods, their ups and downs, their chops and changes, their needs and demands. (Here, I am afraid, I am beginning to talk too vaguely. I do not like writing *about* words, because then I often use bad and wrong and stale and wooly words. What I like to do is to treat words as a craftsman does his wood or stone or what-have-you, to hew, carve, mould, coil, polish and plane them into patterns, sequences, sculptures, fugues of sound expressing some lyrical impulse, some spiritual doubt or conviction, some dimly-realised truth I must try to reach and realise). It was when I was very young, and just at school, that, in my father's study, before homework that was never done, I began to know one kind of writing from another, one kind of goodness, one kind of badness. My first, and greatest, liberty was that of being able to read everything and anything I cared to. I read indiscriminately, and with my eyes hanging out. I could never have dreamt that there were such goings-on in the world between the covers of books, such sand-storms and ice-blasts of words, such slashing of humbug, and humbug too, such staggering peace, such enormous laughter, such and so many blinding bright lights breaking across the just-awaking wits and splashing all over the pages in a million bits and pieces all of which were words, words, words, and each of which was alive forever in its own delight and glory and oddity and light (I must try not to make these supposedly helpful notes as confusing as my poems themselves.) I wrote endless imitations, though I never thought them to be imitations but, rather, wonderfully original things, like eggs laid by tigers. They were imitations of anything I happened to be reading at the time: Sir Thomas Browne, de Quincey, Henry Newbolt, the Ballads, Blake, Baroness Orczy, Marlowe, Chums, the Imagists, the Bible, Poe, Keats, Lawrence, Anon., and Shakespeare. A mixed lot, as you see, and randomly remembered. I tried my callow hand at almost every poetical form. How could I learn the tricks of a trade unless I tried to do them myself? I learned that the bad tricks come easily; and the good ones, which help you to say what you think you wish to say in the most meaningful, moving way, I am still learning. (But in earnest company you must call these tricks by other names, such as technical devices, prosodic experiments, etc.)

The writers, then, who influenced my earliest poems and stories were, quite simply and truthfully, all the writers I was reading at the time, and, as you see from a specimen list higher up the page, they ranged from writers of schoolboy adventure yarns to incomparable and inimitable masters like Blake. That is, when I began, bad writing had as much influence on my stuff as good. The bad influences I tried to remove and renounce bit by bit, shadow by shadow, echo by echo, through trial and error, through delight and disgust and misgiving, as I came to love words more and to hate the heavy hands that knocked them about, the thick tongues that [had] no feel for their multitudinous tastes, the dull and botching hacks who flattened them out into a colourless and insipid paste, the pedants who made them moribund and pompous as themselves. Let me say that the things that first made me love language and want to work *in* it and *for* it were nursery rhymes and folk tales, the Scottish Ballads, a few lines of hymns, the most famous Bible stories and the rhythms of the Bible, Blake's Songs of Innocence, and the quite incomprehensible magical majesty and nonsense of Shakespeare heard, read, and near-murdered in the first forms of my school.

You ask me, next, if it is true that three of the dominant influences on my published prose and poetry are Joyce, the Bible, and Freud. (I purposely say my 'published' prose and poetry, as in the preceding pages I have been talking about the primary influences upon my very first and forever unpublishable juvenilia.) I cannot say that I have been 'influenced' by Joyce, whom I enormously admire and whose Ulysses, and earlier stories I have read a great deal. I think this Joyce question arose because somebody once, in print, remarked on the closeness of the title of my book of short stories, "Portrait of the Artist As a Young Dog" to Joyce's title, "Portrait of the Artist as a Young Man." As you know, the name given to innumerable portrait paintings by their artists is, "Portrait of the Artist as a Young Man"—a perfectly straightforward title. Joyce used the painting-title for the first time as the title of a literary work. I myself made a bit of doggish fun of the *painting*-title and, of course, intended no possible reference to Joyce. I do not think that Joyce has had any hand at all in my writing; certainly, his Ulysses has not. On the other hand, I cannot deny that the shaping of some of my "Portrait" stories might owe something to Joyce's stories in the volume "Dubliners." But then, "Dubliners" was a pioneering work in the world of the short story, and no good storywriter since can have failed, in some way, however little, to have benefited by it.

The Bible, I have referred to in attempting to answer your

first question. Its great stories, of Noah, Jonah, Lot, Moses, Jacob, David, Solomon and a thousand more, I had, of course, known from very early youth; the great rhythms had rolled over me from the Welsh pulpits; and I read, for myself, from Job and Ecclesiastes; and the story of the New Testament is part of my life. But I have never sat down and studied the Bible, never consciously echoed its language, and am, in reality, as ignorant of it as most brought-up Christians. All of the Bible that I use in my work is remembered from childhood, and is the common property of all who were brought up in English-speaking communities. Nowhere, indeed, in all my writing, do I use any knowledge which is not commonplace to any literate person. I *have* used a few difficult words in early poems, but they are easily looked-up and were, in any case, thrown into the poems in a kind of adolescent showing-off which I hope I have now discarded.

And that leads me to the third 'dominant influence': Sigmund Freud. My only acquaintance with the theories and discoveries of Dr. Freud has been through the work of novelists who have been excited by his case-book histories, of popular newspaper scientific-potboilers who have, I imagine, vulgarised his work beyond recognition, and of a few modern poets, including Auden, who have attempted to use psychoanalytical phraseology and theory in some of their poems. I have read only one book of Freud's, "The Interpretation of Dreams", and do not recall having been influenced by it in any way. Again, no honest writer today can possibly avoid being influenced by Freud through his pioneering work into the Unconscious and by the influence of those discoveries on the scientific, philosophic, and artistic work of his contemporaries: but not, by any means, necessarily through Freud's own writing.

To your third question—Do I deliberately utilise devices of rhyme, rhythm, and word-formation in my writing—I must, of course, answer with an immediate, Yes. I am a painstaking, conscientious, involved and devious craftsman in words, however unsuccessful the result so often appears, and to whatever wrong uses I may apply my technical paraphernalia. I use everything and anything to make my poems work and move in the direction I want them to: old tricks, new tricks, puns, portmanteau-words, paradox, allusion, paronomasia, paragram, catachresis, slang, assonantal rhymes, vowel rhymes, sprung rhythm. Every device there is in language is there to be used if you will. Poets have got to enjoy themselves sometimes, and the twisting and convolutions of words, the inventions and contrivances, are all part of the joy that is part of the painful, voluntary work.

Your next question asks whether my use of combinations of words to create something new, "in the Surrealist way," is according to a set formula or is spontaneous.

There is a confusion here, for the Surrealists' set formula *was* to juxtapose the unpremeditated.

Let me make it clearer if I can. The Surrealists—(that is, super-realists, or those who work *above* realism)—were a coterie of painters and writers in Paris, in the nineteen twenties, who did not believe in the conscious selection of images. To put it in another way: They were artists who were dissatisfied with both the realists—(roughly speaking, those who tried to put down in paint and words an actual representation of what they imagined to be the real world in which they lived)—and the impressionists who, roughly speaking again, were those who tried to give an impression of what they imagined to be the real world. The Surrealists wanted to dive into the subconscious mind, the mind below the conscious surface, and dig up their images from there without the aid of logic of reason, and put them down, illogically and unreasonably, in paint and words. The Surrealists affirmed that, as three quarters of the mind was submerged, it was the function of the artist to gather his material from the greatest, submerged mass of the mind rather than from that quarter of the mind which, like the tip of an iceberg, protruded from the subconscious sea. One method the Surrealists used in their poetry was to juxtapose words and images that had no rational relationship; and out of this they hoped to achieve a kind of subconscious, or dream, poetry that would be truer to the real, imaginative world of the mind, mostly submerged, than is the poetry of the conscious mind that relies upon the rational and logical relationship of ideas, objects, and images.

This is, very crudely, the credo of the Surrealists, and one with which I profoundly disagree. I do not mind from where the images of a poem are dragged up; drag them up, if you like, from the nethermost sea of the hidden self; but, before they reach paper, they must go through all the rational processes of the intellect. The Surrealists, on the other hand, put their words down together on paper exactly as they emerge from chaos; they do not shape these words or put theim in order; to them, chaos *is* the shape and order. This seems to me to be exceedingly presumptuous; the Surrealists imagine that whatever they dredge from their subconscious selves and put down in paint or in words must, essentially, be of some interest or value. I deny this. One of the arts of the poet is to make comprehensible and articulate what might emerge from subconscious sources; one of the great main uses of the intellect is to *select,* from the amorphous mass of subconscious images, those that will best further his imaginative purpose, which is to write the best poem he can.

And Question five is, God help us, what is my definition of Poetry?

I myself, do not read poetry for anything but pleasure. I read only the poems I like. This means, of course, that I have to read a lot of poems I don't like before I find the ones I do, but, when I *do* find the ones I do, then all I can say is "Here they are," and read them to myself for pleasure.

Read the poems you like reading. Don't bother whether they're important, or if they'll live. What does it matter what poetry *is,* after all? If you want a definition of poetry, say: "Poetry is what makes me laugh or cry or yawn, what makes my toenails twinkle, what makes me want to do this or that or nothing," and let it go at that. All that matters about poetry is the enjoyment of it, however tragic it may be. All that matters is the eternal movement behind it, the vast undercurrent of human grief, folly, pretension, exaltation, or ignorance, however unlofty the intention of the poem.

You can tear a poem apart to see what makes it technically tick, and say to yourself, when the works are laid out before you, the vowels, the consonants, the rhymes and rhythms, "Yes, this is *it.* This is why the poem moves me so. It is because of the craftsmanship." But you're back again where you began. You're back with the mystery of having been moved by words. The best craftsmanship always leaves holes and gaps in the works of the poem so that something that is *not* in the poem can creep, crawl, flash, or thunder in.

The joy and function of poetry is, and was, the celebration of man, which is also the celebration of God.

David Jones

David Jones, who is an engraver and water colorist, was born in the southeast of England in 1895. In 1921 he became a convert to Roman Catholicism. Although his first work, In Parenthesis, *reflects his experiences with the Welsh Fusileers in World War I, it was not published until 1937.* The Anathemata, *his second and most recent "making," appeared in 1952.*

Poetry is a kind of anamnesis, a recollection and a cherishing. "Our making is dependent on a remembering of some sort. It may be only the remembering of a personal emotion of last Monday-week in the tranquility of next Friday fortnight. But a 'deed' has entered history, in this case our private history, and is therefore valid as matter for our poetry." To become a making or poiesis, *then, the deed must be shown forth as a "thing"; some abstract quality must cause it to have "being" or presence. And it must be offered "not with merely utile, but with significant, intent; that is to say a 're-presenting,' a 'showing again under other forms,' an 'effective recalling' " of the deed must be intended.*

"It is on account of the anthropic sign-making that we first

193

suspect that anthropos has some part in a without-endness," suggests Jones, who believes art to be a religious activity. But it might be objected that under the aspect of religion one tends to identify the sign with the thing signified, whereas in art, considered secularly, they remain discrete. Regarding the Eucharist, for example, it may be believed that bread and wine are, or have become, the body and blood of Christ: the bread and wine are signs no longer. To this Jones would reply that an identification occurs in any case, "for the painter may say to himself: 'This is not a representation of a mountain, it is "mountain" under the form of paint.' Indeed, unless he says this unconsciously or consciously he will not be a painter worth a candle." The same would hold true for poets, whose realities exist under the form of language, just as the body and the blood existed under the form of bread and wine.

The sine qua non *of art, finally—and the hallmark of human activity—is gratuitousness. "Art is the sole intransitive activity of man"; it attests to our humanity as well as our part in divinity. So it is that, with his keen and touching sense of the lineage of some morning's inconsequence, Jones quotes from the Knox translation of Proverbs: "I made play in this world of dust, with the sons of Adam for my play-fellows."*

The Preface to *The Anathemata**

'I have made a heap of all that I could find.' [1] So wrote Nennius, or whoever composed the introductory matter to the *Historia Brittonum*. He speaks of an 'inward wound which was caused by the fear that certain things dear to him, 'should be like smoke dissipated'. Further he says, 'not trusting my own learning, which is none at all, but partly from writings and monuments of the ancient inhabitants of Britain, partly from the annals of the Romans and the chronicles of the sacred fathers, Isidore, Hieronymus, Prosper, Eusebius and from the histories of the Scots and Saxons although our enemies . . . I have lispingly put together this . . . about past transactions, that [this material] might not be trodden under foot.'[2]

Well, although this writing is neither a history of the Britons nor a history of any sort, and although my intentions in writing at

---

* *The Anathemata*—**Chilmark Press.**

[1] The actual words are *coacervavi omne quod inveni,* and occur in *Prologue II* to the *Historia.*

[2] Quoted from the translation of *Prologue I.* See *The Works of Gildas and Nennius, J. A. Giles,* London, 1841.

all could not, I suppose, be more other than were the intentions of Nennius, nevertheless, there is in these two apologies which preface his work something which, in however oblique a fashion, might serve for my apology also.

Part of my task has been to allow myself to be directed by motifs gathered together from such sources as have by accident been available to me and to make a work out of those mixed data.

This, you will say, is, in a sense, the task of any artist in any material, seeing that whatever he makes must necessarily show forth what is his by this or that inheritance.

True, but since, as Joyce is reported to have said, 'practical life or "art" . . . comprehends all our activities from boatbuilding to poetry',[3] the degrees and kinds and complexities of this showing forth of our inheritance must vary to an almost limitless extent:

If one is making a table it is possible that one's relationship to the Battle of Hastings or to the Nicene Creed might have little bearing on the form of the table to be made; but if one is making a sonnet such kinds of relationships become factors of more evident importance.

If one is making a painting of daffodils what is *not* instantly involved? Will it make any difference whether or no we have heard of Persephone or Flora or Blodeuedd?[4]

I am of the opinion that it will make a difference, but would immediately make this reservation: Just as Christians assert that baptism by water 'makes a difference', but that many by desire and without water achieve the benefits of that 'difference', so, without having heard of Flora Dea, there are many who would paint daffodils as though they had invoked her by name.

To continue with these three images, 'which I like', that is, the Battle of Hastings, the Nicene Creed and Flora Dea, and to use them—as counters or symbols merely—of the *kind* of motifs employed in this writing of mine; it is clear that if such-like motifs are one's material, then one is trying to make a shape out of the very things of which one is oneself made; even though, as may well be the case, one may be aware of these things that have made one, by 'desire' only, and not by 'water'—to pursue the analogy used

---

[3] See Gogarty *As I was Going Down Sackville Street,* p. 287. London, 1937.

[4] Blodeuedd, blod-ei-eth, ei as in height, eth as in nether, accent on middle syllable; from *blodau* flowers. The name given in Welsh mythology to the woman made by magical processes from various blossoms.

above.

So that to the question: What is this writing about? I answer that it is about one's own 'thing', which *res* is unavoidably part and parcel of the Western Christian *res,* as inherited by a person whose perceptions are totally conditioned and limited by and dependent upon his being indigenous to this island. In this it is necessarily insular; within which insularity there are the further conditionings contingent upon his being a Londoner, of Welsh and English parentage, of Protestant upbringing, of Catholic subscription.

While such biographical accidents are not in themselves any concern of, or interest to, the reader, they are noted here because they are responsible for most of the content and have had an over-ruling effect upon the form of this writing. Though linguistically 'English monoglot' accurately describes the writer, owing to the accidents above mentioned certain words, terms and occasionally phrases from the Welsh and Latin languages and a great many concepts and motifs of Welsh and Romanic provenance have become part of the writer's *Realien,* within a kind of Cockney setting. Like the elder boy in *The Prioresses Tale,* who knew well the necessity and significance of the hymn, *Alma Redemptoris Mater,* I too might say:

I can no more expounde in this matere
I lerne song, I can but smal grammere.

Seeing that, *as one is so one does,* and that, *making follows being,* it follows that these mixed terms and themes have become part of the making of this writing. But here problems arise and rather grave ones.

The words, 'May they rest in peace' and the words 'Whoso-ever will' might, by some feat of artistry, be so juxtaposed within a context as not only to translate the words 'Requiescant in pace' and 'Quicunque vult' but to evoke the *exact historic overtones and under-tones* of those Latin words. But should some writer find himself unable by whatever ingenuity of formal arrangement or of contextual allusion to achieve this identity of content and identity of evocation, while changing the language, then he would have no alternative but to use the original form. Such a writer's own deficiency in, or ignorance of, the original language, has only a very limited bearing on the matter, seeing that his duty is to consider only the objective appropriateness of this or that term and its emotive impact within a given context. It is of no consequence to the shape of the work how the workman came by the bits of material he used in making that shape. When the workman is dead the only thing that will matter is the work, objectively considered. Moreover, the workman must be dead to himself while engaged upon the work, otherwise we have that sort of 'self-expression' which is as undesirable in the painter or the writer as in the carpenter, the cantor, the half-back, or the cook. Although all this is fairly clear in principle, I have not found it easy to apply in practice. That is to say, I have found it exceptionally hard to decide whether in a given context an 'Whosoever will' is the, so to say, effective sign of a 'Quicunque vult'. Or to give a concrete instance: whether, within its context, my use of the Welsh title 'Gwledig' was avoidable and whether the English translation, 'ruler',[5] could have been so conditioned and juxtaposed as to incant what 'Gwledig' incants. The 'grave problems' referred to a few paragraphs back have mostly arisen over questions of this sort. It must be understood that it is not a question of 'translation' or even of 'finding an equivalent word', it is something much more complex. 'Tsar' will mean one thing and 'Caesar' another to the end of time.

When in the Good Friday Office, the Latin, without any warning, is suddenly pierced by the Greek cry *Agios o Theos,* the Greek-speaking Roman Church of the third century becomes almost visibly present to us.[6] So to juxtapose and condition the English words 'O Holy God' as to make them do what this change from Latin to Greek effects within this particular liturgical setting, would not be at all easy. It is problems of this nature that have occupied me a good deal.

With regard to the actual words in the Welsh language I have

---

[5] Or whatever the translation might be. Anwyl's dictionary gives: lord, king, ruler, sovereign, prince. The word appears to be connected with *gwlad,* country or land and in modern Welsh *gwledig,* used as an adjective, implies something rural or rustic. As a noun it belongs to the early Dark Ages when it was used of important rulers; it was used of Maximus the emperor, it was used by Taliesin, of God.

[6] This passage is, historically, inaccurate, because the Greek words, I am told, cannot be said to be left over from the Greek-speaking Roman Church of the third century, but were introduced later into the Latin rite under Greek influence in, probably, the eighth century. However, the main argument is unaffected.

given the meanings and attempted to give the *approximate* sounds in the notes. Welshmen may smile or be angered at the crudity and amateurishness of these attempts, but something of the sort was necessary, because in some cases a constituent part of the actual form—the assonance—of the writing is affected. I shall give one example of this: I have had occasion to use the word *mamau*. This key-word means 'mothers' and can also mean 'fairies'. Now the Welsh diphthong *au* is pronounced very like the 'ei' diphthong in the English word 'height.'[7] Hence *mamau* can be made to have assonance with the Latin word *nymphae* and the English words 'grey-eyed' and 'dryad', and I have employed these particular correspondences or near correspondences, on page 238; but to the reader unacquainted with the Welsh 'au' sound, the form of this passage would be lost. Over such matters annotation seemed a necessity.

With regard to the Latin terms employed I have noted the liturgical or other contexts. For many readers these notes may appear to be an elucidation of the obvious, but, on the other hand, we are not all equally familiar with the deposits. It is sometimes objected that annotation is pedantic; all things considered in the present instance, the reverse would, I think, be the more true. There have been culture-phases when the maker and the society in which he lived shared an enclosed and common background, where the terms of reference were common to all. It would be an affectation to pretend that such was our situation today. Certainly it would be an absurd affectation in me to suppose that many of the themes I have employed are familiar to all readers, even though they are, without exception, themes derived from our own deposits. When I read in the deposits we have received from ancient Hebrew sources, of Og, king of Bashan, of the Azazel, of Urim and Thummim, I may or may not wish for further information regarding the significance of this ruler, this daemon and this method of divination. Similarly when in my text I have found it necessary to use the words Laverna and Rhiannon, *Dux Britanniarum* and *Ymherawdr, groma* and *hudlath,* it is conceivable that some reader may wish for further information about these two goddesses, two titles and two instruments. I have, therefore, glossed the text in order to

---

[7] For which reason Mr. Aneurin Bevan is known as 'Nye' and not 'New.' The Welsh diphthongs *au* and *eu* have indeed a subtle distinction but not sufficient to affect this matter. The reason being that the Welsh *u* alone has approximately the sound of the English ee in 'bee', hence *au* equals ah + ee.

open up 'unshared backgrounds' (to use an expression coined by Mr. C. S. Lewis),[8] if such they are.

The title-page describes this book as 'fragments of an attempted writing' because that is an exact description of it. It had its beginnings in experiments made from time to time between 1938 and 1945. In a sense what was then written is another book. It has been rewritten, large portions excluded,[9] others added, the whole rearranged and considerably changed more than once. I find, for instance, that what is now sheet 166 of my written MS has at different times been sheet 75 and sheet 7. What is now printed represents parts, dislocated attempts, reshuffled and again rewritten intermittently between 1946 and 1951.

The times are late and get later, not by decades but by years and months. This tempo of change, which in the world of affairs and in the physical sciences makes schemes and data outmoded and irrelevant overnight, presents peculiar and phenomenal difficulties to the making of works, and almost insuperable difficulties to the making of certain kinds of works; as when, for one reason or another, the making of those works has been spread over a number of years. The reason is not far to seek. The artist deals wholly in signs. His signs must be valid, that is valid for him, and, normally, for the culture that has made him. But there is a time factor affecting these signs. If a requisite now-ness is not present, the sign, valid in itself, is apt to suffer a kind of invalidation. This presents most complicated problems to the artist working outside a reasonably static culture-phase. These and kindred problems have presented themselves to me with a particular clarity and an increasing acuteness. It may be that the kind of thing I have been trying to make is no longer makeable in the kind of way in which I have tried to make it.

In the late nineteen-twenties and early 'thirties among my most immediate friends there used to be discussed something that we christened 'The Break'. We did not discover the phenomenon so described; it had been evident in various ways to various people for perhaps a century; it is now, I suppose, apparent to most. Or at least most now see that in the nineteenth century, Western Man moved across a rubicon which, if as unseen as the 38th Parallel,

---

[8] See commentary by C. S. Lewis, 'Williams and the Arthuriad', in *Arthurian Torso*, 1948.

[9] Should it prove possible I hope to make, from this excluded material, a continuation, or Part II of *The Anathemata*.

seems to have been as definitive as the Styx. That much is I think generally appreciated. But it was not the memory-effacing Lethe that was crossed; and consequently, although man has found much to his liking, advantage, and considerable wonderment, he has still retained ineradicable longings for, as it were, the farther shore. The men of the nineteenth century exemplify this at every turn; all the movements betray this if in all kinds of mutually contradictory ways. We are their inheritors, and in however metamorphosed a manner we share their basic dilemmas. 'And how!' as we citizens of the Old Rome say in our new Byzantine lingo from across the Herring Pond.

When in the 'twenties we spoke of this Break it was always with reference to some manifestation of this dilemma *vis-à-vis* the arts—and of religion also, but only in so far as religion has to do with signs, just as have the arts.

That is to say our Break had reference to something which was affecting the entire world of sacrament and sign. We were not how-ever speculating on, or in any way questioning dogma concerning 'The Sacraments'. On the contrary, such dogma was taken by us for granted—was indeed our point of departure. It was with the corollaries, the implications and the analogies of such dogma that we were concerned. Our speculations under this head were upon how increasingly isolated such dogma had become, owing to the turn civilization had taken, affecting signs in general and the whole notion and concept of sign.

Water is called the 'matter' of the Sacrament of Baptism. Is 'two of hydrogen and one of oxygen' that 'matter'? I suppose so. But what concerns us here is whether the poet can and does so juxtapose and condition within a context the formula H_2O as to evoke 'founts', 'that innocent creature', 'the womb of this devine font', 'the candidates', or for that matter 'the narrows' and 'the siluer sea, Which serues it in the office of a wall, Or as a Moat de-fensiue to a house'.

A knowledge of the chemical components of this material water should, normally, or if you prefer it, ideally, provide us with further, deeper, and more exciting significances *via-à-vis* the sacra-ment of water, and also, for us islanders, whose history is so much of water, with other significances relative to that. In Britain, 'water' is unavoidably very much part of the *materia poetica*. It may be felt that these examples are somewhat far-fetched, but I choose them as illustrations only. And if you consider how the men of some epochs have managed to wed widely separated ideas, and to make odd scraps of newly discovered data subserve immemorial themes (cf. the English Metaphysicals?)[10] my examples may not appear all that strained.

Whether there is a radical incompatibility between the world of the 'myths' and the world of the 'formulae', or whether it is a matter only of historic accident, of an unfortunate and fortuitous association of ideas leading to estrangement and misunderstanding, are questions which are continually debated and discussed at every sort of level by 'thinkers' of all shades of opinion. Clearly such questions are most grave but they do not directly concern us here, nor are they, I think, within our competence. What we are here concerned with and which does fall within our experience and competence, is the effect and consequence of such unresolved elements (whatever the cause) upon the making of works at this present time; the effect, that is to say, upon ourselves, here and now. We are concerned only with the actual existence of a lesion of some sort (whether ephemeral or more enduring we do not know), which appears, in part at least, to be in some way bound up with the historic phenomena indicated. And we are concerned with the present effects of these phenomena only in so far as those effects impinge upon, raise problems relative to, inconvenience or impoverish, handicap the free use of, modify the possibilities of, or in any way affect the *materia poetica*.

The reader may object, with regard to some of the problems cited, suggested or implied throughout this preface, that they exist only for those who adhere to, or hanker after, some theological scheme; or are otherwise entangled in conceptions and images carried over from a past pattern of life and culture. Though it is easy enough to see how such an objection might seem both cogent and convenient, it arises from a serious misinterpretation of the nature of the problems in question. In case my terminology may be thought by some to lend itself to some such misinterpretation I shall attempt a further elucidation, because it is, in my view, very necessary to get this matter clear.

---

[10] Who wrote a poetry that was counter-Renaissant, creaturely yet otherworld-ordered, ecstatical yet technically severe and ingenious, concerned with conditions of the psyche, but its images very much of the soma; metaphysical, but not un-intrigued by the physics of the period; English, but well represented by names hardly English; thus still posing interesting questions for those specialists whose business it is to research into that epoch.

It might not be a bad idea to remind ourselves here that the attitude of the artist is necessarily empirical rather than speculative. 'Art is a virtue of the practical intelligence.' All 'artistic' problems are, as such, practical problems. You can but cut the suit according to the cloth. For the artist the question is 'Does it?' rather than 'Ought it?'

The problems of which I speak can neither be brought into existence nor made to vanish by your opinions or mine. Though, of course, what we believe, or think we believe, the temper and nature, the validity or otherwise of those beliefs will largely condition our attitude toward all problems. Our beliefs, seeing that they stand in some relationship to the sum of our perceptions, may enhance or lessen our awareness of the very existence of some of those problems. But the problems themselves are inherent in a cultural or civilization situation, and from problems of such a nature no person of that culture or civilization can escape, least of all the 'poets' of that culture or civilization.

I name the poets in particular, not to round off a phrase, but to state what appears to me to be a fact. The forms and materials which the poet uses, his images and the meanings he would give to those images, his perceptions, what is evoked, invoked or incanted, is in some way or other, to some degree or other, essentially bound up with the particular historic complex to which he, together with each other member of that complex, belongs. But, for the poet, the woof and warp, the texture, feel, ethos, the whole *matière* comprising that complex comprises also, or in part comprises, the actual material of his art. The 'arts' of, e.g., the strategist, the plumber, the philosopher, the physicist, are, no doubt, like the art of the poet, conditioned by and reflective of the particular cultural complex to which their practitioners belong, but neither of these four arts, *with respect to their several causes,* can be said to be occupied with the embodiment and expression of the mythus and deposits comprising that cultural complex. Whereas the art of poetry, even in our present civilizational phase, even in our hyper-Alexandrian and megalopolitan situation, is, in some senses, still so occupied.

T. Gilby, in *Barbara Celarent,* writes 'The formal cause is the specific factor that we seek to capture, the mind is a hunter of forms, *venator formarum*'.

This, I suppose, applies to the 'specific factor' that the art of plumbing has as its formal cause, no less than to that which the art of poetry has. But the particular quarry that the mind of the poet seeks to capture is a very elusive beast indeed. Perhaps we can say that the country to be hunted, the habitat of that quarry, where the 'forms' lurk that he's after, will be found to be part of vast, densely wooded, inherited and entailed domains. It is in that 'sacred wood' that the spoor of those 'forms' is to be tracked. The 'specific factor' to be captured will be pungent with the smell of, asperged with the dew of, those thickets. The *venator poeta* cannot escape that tangled brake. It is within such a topography that he will feel forward, from a find to a check, from a check to a view, from a view to a possible kill: in the morning certainly, but also in the lengthening shadows.

Or, to leave analogy and to speak plain: I believe that there is, in the principle that informs the poetic art, a something which cannot be disengaged from the mythus, deposits, *matière,* ethos, whole *res* of which the poet is himself a product.

My guess is that we cannot answer the question 'What is poetry?' (meaning, What is the nature of poetry?) without some involvement in this mythus, deposit, etc.

We know—it goes without saying—that the question 'What is the material of poetry' cannot be answered without some mention of these same deposits.

We know also, and even more certainly, that this applies to the question 'By what means or agency is poetry?' For one of the efficient causes of which the effect called poetry is a dependant involves the employment of a particular language or languages, and involves that employment at an especially heightened tension. The means or agent is a veritable torcular, squeezing every drain of evocation from the word-forms of that language or languages. And that involves a bagful of mythus before you've said Jack Robinson —or immediately after.

My contention is that all this holds whether the poet practises his art in some 'bardic' capacity and as a person of defined duties and recognized status in an early and simple phase of a culture (the 'morning' in the analogy employed above) or whether he happens to be a person who, for reasons of one sort or another, 'writes poetry' in a late and complex phase of a phenomenally complex civilization (the 'lengthening shadows' in the analogy) the many amenities of which you and I now enjoy.

We are not here considering the advantages or disadvantages to the art of poetry in these two totally other situations. We are noting only that in the latter situation the causes are *still* linked with the deposits.

We are, in our society of today, very far removed from those culture-phases where the poet was explicitly and by profession the custodian, rememberer, embodier and voice of the mythus, etc., of some contained group of families, or of a tribe, nation, people, cult. But we can, perhaps, diagnose something that appears as a constant in poetry by the following consideration: When rulers seek to impose a new order upon any such group belonging to one or other of those more primitive culture-phases, it is necessary for those rulers to take into account the influence of the poets as recalling something loved and as embodying an ethos inimical to the imposition of that new order. Whether the policy adopted is one of suppression or of some kind of patronage, a recognition of possible danger dictates the policy in either case. Leaving aside such political considerations as may cause such recognition under such circumstances, we may still recognize the 'dangerous' element. Poetry is to be diagnosed as 'dangerous' because it evokes and recalls, is a kind of *anamnesis* of, i.e. is an effective recalling of, something loved. In that sense it is inevitably 'propaganda', in that any real formal expression propagands the reality which caused those forms and their content to be. There are also to be considered the contingent and more remote associations which those forms and their content may evoke. There is a sense in which *Barbara Allen* is many times more 'propagandist' than *Rule Britannia*. The more real the thing, the more it will confound their politics. If the dog-rose moves something in the Englishman at a deeper level than the Union Flag it is not only because of the fragile and peculiar beauty of that flower, but also because the poetry of England, drawing upon the intrinsic qualities of the familiar and common June rose, has, by the single image of a rose, managed to recall and evoke, for the English, a June-England association. The first concept being altogether and undeniably lovely, the other also must be lovely! A very satisfactory conclusion. The magic works. But it might prove most adverse magic to an opponent of the thing, idea or complex of sentiments which the word 'England' is patient of comprising.

The problems that confront the poet, as poet, in any given cultural or civilizational phase, no matter what his subjective attitude toward those problems, and though they concern only such elusive matters as the validity of a word, are themselves as objective as is the development of the aero-engine, the fact that my great-uncle William served in the ranks in the Crimea, that the tree outside the window happens to be an acacia, that field-archaeology has changed some of the accents of, e.g., Biblical criticism, that an extension of state-control characterizes the period in which we now live, or that something analogous to that extension is remarked by students of the period of Valens and Valentinian, and that like effects may possibly have like causes.

The poet is born into a given historic situation and it follows that his problems—i.e. his problems as a poet—will be what might be called 'situational problems'.

If, owing to a complex of causes, sable-hair brushes, chinese white and hot-pressed water-colour paper went off the market, you would, if you were a user of such commodities, be faced with a situational problem of a very awkward but fundamentally material sort. Whatever the consolation of philosophy, no attitude of mind would bring back to your workroom the required commodities which the market no longer provided. You would willy-nilly suffer an inconvenience. The effect of that inconvenience *might* be most salutary, might occasion in you a most unsuspected inventiveness. Well, the situational problem which concerns us here is of an equally objective nature, but so far from affecting only the materials of one particular kind of artist, it affects man-the-artist as such, and affects him not at one peripheral point, but crucially. Nevertheless, as with the inconvenienced water-colourist, the 'inconveniences' of our situation may turn out to be, in some respects and for some, 'most salutary'. Indeed there is not wanting evidence that such is the case. And so it is that the present situation presents its own particular difficulties with regard to signs in general and the concept of sign.

The whole complex of these difficulties is primarily felt by the sign-maker, the artist, because for him it is an immediate, day by day, factual problem. He has, somehow or other, to lift up valid signs; that is his specific task.

In practice one of his main problems, one of the matters upon which his judgement is exercised ('The virtue of art is to judge') concerns the validity and availability that constitutes his greatest problem in the present culture-situation.

If the poet writes 'wood' what are the chances that the Wood of the Cross will be evoked? Should the answer be 'None', then it would seem that an impoverishment of some sort would have to be admitted. It would mean that that particular word could no longer be used with confidence to implement, to call up or to set in motion a whole world of content belonging in a special sense to the mythus of a particular culture and of concepts and realities belonging to mankind as such. This would be true irrespective of our beliefs or disbeliefs. It would remain true even if we were of the opinion that it was high time that the word 'wood' should be dissociated from the mythus and concepts indicated. The arts abhor any loppings off of meanings or emptyings out, any lessening of the totality of connotation, any loss of recession and thickness through.

If the painter makes visual forms, the content of which is chairs or chair-ishness, what are the chances that those who regard his painting will run to meet him with the notions 'seat', 'throne', 'session', *cathedra'*, 'Scone', 'on-the-right-hand-of-the-Father', in mind? If this haphazard list is, in some of its accidents, yours and mine, it nevertheless serves, *mutatus mutandis,* for Peloponnesians and for Polynesians too.

It is axiomatic that the function of the artist is to make things *sub specie aeternitatis.*

> **He said 'What's Time? Leave Now for dogs and apes!**
> **Man has For ever'.**

True, but the works of man, unless they are of 'now' and of 'this place', can have no 'for ever'.

The poet may feel something with regard to Penda the Mercian and nothing with regard to Darius the Mede. In itself that is a limitation, it might be regarded as a disproportion; no matter, there is no help—he must work within the limits of his love. There must be no mugging-up, no 'ought to know' or 'try to feel'; for only what is actually loved and known can be seen *sub specie aeternitatis.* The muse herself is adamant about this: she is indifferent to what the poet may wish he could feel, she cares only for what he in fact feels. In this she differs totally from her sister, the 'Queen of the Moral Virtues', who, fortunately for us, is concerned only with our will and intention.

This applies to poets, artefacturers of *opera* of any sort, at any period of human history. But as I see it, we are today so situated that it is pertinent to ask: What for us *is* patient of being 'actually loved and known', where for us is 'this place', where do we seek or find what is 'ours', what *is* available, what *is* valid as material for our effective signs?

Normally we should not have far to seek: the flowers for the muse's garland would be gathered from the ancestral burial-mound

—always and inevitably fecund ground, yielding perennial and familiar blossoms, watered and, maybe, potted, perhaps 'improved', by ourselves. It becomes more difficult when the bulldozers have all but obliterated the mounds, when all that is left of the potting-sheds are the disused hypocausts, and when where was this site and were these foci there is *terra informis*.

To what degree, for instance, is it possible for the 'name' to evoke the 'local habitation' long since gone? I do not raise these questions in order to answer them, for I do not know what the answers may be, but I raise them in order to indicate some of the dilemmas which have been present with me all the time.

When I was a child there was still in vogue the Victorian catch-question 'When is a door not a door?' Today I find that question has gathered to itself unexpected meaning. It has become the keynote of a so to say auto-catechism: When is a door not a door? When is a sign not a sign? When is what was valid no longer valid?'

Such questions and attempts to answer them are in part reflected in the preoccupation with the 'abstract' in the visual arts. This preoccupation, whether mistaken or rewarding, is neither whim nor accident but is determined by historic causes affecting all this whole business of sign and what is signified, now-ness and place-ness and loves and validities of many sorts and kinds.

What goes for tinker goes for tailor; and it is worth noting, for again it is not accidental, that the man who was super-sensitive to the unique and specific possibilities and demands of his own art. should have shown in his attitude toward that art and in that art itself, how analogous are some of the problems that the muse sets for the writer and those she sets for the painter. And further that this artist, while pre-eminently 'contemporary' and indeed 'of the future', was also of all artists the most of site and place. And as for 'the past', as for 'history', it was from the ancestral mound that he fetched his best garlands and Clio ran with him a lot of the way —if under the name of Brigit. So that although most authentically the bard of the shapeless cosmopolis and of the megalopolitan diaspora, he could say.

**Come ant daunce wyt me
In Irelaunde.**

In taking Joyce to illustrate the problem I do so because any problem inherent in the arts today, and in particular in that of writing, is illumined by so doing. Quite irrespective of whether we approve or deprecate his matter or his form or both, Joyce was centrally occupied with the formal problems of art, as exemplified in a particular art and in his own very particular deployment of that art. It is just such *kinds* of artist who alone illustrate the artistic dilemmas of any age. Hopkins, 'as one born out of due time', but before his time (yet how very much *of* his time!) was just such another. And we know how he, Manley Hopkins, stands over so many later artists, saying, in the words of another and preeminent living artist,

And I Tiresias have foresuffered all.

And Browning too might well have his say and continue the quotation,

Enacted on this same divan or bed.

That bed may indeed seem procrustean, for the artist may be stretched upon it

Dead from the waist down

and it is on such a couch that the muse exacts and interrogates, subsequent to

The fine delight that fathers thought.

To take an example from a visual art: Though our presiding spirit were akin to that which presided over the illustrative charm of Beatrix Potter, we should be more than foolish to close our eyes to the existence of Pablo Picasso, because our problems as a visual artist would be bound in some way or other, to some degree or other, to involve matters over which that Spanish Hercules has laboured in more than twelve modes. Behind his untiring inventiveness there is the desire to uncover a valid sign. And that desire is, as I have said, incumbent upon all who practice an art.

A rhyme I associate with St. Thomas More (but perhaps it is not his) runs

The cook that doth to painting fall
I ween he shall prove a fool.

In practice maybe—it all depends. But in idea he will not be proved so foolish as the painter who thinks cookery not subject to the same demands of the muse as is painting or any making that contrives things patient of being 'set up to the gods'.

The foregoing considerations may appear to lack continuity and to run tangent, but they will perhaps indicate something of my attitude toward human works of all sorts and are thus not out of place in an introduction to this attempted sort of work of my own.

I call what I have written *The Anathemata*. (The dictionary puts the accent on the *third* syllable in contradistinction to 'anathemas'.)

It came to have this title in the following way: I knew that in antiquity the Greek word *anathema* (spelt with an epsilon) meant (firstly) something holy but that in the N.T. it is restricted to the opposite sense. While this duality exactly fitted my requirements, the English word 'anathemas', because referring only to that opposite sense, was of no use to me. I recalled, however, that there was the other English plural, 'anathemata', meaning devoted things, and used by some English writers down the centuries, thus preserving in our language the ancient and beneficent meaning; for 'anathemata' comes from *anathema* spelt with an eta, of which the epsilon form is a variant.

It might be said that 'anathemata' precludes 'anathemas' no less than *vice versa,* but considering that the former carries us back to a beneficent original, and the latter only to a particular meaning of a variant of that original, I decided that 'anathemata' would serve my double purpose, even if it did so only by means of a pun.

Subsequent to deciding upon this title, I noted that in a reference to St. John Chrysostom it was said that he described the word as 'things . . . laid up from other things'. And again that in Homer it refers only to delightful things and to ornaments. And further, that it is a word having certain affinities with *agalma,* meaning what is glorious, and so used of statue, image, figure. (Hence our word figure-stone, agalmatolite, called also pagodite because the sacred images or pagodas of Asia are carved in it.) And again in the gospel, after narrating the incident of the widow's mite, St. Luke speaks of the onlookers who admired the 'goodly stones and gifts' that embellished the temple and he uses the word 'anathemata' of those gifts. And in the middle of the last century, an author, commenting on ancient votive offerings—figurines of animals—writes of 'such anathemata being offered by the poor'.

So I mean by my title as much as it can be made to mean, or can evoke or suggest, however obliquely: the blessed things that have taken on what is cursed and the profane things that somehow are redeemed: the delights and also the 'ornaments', both in the primary sense of gear and paraphernalia and in the sense of what simply adorns; the donated and votive things, the things dedicated after whatever fashion, the things in some sense made separate, being 'laid up from other things'; things, or some aspect of them, that partake of the extra-utile and of the gratuitous; things that are the signs of something other, together with those signs that not only have the nature of a sign, but are themselves, under some mode, what they signify. Things set up, lifted up, or in whatever manner made over to the gods.

But here I shall have to recall an ancient distinction as it very much concerns, and is mixed up with, what I include under anathemata.

It is spoken of under the terms *prudentia* and *ars*. With regard to the latter, the 'virtue of art', a compact or shipshape passage occurs in a recent book.[11] This passage concludes thus: 'The emphasis is on the thing to be done, not, as in the moral virtues, on our personal dispositions in doing it.' The one is concerned only for our intentions and dispositions, and the other only for the formal dispositions that comprise an artefact. One cares for us and our final condition, the other for the work and *its* final condition. Our final condition or last end is not yet, whereas our artefacts have their completion now or never. For which reason, while Prudentia is exercised about our intentions, Ars is concerned with the shape of a finished article. She *cannot,* as the other *must,* wait till the Judgement.

The distinction could hardly be greater in all respects—that is what makes the analogies particularly significant. For it emerges that both are concerned with the proper integration and perfection of shape, in the one case that of persons and in the other of perishable things. Both then are concerned with what is patient of being 'devoted', 'laid up from other things', 'consecrated to divine use', made anathemata in some sense or other.

---

[11] A book from which I have already quoted, by Thomas Gilby, O.P.
The distinction compactly put by Fr. Gilby in this passage has indeed been expressed and many of its implications dwelt upon by my friend the late Mr. Eric Gill; and I should like to take this opportunity of acknowledging my indebtedness to those fruitful conversations with Mr. Gill in years gone by, regarding this business of man-the-artist. For he possessed, in conversation, a Socratic quality, which, even in disagreement, tended to clarification.

So that at one end of the scale or Jacob's ladder or song of degrees, we can include, in respect of things offered, those differing coloured marks or spots that boys chalk carefully on their whipping-tops,[12] which, when they whip the top, take on definity and form and appear as revolving circles of rainbow hue. (And if this is not a gift to the muse, then I do not know what is, and a falsity pervades my suppositions and analogies throughout.)

At the other end we can include that which comprises anathemata in *every possible* sense, offerings of both persons and things, including those things over which the minister is directed to say '. . . bless, ascribe to, ratify, make reasonable and acceptable'.[13]

We note that he is not directed to say those words with reference to grapes and wheat,[14] but with reference to things which have already passed under the jurisdiction of the muse, being themselves quasi-artefacts, made according to a *recta ratio* and involving the operation of several arts, as that of the mill, the kneading-board, the oven, the *torcular,* the vat.

So that, leaving aside much else, we could not have the bare and absolute essentials wherewith to obey the command 'Do this for a recalling[15] of me, without artefacture. And where artefacture

---

[12] Or did so forty or fifty years back.

[13] The actual form now in use is: '. . . *benedictam, adscriptam, ratam, rationabilem, acceptabilemque facere digneris'* and is part of the oblational prayers in the Roman mass. As it stands in its Latin form it is only of the fourth century. It is, however, said by liturgical scholars to link with forms in use in the Greek-speaking Roman Church about the beginning of the third century; a date as near to St. John or to 'Boadicea' as are you and I to William Blake or Maréchal Ney.

[14] I seem to recall a passage in *The Shape of the Liturgy* (Dix) where the author, referring to the words 'these thy creatures of bread and wine' in the *Book of Common Prayer,* rightly says (as far as I can remember) that these words suggest that bread and wine are simply fruits of the earth, whereas this is not strictly so. At all events that is the disinction which I wish to emphasize here. It is one which I think has very important implications and corollaries.

[15] Anamnesis. I take leave to remind the reader that this is a key-word in our deposits. The dictionary defines its general meaning as 'the recalling of things past'. But what is the nature of this particular recalling? I append the following quotation as being clear and to the point: 'It (anamnesis) is not quite easy to represent accurately in English, words like "remembrance" or "memorial" having for us a connotation of something *absent* which is only mentally recollected. But in the Scriptures of both the Old and New Testament *anamnesis* and the cognate verb have a sense of "recalling" or "re-presenting" before God an event in the past so that it becomes *here and now operative by its effects.'* Gregory Dix, *The Shape of the Liturgy,* p. 161.

is there is the muse, and those cannot escape her presence who with whatever intention employ the signs of wine and bread. Something has to be made by us before it can become for us his sign who made us. This point he settled in the upper room. No artefacture no Christian religion.[16] Thus far what goes for Mass-house goes for Meeting-house.[17] The muse then is with us all the way—she that has music wherever she goes.

This leads direct to a further point. I have already referred to what this writing 'is about'; but I now wish to add something rather more particularized and somewhat difficult to say.

In a sense the fragments that compose this book are about, or around and about, matters of all sorts which, by a kind of quasi-free association, are apt to stir in my mind at any time and as often as not 'in the time of the Mass'. The mental associations, liaisons, meanderings to and fro, 'ambivalences', asides, sprawl of the pattern, if pattern there is—these thought-trains (or, some might reasonably say, trains of distraction and inadvertence) have been as often as not initially set in motion, shunted or buffered into near sidings or off to far destinations, by some action or word, something seen or heard, during the liturgy. The speed of light, they say, is very rapid—but it is nothing to the agility of thought and its ability to twist and double on its tracks, penetrate recesses and generally nose about. You can go around the world and back again, in and out the meanders, down the history-paths, survey *religio* and *superstitio,* call back many yester-days, but yesterday week ago, or long, long ago, note Miss Weston's last year's Lutetian trimmings and the Roman laticlave on the deacon's Dalmatian tunic, and a lot besides, during those few seconds taken by the presbyter to move from the Epistle to the Gospel side, or while he leans to kiss the board or stone (where are the tokens of the departed) or when he turns to incite the living *plebs* to assist him.

But if the twists and turns that comprise thought are quicker than light, the action of making anything—any artefact or work of any sort—from those thoughts, is, as the tag says, longer.

The mote of dust or small insect seen for an instant in a bend

---

[16] Unless of course we regarded that religion as being *exclusively* concerned with an attitude of mind or state of soul.

[17] Except in some few denominations, e.g. the Society of Friends. Not that these escape either; for they employ forms of some kind and a genuine and very decent procedure. And where there is order and sensitivity to the conserving of a form, there is the muse.

or pale of light, may remind us of the bird that winged swiftly through the lighted mote-hall, and that I suppose cannot but remind us of the northern Witan and that may recall the city of York and that again Canterbury and that the 'blisful briddes', and that Tabard Street, E.C.1, and that London Bridge and that the South Bank and its present abstract artefacts, and that again Battersea, and that the forcing of the river at the Claudian invasion, and that the 'Battersea shield', and that that other abstract art of the La Tène Celts in the British Museum in Bloomsbury, W.C. 1.

This much and much more can be 'thought of' in a second or so. But suppose you have to make the actual journey by London Transport and British Railways, starting from the station down the road (Harrow Met.), keeping strictly to the order of your mental itinerary. It would take you not seconds but many, many hours; I should want some days and a long rest.

Now making a work is not thinking thoughts but accomplishing an actual journey. There are the same tediums: strugglings with awkward shapes that won't fit into the bag, the same mislayings, as of tickets, the missings of connections, the long waits, the misdirections, the packing of this that you don't need and the forgetting of that which you do, and all such botherations, not to speak of more serious mishaps. Until in the end you may perhaps wish you had never observed that mote of dust in the beam from the clerestory light that set you willy-nilly on your journey. You might have been better occupied. You well might. It is not without many such misgivings that I write this introduction to the meanderings that comprise this book.

What I have written has no plan, or at least is not planned. If it has a shape it is chiefly that it returns to its beginning. It has themes and a theme even if it wanders far. If it has a unity it is that what goes before conditions what comes after and *vice versa*. Rather as in a longish conversation between two friends, where one thing leads to another; but should a third party hear fragments of it, he might not know how the talk had passed from the cultivation of cabbages to Melchizedek, king of Salem. Though indeed he might guess.

Which means, I fear, that you won't make much sense of one bit unless you read the lot.

My intention has not been to 'edify' (in the secondary but accepted and customary sense of that word), nor, I think, to persuade, but there is indeed an intention to 'uncover'; which is what a 'mystery' does, for though at root 'mystery' implies a closing, all 'mysteries' are meant to disclose, to show forth something. So that in one sense it *is* meant tc 'edify', i.e. 'to set up'. Otherwise my intentions would not sort very well with the title of my book, *The Anathemata,* 'the things set up, etc.'.

Most of all, perhaps, I could wish of my 'mystery', *misterium* or *ministerium,* that it should give some kind of 'pleasure', for I believe in Poussin's dictum: 'The goal of painting is delight', and as I have already said, it is one of my few convictions that what goes for one art goes for all of 'em, in some sense or other.

To reinforce something already touched upon: I regard my book more as a series of fragments, fragmented bits, chance scraps really, of records of things, vestiges of sorts and kinds of *disciplinae,*[18] that have come my way by this channel or that influence. Pieces of stuffs that happen to mean something to me. and which I see as perhaps making a kind of coat of many colours, such as belonged to 'that dreamer' in the Hebrew myth.[19] Things to which I would give a related form, just as one does in painting a picture. You use the things that are yours to use because they happen to be lying about the place or site or lying within the orbit of your 'tradition'. It is very desirable in the arts to know the meaning of the word ex-orbitant, or there is pastiche or worse.

Of course, in any case, there may well be pastiche, padding, things not gestant and superficialities of all sorts; but all this is inevitable if you get outside of what I believe Blake called the artist's horizon. I have tried to keep inside it. Necessarily within that 'horizon' you will find material of which it could be said

---

18 I use the word *disciplinae* here because I can't think of an English word which covers what I intend: the various modes and traditions of doing this or that, from bowling a hoop to engraving on copper; from 'Kiss in the Ring' to serving at Mass; from forming fours (or threes) to Rolle of Hampole's *Form of Perfect Living;* from Rugby Union Rules to the rules that governed court etiquette in the Welsh medieval codes; from the mixing of water-colours to the mixing of pig-food; from mending the fire to mending the fire-step; from the making of blackbird pie to the making of a king; from the immemorial nursery methods of reminding children that they are not laws to themselves to the three extinguishings of the lighted flax that at his coronation remind the Pontiff Maximus of much the same truth, together with the words, which at each extinguishing they say to him: *Sancte Pater, sic transit gloria mundi.* For in a sense all *disciplinae* are warnings 'This is the way to make the thing, that way won't do at all.'

19 'Myth', see note to page 219.

> **. . . in scole is gret altercacioun**
> **In this matere, and gret disputision**

and, although it is absolutely incumbent upon the artist to use this disputed 'matere', he may be the least qualified to discuss it, nor is it his business, *qua* artist, He has not infrequently to say, quoting from the same clear source of Englishness,

Those been the cokkes wordes and not myne.

Rather than being a seer or endowed with the gift of prophecy he is something of a vicar whose job is legatine—a kind of Servus Servorum to deliver what has been delivered to him, who can neither add to nor take from the deposits. It is not that we mean by 'originality'. There is only one tale to tell even though the telling is patient of endless development and ingenuity and can take on a million variant forms. I imagine something of this sort to be implicit in what Picasso is reported as saying: 'I do not seek, I find.'

I intend what I have written to be said. While marks of punctuation, breaks of line, lengths of line, grouping of words or sentences and variations of spacing are visual contrivances they have here an aural and oral intention. You can't get the intended meaning unless you hear the sound and you can't get the sound unless you observe the score; and pause-marks on a score are of particular importance. Lastly, it is meant to be said with deliberation—slowly as opposed to quickly—but 'with deliberation' is the best rubric for each page, each sentence, each word.

I would especially emphasize this point, for what I have written will certainly lose half what I intend, indeed, it will fail altogether, unless the advice 'with deliberation' is heeded. Each word is meant to do its own work, but each word cannot do its work unless it is given due attention. It was written to be read in that way. And, as I say above, the spacings are of functional importance; they are not there to make the page look attractive—though it would be a good thing should that result also.

'Old Johnny Fairplay all the way from Bómbay . . . the more you put down the more you pick up . . . pây the man his móney.'

In the 1914-18 army there used to be played a proscribed game of chance, and a reiterated form of words, a kind of liturgic refrain heard from among a huddle of players, included the words above quoted.[20] It was part of the ritual of the game and might involve a few centimes or a substantial number of francs; little or much. It seems to me only decent that those should be paid acknowledgment who by some work of theirs have, however obliquely, aided us to make our artefacts. Of course there is the other reflection which 1914-18 painfully recalls, 'No names, no pack-drill', but I think we'll chance it.

First, perhaps, I should mention Mr. Christopher Dawson, to whose writings and conversation I feel especially indebted. Then there is Mr. W. F. Jackson Knight whose particular *numen* or sprite is something of an Ariadne, who pays out more than one length of thread. He, too, would lighten the kitty, had he his due. As it is impossible to write down anything like a complete, or even a representative, list of living or recently living authors to whom I stand indebted in little or much, I shall give fifty names which shall be chosen as they happen to come to mind as I now write: Maurice de la Taille, Oswald Spengler, Jacques Maritain, James Frazer, Jessie Weston, Christopher and Jacquetta Hawkes, Jane Harrison, Gilbert Sheldon, Martin D'Arcy, Louis Duchesne, Louis Gougaud, Gregory Dix, C. H. Cochrane, T. C. Lethbridge, John Edward Lloyd, Ifor Williams, W. F. Grimes, T. Gwynne Jones, A. H. Williams, W. J. Gruffydd, Henry Lewis, T. D. Kendrick, Henri Hubert, Henri Pirenne, R. G. Collingwood with J. N. L. Myres, H. Stuart Jones, Rachel Levy, Cecile O'Rahilly, Laura Keeler, H. M. Chadwick, Margaret Deansley, J. R. R. Tolkien, W. R. Lethaby, S. E. Winbolt, Benjamin Farrington, A. T. Mahan, E. G. R. Taylor, Géza Róheim, C. C. Martindale, Friedrich von Hügel, A. W. F. Blunt, E. C. Blackman, K. E. Kirk, T. Neville George with Bernard Smith, Dora Ware with Betty Beatty, E. K. Chambers, F. M. Powicke, J. Livingstone Lowes, O. G. S. Crawford, A. W. Wade Evans, Gordon Home, A. M. Hocart, but I'm afraid I've exceeded the fifty and must stop.

Some on this brief, arbitrary and very chancy list are recalled perhaps on account of a few informative diagrams or clarifying passages. Some have been deliberately consulted to check up on a half-remembered matter, others have been influential in a more pervasive way. Some are gratefully remembered for a popular, modest, concise, elementary textbook such as *A Short Dictionary*

---

[20] The middle fragment may be inaccurate as it is thirty-four years since I last heard it.

of Architecture including some Common Building Terms by Ware and Beatty. Others for crucial and great works such as Père de la Taille's thesis on the relationship of what was done in the Supperroom with what was done on the Hill and the further relationship of these doings with what is done in the Mass.[21]

Others are recalled for bringing a less tired vision to bear on this matter or that, such as the late Gilbert Sheldon in *The Transition from Roman Britain to Christian England*. Others again for works of natural science or of specialist research, such as the contributions of B. Smith and T. N. George to the *British Regional Geology* series, or E. G. R. Taylor's articles on classical and medieval seafaring that she contributed to *The Journal of the Institute of Navigation,* edited by Mr. M. W. Richey; or the monograph by Laura Keeler of the University of California, entitled *Geoffrey of Monmouth and the Late Latin Chroniclers*.

I have not included here any of those whose influence I associate chiefly with the 'form' of what I have written. It is confined to those whose works have had a bearing on the 'content' only, or principally so. The intention here is to acknowledge information and data.

There are, however, many others to whom I may be as, or more, indebted. Who should say how much may be owing to a small textbook on botany; a manual of seamanship; various items in the magazine *Wales* edited by Mr. Keidrych Rhys; a guide to the Isle of Wight; a child's picture-book of prehistoric fauna; a guide-book to the parish church of Cilcain, Flintshire, by a local antiquary, 1912; a glossy 1949 bookstall purchase on the pontifex Isambard Kingdom Brunel; a brochure on the composition and permanence of colours; a pamphlet on the prevention of collisions at sea; a paper read before a London conference of psychologists; the text of a guide to a collection of Welsh samplers and embroideries; a catalogue of English china or plate; a neglected directive from Rome on the use of the Chant; a reference in *The Times* to the cry of a bittern in Norfolk, or to the bloom on a thorn-bush in Herefordshire, or to an Homeric find on Karatepe ridge?

---

[21] I have not read, nor am I able to read, the original work in Latin, entitled *Mysterium Fidei;* but an outline of his thesis appeared in English by de la Taille in 1934 and it is to this that I refer. There was also *The Mass and the Redemption* by Fr. D'Arcy, again elucidating in English the same theme.

Since first hearing of this thesis in *c.* 1923, I was drawn to what seemed, to my untrained mind, its integration and creativity, and it seemed to illumine things outside its immediate theological context.

Then there are the conversations that have had a direct and immediate bearing of some kind. Among many such I call to mind talks with the late Eric Burrows, and with Richard Kehoe and Bernard Wall.

I thank all those many old or more recent friends who have assisted me in many various ways and by kindnesses, tolerances and understandings of all sorts.

As in writing the preface to *In Parenthesis* fourteen years ago, I must again especially thank my friend Mr. Harman Grisewood for his encouragement and for his critical assistance whenever it was sought, over the form here or the content there.

Others of whose help I am *particularly* sensible, I fear I shall have to leave unnamed, rather than omit any. These include some of my nearest friends, and I am grateful to them all.[22]

I have already given a random list of some few contemporary 'authorities' to whom I know myself indebted, but there are the more formidable and more forming creditors of the past. I shall not attempt to make a list of them, whether they were living in the world of Kipling's khaki *limes,* or in the world of R. T. McMullen (who circumnavigated the Island in the Jubilee Year), or in the world of Heinrich Schliemann (who digged nine sites down in Helen's laughless rock) or in that of Cruikshank's Boz, or that of Smith the lexicographer. Or in the period of 'poor Smart' (for whom, Alleluia!), or of John Gay, or of Herbert of Cherbury, or of Stow the Londoner, or of Adam of Usk, or of Langland the Englishman, or of Duns the Scot and the Angel from Aquin; or of those various Chrétiens who French-polished the *matière de Bretagne* (confounding the topography and playing Old Harry with the persons, for all the perfections of their art) or of Gerald the Welshman, or of Anselm the Italian. Then there are the basic things: the early mixed racial deposits, the myth (mythus)[23] that is specifically of this Island, and the Christian

---

22 Nor can I neglect to mention those doctors, necessarily unnamed, and nurses who, by the practice of their arts, aided me to re-continue the practice of mine.

23 I prefer 'myth' to 'mythus', but owing to such sentences as 'She said she'd got some fags, but it was a pure myth' the meaning of 'myth' is liable to misunderstanding even in the most serious connections.

Unfortunately *The Shorter Oxford English Dictionary* (1933) defines 'myth' as 'A purely fictitious narrative, etc.' Yet we sing in the Liturgy '*Teste David cum Sibylla*' and clearly the Sibyl belongs to what, for the Christian Church, is an extra-revelational body of tradition. But such bodies of tradi-

Liturgy, and the Canon of Scripture, and the Classical deposits. I list these four thus for mere convenience. Clearly they comprise in our tradition a great complex of influences and interactions which have conditioned us all. To say that one draws upon such deposits does not imply erudition; it suggests only that these form the *materia* that we *all* draw upon, whether we know it or not, to this degree or that, in however roundabout a way, whether we are lettered or illiterate, Christian or post-Christian, or anti-Christian.

Then there are the living, dying, or dead traditions in which one has oneself participated or heard of with one's own ears from one's own parents or near relatives or immediate forebears. These things received in childhood are of course fragments or concomitants only of the whole above-mentioned complex. I am thinking only of the means whereby those concomitants and fragments reached me. I am speaking of channels only, but of immediate channels and such as condition all that passes through them, and which condition also one's subsequent attitude to all the rest. These I judge to be of the most primary importance. It is through them that 'all the rest' is already half sensed long before it is known. If ever it is known. You smell a rat or two pretty early on.

It so happens that whereas I did drawings from five years onwards I was very stupid in learning to read and found it hard at nine and subsequently. On more than one occasion I recall paying my sister a penny to read to me. There was in those days a children's pink paper-covered series called Books for the Bairns and one of that series dealt with King Arthur's knights (including the story of the Knight of the Sparrowhawk) and that was the book I most liked hearing read. And then *The Lays of Ancient Rome* became a favourite. I used to try to read, or rather turn over the pages of, Jewel's *Apology,* partly I think because that was in full calf, which I thought grand. Also there was Keble's *Christian Year* with illustrations by Johann Friedrich Overbeck.

Then my father sometimes read Bunyan aloud. Then there

---

tion are not to be described as 'purely fictitious', yet they are certainly properly described as 'myth.' I choose this example from among innumerable others, because of the accepted rule that the public prayer of an institution is a sure gauge to the mind of the institution that employs that prayer. I don't mind the rather academic 'mythus' but I don't see why we should have the English form 'myth' permanently separated from its primal innocence, from the Greek *mythos,* which, I understand, means a word uttered, something told. Then we should rightly speak of the myth of the Evangel, a myth devoid of the fictitious, an utterance of the Word, a 'pure myth.'

was the attempt to imitate the sounds when he sang *Mae hen wlad fy nhadau* or *Ar hyd y nos*. But without success. A failure which has pursued me. And then there were the reproductions of two or three thirteenth-century drawings of Welsh foot-soldiers in J. R. Green's *Short History of the English People*. These were a particular delight to me. And what lively drawings they in fact are. The draughtsman undoubtedly got the Welsh 'look'.[24]

It would seem that whether or no 'old friends are the best', they appear, in some ways, to be stayers.

It may be yesterday only that you heard of the significance of *The Epistle of Clement* and but a few years back that the other Clement's *Exhortation to the Greeks* was recommended to you by a perceptive cousin. But it was very many years ago that you wondered what Clement had to do with Danes. And it was much longer still ago that an aunt initiated you into 'Oranges and Lemons'. She may have been evasive when asked, 'Aunty, what's Clemens?' but she was handing down a traditional form and starting up in you a habit of 'recalling'. For names linger, especially when associated with some sort of *disciplina ludi*. They go into your word-hoard, whether or no you ever attempted to unlock it. No need to say anything further here of those channels, those creditors, for the book itself is meant to pay a farthing or two of that inescapable great debt.

I have a last point that I wish to get clear. Although in the notes to the text and in this apology I refer to or cite various authorities and sources, that does not mean that this book has

---

24 The originals are, I believe, in a collection called 'Liber A' in the Public Records Office. In the thirteenth century it was customary to give documents a marginal device for purposes of cataloguing, and for those dealing with Wales the official device was a Welsh bowman or a Welsh spearman. As far as I know these are among the very few visual representations of Welshmen from A.D. 400 to 1282 and after. There are just a few other indications, but very, very few. So that these drawings are of unusual interest. The lack of visual representation is one of the most distressing things about all matters touching the Welsh past. There are innumerable references to clothes and arms in the written deposits, as in the *Gododdin* and in the Welsh Laws and in the vivid descriptions of Giraldus, but we have no visual counterpoint to any of this. We would like to know what Maelgwn Gwynedd or Hywel the Good *looked* like; in what did the cut of their coats differ from that of those worn by Chilperic or Henry the Fowler, their respective near contemporaries? A single drawing is more objective than whole pages of descriptive writing. So that we are greatly indebted to these thirteenth-century English clerks who sketched the appropriate marginal signs on the *Littera Wallie* and the *Scripta Wallie*.

any pretensions whatever of a didactic nature. I refer to those sources only to elucidate a background. As often as not I have no means of judging the relative accuracy of these data. I refer to them only as a traveller might, in making a song or story about a journey he had taken from his home through far places and back. He may have been impressed by the clarity of a waterfall here, by the courage and beauty of the inhabitants there, or by the note of a bird elsewhere. And these phenomena would be deployed throughout his song as providing part of the content and affecting the form of that song. Such a person *might* choose to gloss what he was writing, or to break off from his narrative in order to tell his audience what the locals averred of those falling waters, or what the anthropologists had established with regard to the ancestry of those inhabitants, or how the ornithologists maintained that that bird-song was the song of no bird known to them. Such glosses might be made in order to explain some 'how' or 'why' of the relevant text.

The notes, because they so often concern the *sounds* of the words used in the text, and are thus immediately relevant to its *form,* are printed along with it, rather than at the back of the book. But this easy availability would be a disadvantage if it distracted attention from the work itself. So I ask the reader *when actually engaged upon the text,* to consult these glosses mainly or only on points of pronunciation. For other purposes they should be read separately.

Words in Latin follow a 'modern' pronunciation: *c* and *g* hard, *ae* as *i* in wine. This rule is important as it affects the consonance and sometimes the rhyme. Exception may be made in quotations from the Liturgy where softenings would occur, but this affects a dozen words only throughout.

Robert Lowell

Robert Lowell was born in Boston, Massachusetts, on March 1, 1917. He majored in classics at Kenyon College and in 1940 became a convert to Roman Catholicism. During the Second World War Lowell was a conscientious objector, for which he served a term in jail.

His earlier poetry—Catholic, visionary, oratorical—is notable for the intense concretion of its images, many of which are felt rather than visualized: they impress the mind so as to consolidate what the eyes alone could never perceive. And, once the phrase has been introduced, it is difficult to dissociate those poems from Wallace Stevens's dictum to set up "the rugged black, the image." Much of their power derives from Lowell's informed sense of history and evil, although his sense of evil may slip into a habit of violence. In Imitations, *a collection of foreign poems regenerated into English, violence is sometimes used as a principle governing the selection of images; his awesome version of Eugenio Montale's* La casa dei doganieri *is so reconceived that "Ed io non so chi va e* chi resta" *("And I do not know who goes and who stays")* *becomes:*

I have no way of knowing
who forces an entrance.

Beginning with Life Studies, *a series of original poems, Lowell has given over the resounding pentameters of his earlier poetry for increasingly high-strung, nervous rhythms, attempting also to transmute family history and autobiography into a bitable image of the whole of contemporary society. Simultaneously he has appealed to brute things, as distinguished from the ideas of things, for the substance of his poems. However, his chief means of revealing theme and attitude is not direct statement sprinkled with illustrations, but the presentation of those "things" under a highly colored or biased overlay of language. In this way symbolic significance is woven about the most casual details.*

At other times the symbolic impetus behind a poem may even manifest itself through proper nouns. "Nautilus Island" is not merely a place name, for example, but must function symbolically as "a spiral chambered shell pearly on the inside"; thus an inhabitant of the island is analogous to a skunk with its head wedged in a cup of sour cream, or an ostrich with its head buried in the sand. Otherwise, things or images of things may take on characteristic burdens of the epigram, as when the state becomes "a diver under a glass bell." Or they may combine with puns to perform the same service, as when Czar Lepke of Murder Incorporated *concentrates on the electric chair—*

hanging like an oasis in his air
of lost connections . . . .

An Interview*

INTERVIEWER: What are you teaching now?

LOWELL: I'm teaching one of these poetry-writing classes and a course in the novel. The course in the novel is called Practical Criticism. It's a course I teach every year, but the material changes. It could be anything from Russian short stories to Baudelaire, a study of the New Critics, or just fiction. I do whatever I happen to be working on myself.

INTERVIEWER: Has your teaching over the last few years meant anything to you as a writer?

LOWELL: It's meant a lot to me as a human being, I think. But my teaching is part time and has neither the merits nor the burdens of real teaching. Teaching is entirely different from writing. You're always up to it, or more or less up to it; there's no

* **From** *Writers at Work: The Paris Review Interviews, Second Series,* **ed. by Malcolm Cowley. The interviewer is Frederick Seidel.**

225

question of it's clogging, of it's not coming. It's much less subjective, and it's a very pleasant pursuit in itself. In the kind of teaching I do, conversational classes, seminars, if the students are good, which they've been most of the time, it's extremely entertaining. Now, I don't know what it has to do with writing. You review a lot of things that you like, and you read things that you haven't read or haven't read closely, and read them aloud, go into them much more carefully than you would otherwise; and that must teach you a good deal. But there's such a jump from teaching to writing.

INTERVIEWER: Well, do you think the academic life is liable to block up the writer-professor's sensitivity to his own intuitions?

LOWELL: I think it's impossible to give a general answer. Almost all the poets of my generation, all the best ones, teach. I only know one, Elizabeth Bishop, who doesn't. They do it for a livelihood, but they also do it because you can't write poetry all the time. They do it to extend themselves, and I think it's undoubtedly been a gain to them. Now the question is whether something else might be more of a gain. Certainly the danger of teaching is that it's much too close to what you're doing—close and not close. You can get expert at teaching and be crude in practice. The revision, the consciousness that tinkers with the poem—that has something to do with teaching and criticism. But the impulse that starts a poem and makes it of any importance is distinct from teaching.

INTERVIEWER: And protected, you think, from whatever you bring to bear in the scrutiny of parts of poems and aspects of novels, etc.?

LOWELL: I think you have to tear it apart from that. Teaching may make the poetry even more different, less academic than it would be otherwise. I'm sure that writing isn't a craft, that is, something for which you learn the skills and go on turning out. It must come from some deep impulse, deep inspiration. That can't be taught, it can't be what you use in teaching. And you may go further afield looking for that than you would if you didn't teach. I don't know, really; the teaching probably makes you more cautious, more self-conscious, makes you write less. It may make you bolder when you do write.

INTERVIEWER: You think the last may be so?

LOWELL: The boldness is ambiguous. It's not only teaching, it's growing up in this age of criticism which we're all so conscious of, whether we like it or don't like it, or practice it or don't practice it. You think three times before you put a word down, and ten times about taking it out. And that's related to boldness; if you put words down they must do something, you're not going to put clichés. But then it's related to caution; you write much less.

INTERVIEWER: You yourself have written very little criticism, haven't you? You did once contribute to a study of Hopkins.

LOWELL: Yes, and I've done a few omnibus reviews. I do a review or two a year.

INTERVIEWER: You did a wonderful one of Richards' poems.

LOWELL: I felt there was an occasion for that, and I had something to say about it. Sometimes I wish I did more, but I'm very anxious in criticism not to do the standard analytical essay. I'd like my essay to be much sloppier and more intuitive. But my friends are critics, and most of them poet-critics. When I was twenty and learning to write, Allen Tate, Eliot, Blackmur, and Winters, and all those people were very much news. You waited for their essays, and when a good critical essay came out it had the excitement of a new imaginative work.

INTERVIEWER: Which is really not the case with any of the critics writing today, do you think?

LOWELL: The good critics are almost all the old ones. The most brilliant critic of my generation, I think, was Jarrell, and he in a way connects with the older generation. But he's writing less criticism now than he used to.

INTERVIEWER: In your schooling at St. Mark's and Harvard— we can talk about Kenyon in a minute—were there teachers or friends who had an influence on your writing, not so much by the example of their own writing as by personal supervision or direction —by suggesting certain reading, for instance?

LOWELL: Well, my school had been given a Carnegie set of art books, and I had a friend, Frank Parker, who had great talent as a painter but who'd never done it systematically. We began reading the books and histories of art, looking at reproductions, tracing the Last Supper on tracing paper, studying dynamic symmetry, learning about Cézanne, and so on. I had no practical interest in painting, but that study seemed rather close to poetry. And from there I began. I think I read Elizabeth Drew or some such book on modern poetry. It had free verse in it, and that seemed very simple to do.

INTERVIEWER: What class were you in then?

LOWELL: It was my last year. I'd wanted to be a football player very much, and got my letter but didn't make the team. Well, that was satisfying but crushing too. I read a good deal, but had never written. So this was a recoil from that. Then I had some luck in that Richard Eberhart was teaching there.

INTERVIEWER: I'd thought he'd been a student there with you.

LOWELL: No, he was a young man about thirty. I never had him in class, but I used to go to him. He'd read aloud and we'd talk, he was very pleasant that way. He'd smoke honey-scented tobacco, and read Baudelaire and Shakespeare and Hopkins—it made the thing living—and he'd read his own poems. I wrote very badly at first, but he was encouraging and enthusiastic. That probably was decisive, that there was someone there whom I admired who was engaged in writing poetry.

INTERVIEWER: I heard that a very early draft of "The Drunken Fisherman" appeared in the St. Mark's magazine.

LOWELL: No, it was the Kenyon college magazine that published it. The poem was very different then. I'd been reading Winters, whose model was Robert Bridges, and what I wanted was a rather distant, quiet classical poem without any symbolism, It was in four-foot couplets as smooth as I could write them. The *Kenyon Review* had published a poem of mine and then they'd stopped. This was the one time they said, if you'd submitted this we'd have taken it.

INTERVIEWER: Then you were submitting other poems to the Review?

LOWELL: Yes, and that poem was rather different from anything else I did. I was also reading Hart Crane and Thomas and Tate and Empson's *Seven Types of Ambiguity;* and each poem was more difficult than the one before, and had more ambiguities. Ransom, editing the *Kenyon Review,* was impressed, but didn't want to publish them. He felt they were forbidding and clotted.

INTERVIEWER: But finally he did come through.

LOWELL: Well, after I'd graduated. I published when I was a junior, then for about three years no magazine would take anything I did. I'd get sort of pleasant letters—"One poem in this group interests us, if you can get seven more." At that time it took me about a year to do two or three poems. Gradually I just stopped, and really sort of gave it up. I seemed to have reached a great impasse. The kind of poem I thought was interesting and would work on became so cluttered and overdone that it wasn't really poetry.

INTERVIEWER: I was struck on reading *Land of Unlikeness* by the difference between the poems you rejected for *Lord Weary's*

Castle and the few poems and passages that you took over into the new book.

LOWELL: I think I took almost a third, but almost all of what I took was rewritten. But I wonder what struck you?

INTERVIEWER: One thing was that almost all the rejected poems seemed to me to be those that Tate, who in his introduction spoke about two kinds of poetry in the book, said were the more strictly religious and strictly symbolic poems, as against the poems he said were perhaps more powerful because more experienced or relying more on your sense of history. What you took seemed really superior to what you left behind.

LOWELL: Yes, I took out several that were paraphrases of early Christian poems, and I rejected one rather dry abstraction, then whatever seemed to me to have a messy violence. All the poems have religious imagery, I think, but the ones I took were more concrete. That's what the book was moving toward: less symbolic imagery. And as I say, I tried to take some of the less fierce poems. There seemed to be too much twisting and disgust in the first book.

INTERVIEWER: I wondered how wide your reading had been at the time, I wondered when I read in Tate's introduction that the stanza in one of your poems was based on the stanza in "The Virginian Voyages," whether someone had pointed out Drayton's poem to you.

LOWELL: Tate and I started to make an anthology together. It was a very interesting year I spent with Tate and his wife. He's a poet who writes in spurts, and he had about a third of a book. I was going to do a biography of Jonathan Edwards and he was going to write a novel, and our wives were going to write novels. Well, the wives just went humming away. "I've just finished three pages," they'd say at the end of the day; and their books mounted up. But ours never did, though one morning Allen wrote four pages to his novel, very brilliant. We were in a little study together separated by a screen. I was heaping up books on Jonathan Edwards and taking notes, and getting more and more numb on the subject, looking at old leather-bound volumes on freedom of the will and so on, and feeling less and less a calling. And there we stuck. And then we decided to make an anthology together. We both liked rather formal, difficult poems, and we were reading particularly the Sixteenth and Seventeenth centuries. In the evening we'd read aloud, and we started a card catalogue of what we'd make for the anthology. And then we started writing. It seems to me we took old models like Drayton's Ode—Tate wrote a poem called "The Young Proconsuls of the Air" in that stanza. I think there's a trick to formal poetry. Most poetry is very formal, but when a modern poet is formal he gets more attention for it than old poets did. Somehow we've tried to make it look difficult. For example, Shelley can just rattle off terza rima by the page, and it's very smooth, doesn't seem an obstruction to him—you sometimes wish it were more difficult. Well, someone does that today and in modern style it looks as though he's wrestling with every line and may be pushed into confusion, as though he's having a real struggle with form and content. Marks of that are in the finished poem. And I think both Tate and I felt that we wanted our formal patterns to seem a hardship and something that we couldn't rattle off easily.

INTERVIEWER: But in *Lord Weary's Castle* there were poems moving toward a sort of narrative calm, almost a prose calm— "Katherine's Dream," for example, or the two poems on texts by Edwards, or "The Ghost"—and then, on the other hand, poems in which the form was insisted upon and maybe shown off, and where the things that were characteristic of your poetry at that time—the kind of enjambments, the rhyming, the meters, of course—seem willed and forced, so that you have a terrific log jam of stresses, meanings, strains.

LOWELL: I know one contrast I've felt, and it takes different forms at different times. The ideal modern form seems to be the novel and certain short stories. Maybe Tolstoi would be the perfect example—his work is imagistic, it deals with all experience, and there seems to be no conflict of the form and content. So one thing is to get into poetry that kind of human richness in rather simple descriptive language. Then there's another side of poetry: compression, something highly rhythmical and perhaps wrenched into a small space. I've always been fascinated by both these things. But getting it all on one page in a few stanzas, getting it all done in as little space as possible, revising and revising so that each word and rhythm though not perfect is pondered and wrestled with—you can't do that in prose very well, you'd never get your book written. "Katherine's Dream" was a real dream. I found that I shaped it a bit, and cut it, and allegorized it, but still it was a dream someone had had. It was material that ordinarily, I think, would go into prose, yet it would have had to be much longer or part of something much longer.

INTERVIEWER: I think you can either look for forms, you can

do specific reading for them, or the forms can be demanded by what you want to say. And when the material in poetry seems under almost unbearable pressure you wonder whether the form hasn't cookie-cut what the poet wanted to say. But you chose the couplet, didn't you, and some of your freest passages are in couplets.

LOWELL: The couplet I've used is very much like the couplet Browning uses in "My Last Duchess," in *Sordello,* run-on with its rhymes buried. I've always, when I've used it, tried to give the impression that I had as much freedom in choosing the rhyme word as I had in any of the other words. Yet they were almost all true rhymes, and maybe half the time there'd be a pause after the rhyme. I wanted something as fluid as prose; you wouldn't notice the form, yet looking back you'd find that great obstalces had been climbed. And the couplet is pleasant in this way—once you've got your two lines to rhyme, then that's done and you can go on to the next. You're not stuck with the whole stanza to round out and build to a climax. A couplet can be a couplet or can be split and left as one line, or it can go on for a hundred lines; any sort of compression or expansion is possible. And that's not so in a stanza. I think a couplet's much less lyrical than a stanza, closer to prose. Yet it's an honest form, its difficulties are in the open. It really is pretty hard to rhyme each line with the one that follows it.

INTERVIEWER: Did the change of style in *Life Studies* have something to do with working away from that compression and pressure by way of, say, the kind of prose clarity of "Katherine's Dream"?

LOWELL: Yes. By the time I came to *Life Studies* I'd been writing my autobiography and also writing poems that broke meter. I'd been doing a lot of reading aloud. I went on a trip to the West Coast and read at least once a day and sometimes twice for fourteen days, and more and more I found that I was simplifying my poems. If I had a Latin quotation I'd translate it into English. If adding a couple of syllables in a line made it clearer I'd add them, and I'd make little changes just impromptu as I read. That seemed to improve the reading.

INTERVIEWER: Can you think of a place where you added a syllable or two to an otherwise regular line?

LOWELL: It was usually articles and prepositions that I added, very slight little changes, and I didn't change the printed text. It was just done for the moment.

INTERVIEWER: Why did you do this? Just because you thought

the most important thing was to get the poem over?

LOWELL: To get it over, yes. And I began to have a certain disrespect for the tight forms. If you could make it easier by adding syllables, why not? And then when I was writing *Life Studies,* a good number of the poems were started in very strict meter, and I found that, more than the rhymes, the regular beat was what I didn't want. I have a long poem in there about my father, called "Commander Lowell," which actually is largely in couplets, but I originally wrote perfectly strict four-foot couplets. Well, with that form it's hard not to have echoes of Marvell. That regularity just seemed to ruin the honesty of sentiment, and became rhetorical; it said, "I'm a poem"—though it was a great help when I was revising having this original skeleton. I could keep the couplets where I wanted them and drop them where I didn't; there'd be a form to come back to.

INTERVIEWER: Had you originally intended to handle all that material in prose?

LOWELL: Yes. I found it got awfully tedious working out transitions and putting in things that didn't seem very important but were necessary to the prose continuity. Also I found it hard to revise. Cutting it down into small bits, I could work on it much more carefully and make fast transitions. But there's another point about this mysterious business of prose and poetry, form and content, and the reasons for breaking forms. I don't think there's any very satisfactory answer. I seesaw back and forth between something highly metrical and something highly free; there isn't any one way to write. But it seems to me we've gotten in a sort of Alexandrian age. Poets of my generation and particularly younger ones have gotten terribly proficient at these forms. They write a very musical, difficult poem with tremendous skill, perhaps there's never been such skill. Yet the writings seem divorced from culture somehow. It's become too much something specialized that can't handle much experience. It's a craft, purely a craft, and there must be some breakthrough back into life. Prose is in many ways better off than poetry. It's quite hard to think of a young poet who has the vitality, say, of Salinger or Saul Bellow. Yet prose tends to be very diffuse. The novel is really a much more difficult form than it seems; few people have the wind to write anything that long. Even a short story demands almost poetic perfection. Yet on the whole prose is less cut off from life than poetry is. Now, some of this Alexandrian poetry is very brilliant, you would not have it changed at all.

But I thought it was getting increasingly stifling. I couldn't get any experience into tight metrical forms.

INTERVIEWER: So you felt this about your own poetry, your own technique, not just about the general condition of poetry?

LOWELL: Yes, I felt that the meter plastered difficulties and mannerisms on what I was trying to say to such an extent that it terribly hampered me.

INTERVIEWER: This then explains, in part anyway, your admiration for Elizabeth Bishop's poetry. I know that you've said the qualities and the abundance of its descriptive language reminded you of the Russian novel more than anything else.

LOWELL: Any number of people are guilty of writing a complicated poem that has a certain amount of symbolism in it and really difficult meaning, a wonderful poem to teach. Then you unwind it and you feel that the intelligence, the experience, whatever goes into it, is skin-deep. In Elizabeth Bishop's "Man-Moth" a whole new world is gotten out and you don't know what will come after any one line. It's exploring. And it's as original as Kafka. She's gotten a world, not just a way of writing. She seldom writes a poem that doesn't have that exploratory quality; yet it's very firm, it's not like beat poetry, it's all controlled.

INTERVIEWER: What about Snodgrass? What you were trying to do in *Life Studies* must have something to do with your admiration for his work.

LOWELL: He did these things before I did, though he's younger than I am and had been my student. He may have influenced me, though people have suggested the opposite. He spent ten years at the University of Iowa, going to writing classes, being an instructor; rather unworldly, making little money, and specializing in talking to other people writing poetry, obsessed you might say with minute technical problems and rather provincial experience—and then he wrote about just that. I mean, the poems are about his child, his divorce, and Iowa City, and his child is a Dr. Spock child—all handled in expert little stanzas. I believe that's a new kind of poetry. Other poems that are direct that way are slack and have no vibrance. His experience wouldn't be so interesting and valid if it weren't for the whimsy, the music, the balance, everything revised and placed and pondered. All that gives light to those poems on agonizing subjects comes from the craft.

INTERVIEWER: And yet his best poems are all on the verge of being slight and even sentimental.

LOWELL: I think a lot of the best poetry is. Laforgue—it's hard to think of a more delightful poet, and his prose is wonderful too. Well, it's on the verge of being sentimental, and if he hadn't dared to be sentimental he wouldn't have been a poet. I mean, his inspiration was that. There's some way of distinguishing between false sentimentality, which is blowing up a subject and giving emotions that you don't feel, and using whimsical, minute, tender, small emotions that most people don't feel but which Laforgue and Snodgrass do. So that I'd say he had pathos and fragility—but then that's a large subject too. He has fragility along the edges and a main artery of power going through the center.

INTERVIEWER: Some people were disappointed with *Life Studies* just because earlier you had written a kind of heroic poetry, an American version of heroic poetry, of which there had been none recently except your own. Is there any chance that you will go back to that?

LOWELL: I don't think that a personal history can go on forever, unless you're Walt Whitman and have a way with you. I feel I've done enough personal poetry. That doesn't mean I won't do more of it, but I don't want to do more now. I feel I haven't gotten down all my experience, or perhaps even the most important part, but I've said all I really have much inspiration to say, and more would just dilute. So that you need something more impersonal, and other things being equal it's better to get your emotions out in a Macbeth than in a confession. Macbeth must have tons of Shakespeare in him. We don't know where, nothing in Shakespeare's life was remotely like Macbeth, yet he somehow gives the feeling of going to the core of Shakespeare. You have much more freedom that way than you do when you write an autobiographical poem.

INTERVIEWER: These poems, I gather from what you said earlier, did take as much working over as the earlier ones.

LOWELL: They were just as hard to write. They're not always factually true. There's a good deal of tinkering with fact. You leave out a lot, and emphasize this and not that. Your actual experience is a complete flux. I've invented facts and changed things, and the whole balance of the poem was something invented. So there's a lot of artistry, I hope, in the poems. Yet there's this thing: if a poem is autobiographical—and this is true of any kind of autobiographical writing and of historical writing—you want the reader to say, this is true. In something like Macaulay's *History of England* you think you're really getting William III. That's as good as a good plot in a novel. And so there was always that standard of truth which you wouldn't ordinarily have in poetry—the reader was to believe he was getting the *real* Robert Lowell.

INTERVIEWER: I wanted to ask you about this business of taking over passages from earlier poems and rewriting them and putting them in new contexts. I'm thinking of the passage at the end of the "Cistercians in Germany," in *Land of Unlikeness,* which you rewrote into those wonderful lines that end "At the Indian Killer's Grave." I know that Hart Crane rewrote early scraps a great deal and used most of the rewrites. But doesn't doing this imply a theory of poetry that would talk much more about craft than about experience?

LOWELL: I don't know, it's such a miracle if you get lines that are halfway right; it's not just a technical problem. The lines must mean a good deal to you. All your poems are in a sense one poem, and there's always the struggle of getting something that balances and comes out right, in which all parts are good, and that has experience that you value. And so if you have a few lines that shine in a poem or are beginning to shine, and they fail and get covered over and drowned, maybe their real form is in another poem. Maybe you've mistaken the real inspiration in the original poem and they belong in something else entirely. I don't think that violates experience. The "Cistercians" wasn't very close to me, but the last lines seemed felt; I dropped the Cistercians and put a Boston graveyard in.

INTERVIEWER: But in Crane's "Ode to an Urn," a poem about a personal friend, there are lines which originally applied to something very different, and therefore, in one version or the other, at least can't be called personal.

LOWELL: I think we always bring over some unexplained obscurities by shifting lines. Something that was clear in the original just seems odd and unexplained in the final poem. That can be quite bad, of course; but you always want—and I think Chekhov talks about this—the detail that you can't explain. It's just there. It seems right to you, but you don't have to have it; you could have something else entirely. Now if everything's like that you'd just have chaos, but a few unexplained difficult things—they seem to be the life-blood of variety—they may work. What may have seemed a little odd, a little difficult in the original poem, gets a little more difficult in a new way in the new poem. And that's purely accidental, yet you may gain more than you lose—a new suggestiveness and magic.

INTERVIEWER: Do you revise a very great deal?

LOWELL: Endlessly.

INTERVIEWER: You often use an idiom or a very common phrase either for the sake of irony or to bear more meaning than it's customarily asked to bear—do these come late in the game, do you have to look around for them?

LOWELL: They come later because they don't prove much in themselves, and they often replace something that's much more formal and worked-up. Some of my later poetry does have this quality that the earlier doesn't: several lines can be almost what you'd say in conversation. And maybe talking with a friend or with my wife I'd say, "This doesn't sound quite right," and sort of reach in the air as I talked and change a few words. In that way the new style is easier to write; I sometimes fumble out a natural sequence of lines that will work. But a whole poem won't come that way; my seemingly relaxed poems are just about as hard as the very worked-up ones.

INTERVIEWER: That rightness and familiarity, though, is in "Between the Porch and the Altar" in several passages which are in couplets.

LOWELL: When I am writing in meter I find the simple lines never come right away. Nothing does. I don't believe I've ever written a poem in meter where I've kept a single one of the original lines. Usually when I was writing my old poems I'd write them out in blank verse and then put in the rhymes. And of course I'd change the rhymes a lot. The most I could hope for at first was that the rhymed version wouldn't be much inferior to the blank verse. Then the real work would begin, to make it something much better than the original out of the difficulties of the meter.

INTERVIEWER: Have you ever gone as far as Yeats and written out a prose argument and then set down the rhymes?

LOWELL: With some of the later poems I've written out prose versions, then cut the prose down and abbreviated it. A rapidly written prose draft of the poem doesn't seem to do much good, too little pain has gone into it; but one really worked on is bound to have phrases that are invaluable. And it's a nice technical problem: how can you keep phrases and get them into meter?

INTERVIEWER: Do you usually send off your work to friends before publishing it?

LOWELL: I do it less now. I always used to do it, to Jarrell and one or two other people. Last year I did a lot of reading with Stanley Kunitz.

INTERVIEWER: At the time you were writing the poems for *Lord Weary's Castle,* did it make a difference to you whether the poet to whom you were sending your work was Catholic?

LOWELL: I don't think I ever sent any poems to a Catholic. The person I was closest to then was Allen Tate, who wasn't a Catholic at the time; and then later it became Jarrell, who wasn't at all Catholic. My two close Catholic writer friends are prose writers, J. F. Powers and Flannery O'Connor, and they weren't interested in the technical problems of poems.

INTERVIEWER: So you feel that the religion is the business of the poem that it's in and not at all the business of the Church or the religious person.

LOWELL: It shouldn't be. I mean, a religion ought to have objective validity. But by the time it gets into a poem it's so mixed up with technical and imaginative problems that the theologian, the priest, the serious religious person isn't of too much use. The poem is too strange for him to feel at home and make any suggestions.

INTERVIEWER: What does this make of the religious poem as a religious exercise?

LOWELL: Well, it at least makes this: that the poem tries to be a poem and not a piece of artless religious testimony. There is a drawback. It seems to me that with any poem, but maybe particularly a religious one where there are common interests, the opinion of intelligent people who are not poets ought to be useful. There's an independence to this not getting advice from religious people and outsiders, but also there's a narrowness. Then there is a question whether my poems are religious, or whether they just use religious imagery. I haven't really any idea. My last poems don't use religious imagery, they don't use symbolism. In many ways they seem to me more religious than the early ones, which are full of symbols and references to Christ and God. I'm sure the symbols and the Catholic framework didn't make the poems religious experiences. Yet I don't feel my experience changed very much. It seems to me it's clearer to me now than it was then, but it's very much the same sort of thing that went into the religious poems—the same sort of struggle, light and darkness, the flux of experience. The morality seems much the same. But the symbolism is gone; you couldn't possibly say what creed I believed in. I've wondered myself often. Yet what made the earlier poems valuable seems to be some recording of experience, and that seems to be what makes the later ones.

INTERVIEWER: So you end up saying that the poem does have some integrity and can have some beauty apart from the beliefs expressed in the poem.

LOWELL: I think it can only have integrity apart from the beliefs; that no political position, religious position, position of generosity, or what have you, can make a poem good. It's all to the good if a poem *can* use politics, or theology, or gardening, or anything that has its own validity aside from poetry. But these things will never *per se* make a poem.

INTERVIEWER: The difficult question is whether when the beliefs expressed in a poem are obnoxious the poem as a whole can be considered to be beautiful—the problem of the *Pisan Cantos*.

LOWELL: The *Pisan Cantos* are very uneven, aren't they? If you took what most people would agree are maybe the best hundred passages, would the beliefs in those passages be obnoxious? I think you'd get a very mixed answer. You could make quite a good case for Pound's good humor about his imprisonment, his absence of self-pity, his observant eye, his memories of literary friends, for all kinds of generous qualities and open qualities and lyrical qualities that anyone would think were good. And even when he does something like the death of Mussolini, in the passage that opens the *Pisan Cantos,* people debate about it. I've talked to Italians who were partisans, and who said that this is the only poem on Mussolini that's any good. Pound's quite wily often: Mussolini hung up like an ox—his brutal appearance. I don't know whether you could say the beliefs there are wrong or not. And there are other poems that come to mind: in Eliot, the Jew spelled with a small j in "Gerontion," is that anti-Semitism or not? Eliot's not anti-Semitic in any sense, but there's certainly a dislike of Jews in those early poems. Does he gain in the fierceness of writing his Jew with a small j? He says you write what you have to write and in criticism you can say what you think you should believe in. Very ugly emotions perhaps make a poem.

INTERVIEWER: You were on the Bollingen Committee at the time the award was made to Pound. What did you think of the great ruckus?

LOWELL: I thought it was a very simple problem of voting for the best book of the year; and it seemed to me Pound's was. I thought the *Pisan Cantos* was the best writing Pound had ever done, though it included some of his worst. It is a very mixed book: that was the question. But the consequences of not giving the best book of the year a prize for extraneous reasons, even terrible ones in a sense—I think that's the death of art. Then you have Pasternak suppressed and everything becomes stifling. Particularly in a strong country like ours you've got to award things objectively and not let the beliefs you'd like a man to have govern your choice. It was very close after the war, and anyone must feel that the poetry award was a trifling thing compared with the concentration camps. I actually think they were very distant from Pound. He had no political effect whatsoever and was quite eccentric and impractical. Pound's social credit, his Fascism, all these various things, were a tremendous gain to him; he'd be a very Parnassan poet without them. Even if they're bad beliefs—and some were bad, some weren't, and some were just terrible, of course—they made him more human and more to do with life, more to do with the times. They served him. Taking what interested him in these things gave a kind of realism and life to his poetry that it wouldn't have had otherwise.

INTERVIEWER: Did you become a translator to suit your own needs or because you wanted to get certain poems, most of them not before translated, into English? Or was it a matter of both, as I suppose it usually is, and as it was for Pound?

LOWELL: I think both. It always seemed to me that nothing very close to the poems I've translated existed in English; and on the other hand, there was some kind of closeness, I felt a kinship. I felt some sort of closeness to the Rilke and Rimbàud poems I've translated, yet they were doing things I couldn't do. They were both a continuation of my own bias and a release from myself.

INTERVIEWER: How did you come to translate Propertius—in fact, how did you come to have such a great interest in Roman history and Latin literature?

LOWELL: At Harvard my second year I took almost entirely English courses—the easiest sort of path. I think that would have been a disaster. But before going to Kenyon I talked to Ford Madox Ford and Ransom, and Ransom said you've just got to take philosophy and logic, which I did. The other thing he suggested was classics. Ford was rather flippant about it, said of course you've got to learn classics, you'll just cut yourself off from humanity if you don't. I think it's always given me some sort of yardstick for English. And then the literature was amazing, particularly the Greek; there's nothing like Greek in English at all. Our plays aren't formally at all like Aeschylus and Sophocles. Their whole inspiration was unbelievably different, and so different that you could hardly think of even the attempt to imitate them, great as their prestige was. That something like *Antigone* or *Oedipus* or the great Achilles moments in the *Iliad* would be at the core of a literature is incredible for anyone brought up in an English culture—Greek wildness and sophistication all different, the women different, everything. Latin's of course much closer. English is a half-Latin language, and we've done our best to absorb the Latin literature. But a Roman poet is much less intellectual than the Englishman, much less abstract. He's nearer nature somehow—somewhat what we feel about a Frenchman but more so still. And yet he's very sophisticated. He has his way of doing things, though the number of forms he explored is quite limited. The amount he could take from the Greeks and yet change is an extraordinary piece of firm discipline. Also, you take almost any really good Roman poet—Juvenal, or Vergil, or Propertius, Catullus—he's much more raw and direct than anything in English, and yet he has this blocklike formality. The Roman frankness interests me. Until recently our literature hasn't been as raw as the Roman, translations had to have stars. And their history has a terrible human frankness that isn't customary with us—corrosive attacks on the establishment, comments on politics and the decay of morals, all felt terribly strongly, by poets as well as historians. The English writer who reads the classics is working at one thing, and his eye is on something else that can't be done. We will always have the Latin and Greek classics, and they'll never be absorbed. There's something very restful about that.

INTERVIEWER: But, more specifically, how did Latin poetry—your study of it, your translations—affect your measure of English poetry?

LOWELL: My favorite English poetry was the difficult Elizabethan plays and the Metaphysicals, then the nineteenth century, which I was aquiver about and disliked but which was closer to my writing than anything else. The Latin seemed very different from either of these. I immediately saw how Shelley wasn't like Horace and Vergil or Aeschylus—and the Latin was a mature poetry, a realistic poetry, which didn't have the contortions of the Metaphysicals. What a frail, bony, electric person Marvell is compared with Horace!

INTERVIEWER: What about your adaptation of Propertius?

LOWELL: I got him through Pound. When I read him in Latin I found a kind of Propertius you don't get in Pound at all. Pound's Propertius is a rather Ovidian figure with a great deal of Pound's fluency and humor and irony. The actual Propertius is a very excited, tense poet, rather desperate; his line is much more like parts of Marlowe's *Faustus*. And he's of all the Roman poets the most like a desperate Christian. His experiences, his love affair with Cynthia, are absolutely rending, destroying. He's like a fallen Christian.

INTERVIEWER: Have you done any other translations of Latin poems?

LOWELL: I did a monologue that started as a translation of Vergil and then was completely rewritten, and there are buried translations in several other poems. There's a poem called "To Speak of Woe That Is in Marriage" in my last book that started as a translation of Catullus. I don't know what traces are left, but it couldn't have been written without the Catullus.

INTERVIEWER: You've translated Pasternak. Do you know Russian?

LOWELL: No, I have rewritten other English translations, and seldom even checked with Russian experts. I want to get a book of translations together. I read in the originals, except for Russian, but I have felt quite free to alter things, and I don't know that Pasternak would look less close than the Italian, which I have studied closely. Before I publish, I want to check with a Russian expert.

INTERVIEWER: Can I get you back to Harvard for a minute? Is it true you tried out for the Harvard *Advocate,* did all the dirty work for your candidacy, and then were turned down?

LOWELL: I nailed a carpet down. I forget who the editor was then, but he was a man who wrote on Frost. At that time people who wrote on Frost were quite different from the ones who write on him now; they tended to be conservative, out of touch. I wasn't a very good writer then, perhaps I should have been turned down. I was trying to write like William Carlos Williams, very simple, free verse, imagistic poems. I had a little group I was very proud of which was set up in galleys; when I left Harvard it was turned down.

INTERVIEWER: Did you know any poets at the time?

LOWELL: I had a friend, Harry Brown, who writes dialogue for movies and has been in Hollywood for years. He was a terribly promising poet. He came to Harvard with a long correspondence with Harriet Monroe and was much more advanced than anyone else. He could write in the style of Auden or Webster or Eliot or Crane. He'd never graduated from high school, and wasn't a student, but he was the person I felt closest to. My other friends weren't writers.

INTERVIEWER: Had you met any older poets—Frost, for instance, who must have been around?

LOWELL: I'd gone to call on Frost with a huge epic on the First Crusade, all written out in clumsy longhand on lined paper. He read a page of that and said, "You have no compression." Then he read me a very short poem of Collins, "How Sleep the Brave," and said, "That's not a great poem, but it's not too long." He was very kindly about it. You know his point about the voice coming into poetry: he took a very unusual example of that, the opening of *Hyperion*; the line about the Naiad, something about her pressing a cold finger to her cold lips, which wouldn't seem like a voice passage at all. And he said, "Now Keats comes alive here." That was a revelation to me; what had impressed me was the big Miltonic imitation in *Hyperion*. I don't know what I did with that, but I recoiled and realized that I was diffuse and monotonous.

INTERVIEWER: What decided you to leave Harvard and go to Kenyon?

LOWELL: I'd made the acquaintance of Merrill Moore, who'd been at Vanderbilt and a Fugitive. He said that I ought to study with a man who was a poet. He was very close to Ransom, and the plan was that I'd go to Vanderbilt; and I would have, but Ransom changed to Kenyon.

INTERVIEWER: I understand you left much against the wishes of your family.

LOWELL: Well, I was getting quite morose and solitary, and they sort of settled for this move. They'd rather have had me a genial social Harvard student, but at least I'd be working hard this way. It seemed to them a queer but orderly step.

INTERVIEWER: Did it help you that you had had intellectual and literary figures in your family?

LOWELL: I really didn't know I'd had them till I went to the South. To my family, James Russell Lowell was the ambassador to England, not a writer. Amy seemed a bit peculiar to them. When I began writing I think it would have been unimaginable to take either Amy or James Russell as models.

INTERVIEWER: Was it through Ransom that you met Tate?

LOWELL: I met them at more or less the same time, but actually stayed with Tate before I knew Ransom very well.

INTERVIEWER: And Ford Madox Ford was there at some time, wasn't he?

LOWELL: I met Ford at a cocktail party in Boston and went to dinner with him at the Athens Olympia. He was going to visit the Tates, and said, "Come and see me down there, we're all going to Tennessee." So I drove down. He hadn't arrived, so I got to know the Tates quite well before his appearance.

INTERVIEWER: Staying in a pup-tent.

LOWELL: It's a terrible piece of youthful callousness. They had one Negro woman who came in and helped, but Mrs. Tate was doing all the housekeeping. She had three guests and her own family, and was doing the cooking and writing a novel. And this young man arrived, quite ardent and eccentric. I think I suggested that maybe I'd stay with them. And they said, "We really haven't any room, you'd have to pitch a tent on the lawn." So I went to Sears, Roebuck and got a tent and rigged it on their lawn. The Tates were too polite to tell me that what they'd said had been just a figure of speech. I stayed two months in my tent and ate with the Tates.

INTERVIEWER: And you were showing him your work all the while.

LOWELL: Oh, I became converted to formalism and changed my style from brilliant free verse, all in two months. And everything was in rhyme, and it still wasn't any good. But that was a great incentive. I poured out poems and went to writers' conferences.

INTERVIEWER: What about Ford?

LOWELL: I saw him out there and took dictation from him for a while. That was hell, because I didn't know how to type. I'd take the dictation down in longhand, and he rather mumbled. I'd ask him what he'd said, and he'd say, "Oh, you have no sense of prose rhythm," and mumble some more. I'd get most of his words, then I'd have to improvise on the typewriter.

INTERVIEWER: So for part of Ford's opus we're indebted to you.

LOWELL: A handful of phrases in *The March of Literature,* on the Provençal poets.

INTERVIEWER: That was the summer before you entered Kenyon; but most of the poems in *Land of Unlikeness* were written after you'd graduated, weren't they?

LOWELL: Yes, they were almost all written in a year I spent

with the Tates, though some of them were earlier poems rewritten. I think becoming a Catholic convert had a good deal to do with writing again. I was much more interested in being a Catholic than in being a writer. I read Catholic writers but had no intention of writing myself. But somehow, when I started again, I won't say the Catholicism gave me subject matter, but it gave me some kind of form, and I could begin a poem and build it to a climax. It was quite different from what I'd been doing earlier.

INTERVIEWER: Why, then, did you choose to print your work in the small liberal magazines whose religious and political positions were very different from yours? Have you ever submitted to the *New Yorker* or the *Atlantic Monthly?*

LOWELL: I think I may have given something to the *Atlantic* on Santayana; the *New Yorker* I haven't given anything. I think the *New Yorker* does some of the best prose in the country, in many ways much more interesting than the quarterlies and little magazines. But poems are lost in it; there's no table of contents, and some of their poetry is light verse. There's no particular continuity of excellence. There just seems no point in printing there. For a while the little magazines, whose religious-political positions *were* very different from mine, were the only magazines that would publish me, and I feel like staying with them. I like magazines like the *New Statesman,* the *Nation,* the *New Republic*—something a little bit off the track.

INTERVIEWER: Just because they are off the track?

LOWELL: I think so. A political position I don't necessarily agree with which is a little bit adverse seems to me just more attractive than a time-serving, conventional position. And they tend to have good reviews, those magazines. I think you write for a small audience, an ardent critical audience. And you know Graves says that poets ought to take in each other's washing because they're the only responsible audience. There's a danger to that—you get too specialized—but I pretty much agree that's the audience you do write for. If it gets further, that's all fine.

INTERVIEWER: There is, though, a certain inbred, in-group anemia to those magazines, at least to the literary quarterlies. For instance, it would have been almost inconceivable for *Partisan Review,* which is the best of them, I think, to give your last book a bad review or even a sharp review.

LOWELL: I think no magazine likes to slam one of its old contributors. *Partisan* has sometimes just not reviewed a book by someone they liked very much and their reviewer didn't. I know Shapiro has been attacked in *Partisan* and then published there, and other people have been unfavorably reviewed and made rather a point of sending them something afterwards. You want to feel there's a certain degree of poorer writing that wouldn't get published in the magazine your work appears in. The good small magazine may publish a lot of rather dry stuff, but at least it's serious, and if it's bad it's not bad by trying to be popular and put something over on the public. It's a wrenched personal ineptitude that will get published rather than a public slickness. I think that has something to do with good reviews coming out in the magazine. We were talking about *Partisan's* not slamming one of its contributors, but *Partisan* has a pretty harsh, hard standard of reviewing, and they certainly wouldn't praise one of their contributors who'd gone to pot.

INTERVIEWER: What poets among your contemporaries do you most admire?

LOWELL: The two I've been closest to are Elizabeth Bishop— I spoke about her earlier—and Jarrell, and they're different. Jarrell's a great man of letters, a very informed man, and the best critic of my generation, the best professional poet. He's written the best war poems, and those poems are a tremendous product of our culture, I feel. Elizabeth Bishop's poems, as I said, are more personal, more something she did herself, and she's not a critic but has her own tastes, which may be very idiosyncratic. I enjoy her poems more than anybody else's. I like some of Shapiro very much, some of Roethke and Stanley Kunitz.

INTERVIEWER: What about Roethke, who tries to do just about everything you don't try to do?

LOWELL: We've read to each other and argued, and may be rather alike in temperament actually, but he wants a very musical poem and always would quarrel with my ear as I'd quarrel with his eye. He has love poems and childhood poems and startling surrealistic poems, rather simple experience done with a blaze of power. He rejoices in the rhetoric and the metrics, but there's something very disorderly working there. Sometimes it will smash a poem and sometimes it will make it. The things he knows about I feel I know nothing about, flowers and so on. What we share, I think, is the exultant moment, the blazing out. Whenever I've tried to do anything like his poems, I've felt helpless and realized his mastery.

INTERVIEWER: You were apparently a very close friend of Delmore Schwartz's.

LOWELL: Yes, and I think that I've never met anyone who has

somehow as much seeped into me. It's a complicated personal thing to talk about. His reading was very varied, Marx and Freud and Russell, very catholic and not from a conservative position at all. He sort of grew up knowing those things and has a wonderful penetrating humorous way of talking about them. If he met T. S. Eliot his impressions of Eliot would be mixed up with his impressions of Freud and what he'd read about Eliot; all these things flowed back and forth in him. Most of my writer friends were more specialized and limited than Schwartz, most of them took against-the-grain positions which were also narrow. Schwartz was a revelation. He felt the poet who had experience was very much better than the poet with polish. Wordsworth would interest him much more than Keats—he wanted openness to direct experience. He said that if you got people talking in a poem you could do anything. And his own writing, *Coriolanus* and *Shenandoah,* is interesting for that.

INTERVIEWER: Isn't this much what you were saying about your own hopes for *Life Studies?*

LOWELL: Yes, but technically I think that Delmore and I are quite different. There have been very few poets I've been able to get very much from technically. Tate has been one of the closest to me. My early poems I think grew out of my admiration for his poems.

INTERVIEWER: What about poets in the past?

LOWELL: It's hard for me to imitate someone; I'm very self-conscious about it. That's an advantage perhaps—you don't become too imitative—but it's also a limitation. I tremble when I feel I'm being like someone else. If it's Rilke or Rimbaud or Propertius, you know the language is a big bar and that if you imitate you're doing something else. I've felt greater freedom that way. I think I've tried to write like some of the Elizabethans.

INTERVIEWER: And Crane? You said you had read a good deal of Crane

LOWELL: Yes, but his difficult style is one I've never been able to do much with. He can be very obscure and yet write a much more inspired poem than I could by being obscure. There's a relationship between Crane and Tate, and for some reason Tate was much easier for me. I could see how Tate was done, though Tate has a rhythm than I've never been able to imitate. He's much more irregular than I am, and I don't know where the rhythm comes from, but I admire it very much. Crane said somewhere that he could write five or six good lines but Tate could write twelve that would hang together, and you'd see how the twelve were built. Tate was somehow more of a model: he had a lot of wildness and he had a lot of construction. And of course I knew him and never knew Crane. I think Crane is the great poet of that generation. He got out more than anybody else. Not only is it the tremendous power there, but he somehow got New York City; he was at the center of things in the way that no other poet was. All the chaos of his life missed getting sidetracked the way other poets' did, and he was less limited than any other poet of his generation. There was a fullness of experience; and without that, if you just had his mannerisms, and not his rather simple writing—which if done badly would be sentimental merely—or just his obscure writing, the whole thing would be merely verbal. It isn't with Crane. The push of the whole man is there. But his style never worked for me.

INTERVIEWER: But something of Crane does seem to have gotten into your work—or maybe it's just that sense of power thrashing about. I though it had come from a close admiring reading of Crane.

LOWELL: Yes, some kind of wildness and power that appeals to me, I guess. But when I wrote difficult poems they weren't meant to be difficult, though I don't know that Crane meant his to be. I wanted to be loaded and rich, but I thought the poems were all perfectly logical. You can have a wonderful time explaining a great poem like "Voyages II," and it all can be explained, but in the end it's just a love poem with a great confusion of images that are emotionally clear; a prose paraphrase wouldn't give you any impression whatever of the poem. I couldn't do that kind of poem, I don't think; at least I've never been able to.

INTERVIEWER: You said that most of the writers you've known have been against the grain. What did you mean?

LOWELL: When I began writing most of the great writers were quite unpopular. They hadn't reached the universities yet, and their circulation was small. Even Eliot wasn't very popular then. But life seemed to be there. It seemed to be one of those periods when the lid was still being blown. The great period of blowing the lid was the time of Schönberg and Picasso and Joyce and the early Eliot, where a power came into the arts which we perhaps haven't had since. These people were all rather traditional, yet they were stifled by what was being done, and they almost wrecked things to do their great works—even rather minor but very good writers such as Williams or Marianne Moore. Their kind of protest and queerness has hardly been repeated. They're wonderful writers. You wouldn't see anyone as strange as Marianne Moore again, not for a long while. Conservative and Jamesian as she is, it was a terrible, private, and strange revolutionary poetry. There isn't the motive to do that now. Yet those were the classics, and it seems to me they were all against the grain, Marianne Moore as much as Crane. That's where life was for the small audience. It would be a tremendous subject to say whether the feelings were against the grain too, and whether they were purifying, nihilistic, or both.

INTERVIEWER: Have you had much contact with Eliot?

LOWELL: I may have seen him a score of times in my life, and he's always been very kind. Long before he published me he had some of my poems in his files. There's some kind of New England connection.

INTERVIEWER: Has he helpfully criticized your work?

LOWELL: Just very general criticism. With the first book of mine Faber did he had a lot of little questions about punctuation, but he never said he liked this or disliked that. Then he said something about the last book—"These are first-rate, I mean it"—something like that that was very understated and gratifying. I feel Eliot's less tied to form than a lot of people he's influenced, and there's a freedom of the twenties in his work that I find very sympathetic. Certainly he and Frost are the great New England poets. You hardly think of Stevens as New England, but you have to think of Eliot and Frost as deeply New England and puritanical. They're a continuation and a criticism of the tradition, and they're probably equally great poets. Frost somehow put life into a dead tradition. His kind of poetry must have seemed almost unpublishable, it was so strange and fresh when it was first written. But still it was old-fashioned poetry and really had nothing to do with modern writing—except that he is one of the greatest modern writers. Eliot was violently modern and unacceptable to the traditionalist. Now he's spoken of as a literary dictator, but he's handled his position with wonderful sharpness and grace, it seems to me. It's a narrow position and it's not one I hold particularly, but I think it's been held with extraordinary honesty and finish and development. Eliot has done what he said Shakespeare had done: all his poems are one poem, a form of continuity that has grown and snowballed.

INTERVIEWER: I remember Jarrell in reviewing *Mills of the*

Kavanaughs said that Frost had been doing narrative poems with ease for years, and that nobody else had been able to catch up.

LOWELL: And what Jarrell said is true: nobody except Frost can do a sort of Chaucerian narrative poem that's organized and clear. Well, a lot of people do them, but the texture of their verse is so limp and uninspired. Frost does them with great power. Most of them were done early, in that *North of Boston* period. That was a miracle, because except for Robinson—and I think Frost is a very much greater poet than Robinson—no one was doing that in England or America.

INTERVIEWER: But you hadn't simply wanted to tell a story in *Mills of the Kavanaughs*.

LOWELL: No, I was writing an obscure, rather Elizabethan, dramatic and melodramatic poem. I don't know quite how to describe this business of direct experience. With Browning, for instance, for all his gifts—and there is almost nothing Browning couldn't use—you feel there's a glaze between what he writes and what really happened, you feel the people are made up. In Frost you feel that's just what the farmers and so on were like. It has the virtue of a photograph but all the finish of art. That's an extraodinary thing; almost no other poet can do that now.

INTERVIEWER: What do you suppose are the qualities that go into that ability?

LOWELL: I don't know. Prose writers have it much more, and quite a few prose writers have it. It's some kind of sympathy and observation of people. It's the deep, rather tragic poems that I value most. Perhaps it's been overdone with Frost, but there's an abundance and geniality about those poems that isn't tragic. With this sense of rhythm and words and composition, and getting into his lines language that is very much like the language he speaks— which is also a work of art, much better than other people's ordinary speech and yet natural to him; he has that continuity with his ordinary self and his poetic self—he's made what with anyone else would be just flat. A very good prose writer can do this and make something of it. You get it quite often in Faulkner. Though he's an Elizabethan sort of character, rather unlike Frost, he can get this amazing immediacy and simplicity. When it comes to verse the form is so hard that all of that gets drained out. In a very conventional old-fashioned writer, or someone who's trying to be realistic but also dramatic and inspired, though he may remain a good poet, most of that directness and realism goes. It's hard for Eliot to be direct that way, though you get it in bits of the *Wasteland*, that marvelous Cockney section. And he can be himself; I feel Eliot's real all through the *Quartets*. He can be very intelligent or very simple there, and *he's* there, but there are no other people in the *Quartets*.

INTERVIEWER: Have many of your poems been taken from real people and real events?

LOWELL: I think, except when I've used myself or occasionally named actual people in poems, the characters are purely imaginary. I've tried to buttress them by putting images I've actually seen and in direct ways getting things I've actually experienced into the poem. If I'm writing about a Canadian nun the poem may have a hundred little bits of things I've looked at, but she's not remotely anyone I've ever known. And I don't believe anybody would think my nun was quite a real person. She has a heart and she's alive, I hope, and she has a lot of color to her and drama, and has some things that Frost's characters don't, but she doesn't have their wonderful quality of life. His Witch of Coös is absolutely there. I've gathered from talking to him that most of the *North of Boston* poems came from actual people he knew shuffled and put together. But then it's all-important that Frost's plots are so extraordinary, so carefully worked out though it almost seems that they're not there. Like some things in Chekhov, the art is very well hidden.

INTERVIEWER: Don't you think a large part of it is getting the right details, symbolic or not, around which to wind the poem tight and tighter?

LOWELL: Some bit of scenery or something you've felt. Almost the whole problem of writing poetry is to bring it back to what you really feel, and that takes an awful lot of maneuvering. You may feel the doorknob more strongly than some big personal event, and the doorknob will open into something that you can use as your own. A lot of poetry seems to me very good in the tradition but just doesn't move me very much because it doesn't have personal vibrance to it. I probably exaggerate the value of it, but it's precious to me. Some little image, some detail you've noticed—you're writing about a little country shop, just describing it, and your poem ends up with an existentialist account of your experience. But it's the shop that started it off. You didn't know why it meant a lot to you. Often images and often the sense of the beginning and end of a poem are all you have—some journey to be gone through between those things; you know that, but you don't know the details. And that's marvelous; then you feel the poem will come out. It's a terrible struggle, because what you really feel hasn't got the form, it's not what you can put down in a poem. And the poem you're equipped to write concerns nothing that you care very much about or have much to say on. Then the great moment comes when there's enough resolution of your technical equipment, your way of constructing things, and what you can make a poem out of, to hit something you really want to say. You may not know you have it to say.

McGraw-Hill Paperbacks in Literature

McGraw-Hill Paperbacks in Criticism

Catalog

If you are interested in a list of fine Paperback
books, covering a wide range of subjects
and interests, send your name and address,
requesting your free catalog, to:

McGraw-Hill Paperbacks
330 West 42nd Street
New York, New York 10036